Ethan Allen Hitchcock

# Swedenborg, a hermetic philosopher:

Being a sequel to Remarks on alchemy and the alchemists. Showing that Emanuel Swedenborg was a hermetic philosopher and that his writings may be interpreted from the point of view of hermetic philosophy

Ethan Allen Hitchcock

**Swedenborg, a hermetic philosopher:**
*Being a sequel to Remarks on alchemy and the alchemists. Showing that Emanuel Swedenborg was a hermetic philosopher and that his writings may be interpreted from the point of view of hermetic philosophy*

ISBN/EAN: 9783337724443

Printed in Europe, USA, Canada, Australia, Japan

Cover: Foto ©ninafisch / pixelio.de

More available books at **www.hansebooks.com**

# SWEDENBORG,

## A HERMETIC PHILOSOPHER.

BEING A SEQUEL TO

REMARKS ON ALCHEMY AND THE ALCHEMISTS.

SHOWING THAT

EMANUEL SWEDENBORG WAS A HERMETIC PHILOSOPHER,
AND THAT HIS WRITINGS MAY BE INTERPRETED
FROM THE POINT OF VIEW OF

## HERMETIC PHILOSOPHY.

WITH A

CHAPTER COMPARING SWEDENBORG AND SPINOZA.

BY THE AUTHOR OF

REMARKS ON ALCHEMY AND THE ALCHEMISTS.

*Ethan Allen Hitchcock*

"One truth openeth the way to another."

NEW YORK:

PUBLISHED BY JAMES MILLER,

SUCCESSOR TO C. S. FRANCIS,

522 BROADWAY.

1865.

# ADVERTISEMENT.

THE writer of the following pages desires to say that, in preparing the work, it has been no part of his design to express his individual opinions upon the topics discussed. His purpose has been to suggest the opinions of others, especially of a class of men scarcely recognized as existing in the world. The art they profess, called after the name of Hermes, *Hermetic* Philosophy, is so little known at the present day that the name of it by no means indicates it. The adepts profess to be, or to have been, in possession of a secret, which they call the *gift of God*. The art has been prosecuted under many names, among which are Alchemy, Astrology, and even Chiromancy, as well as Geomancy, Magic, &c., under all of which names it has had *deluded* followers, who have been deceived, as those who claim to be true artists say, not by the art itself, which never "did betray the heart that loved it," but by their own selfish passions, which play the *Asmodeus* with so many that the few who escape delusion are mystical, not to say mythical, beings who are supposed to have lived upon dreams.

I propose now, without pretending to solve the problem, to suggest the true difficulty in the study, which I take to be this, that the *Alpha* in the art is also the *Omega*, and the Omega the Alpha, and the two are one. Hence the difficulty is something like that of finding the commencement of a circle. Another mode of suggesting the difficulty is by saying that the object is analogous to an attempt to discover the place of that force in nature called gravity or gravitation. In mechanical calculations this force or power is referred to a certain centre, called the centre of gravity; yet every one knows that the absolute centre is a mere point and physically nothing at all, yet there is no particle of matter free from the influence of this power, and every, the most infinitesimal particle, has its own centre. So is it with what the Hermetic philosophers call their *Mercury*, which they say is everywhere seen in action, but nowhere in essence.

I am aware of the fact that some speculative spiritualists of the present day have much to say of what they call *imponderables*, but I am not as yet convinced that any *actual thing* in the universe can be an imponderable, except possibly those invisible things called *thoughts* and *affections ;* yet even these, in some sense, seem to be the most powerful and ponderable of influences, moving the entire being of man in spite of prejudices and of ignorance the most absolute and immovable in themselves.

It is to little or no purpose to give a mere name to a subtle influence whose mode of action is unknown, and whose existence is only recognized through an observation of disconnected effects, our knowledge of which is chaotic and remains chaotic because no *principle* of action is discovered, and yet, how many of us know what life is, except precisely in this way? We see it everywhere, "the birds of the air fly with it, the fishes of the sea swim with it, we carry it about with us everywhere," yet we know not what it is.

Let it be merely supposed now, that a recluse proposes to himself the problem, What is Life?— but, as this word is common and is imagined to carry some meaning with it, while yet the student enters upon the study confessing his ignorance, it is thought convenient to assume another name. Let it then be called *Mercury,* from some remote analogy of this sort; that, if a small portion of this mineral be dashed upon a smooth extended surface, it will separate into an infinity of little globules, each one of which has the entire properties of the whole, and like

so many mirrors reflects so many *universes*, all similar to each other.

Any other word in place of Mercury, as Salt for
example, may be used, or a word may be invented
without any meaning at all, as *Hileg*, to represent the
subject sought for, which is to be found not by the
mere definition of a word, but by the properties or
*principles* of the thing, which are to be admitted, not
upon authority, but by observation and experience
in life, always keeping in view "the possibility of nature," on the principle that though the artist may err,
"nature when rightly handled cannot err."

With these preliminary remarks I shall proceed
to the object I have in view.

E. A. H.

New York, *August*, 1858.

# SWEDENBORG,

## A HERMETIC PHILOSOPHER.

---

### CHAPTER I.

It is more than probable that, on reading the title-page of the following work, some may ask, what is meant by Hermetic philosophy? I think proper, therefore, to premise a few words on that subject, not to explain it in detail, but to indicate some of its principal features.

I published last year a small volume of *Remarks upon Alchemy,** the object of which was to show that the so-called Philosopher's Stone, so much sought after by the Alchemists of the Middle Ages, was a mere symbol, the genuine Alchemists being in fact Hermetic philosophers—a class of men who have never

---

* *Remarks on Alchemy and the Alchemists*, &c.: Crosby, Nichols & Co.  Boston, 1857.

been clearly defined to the general reader, owing, in great part, no doubt, to the nature of their studies and convictions. Many attempts, indeed, have been made to unveil them, and to describe their philosophy, but without results, so far as I have seen; the subject being so remote from the ordinary avocations of life, and because also of the common prepossessions of man in respect to what constitutes the true knowledge of God, and the beatitude of man.

In my *Remarks*, I did not attempt to point out precisely the nature of this philosophy, as such an attempt would have been the height of presumption. That which I chiefly intended, was simply to show from Alchemic books, some of the conditions set forth by the Alchemists themselves, though very mystically and obscurely, as indispensably requisite in him who would possess the philosopher's stone.

A mere accident—a very casual circumstance —some three or four years ago, threw into my hands a small volume on Alchemy, the preface to which alone satisfied me that there must have been two classes of Alchemists: and the perusal of the book assured me that, while some "money-loving sots" employed themselves in experiments upon all sorts of metals and other materials in search of gold, there was another class of men in pursuit of the philosopher's stone by very different means:—by devout contemplation upon the nature of God and of man—upon the human soul and its capacity for knowledge, for happiness, and for immortality;—and the object was a discovery of the means for attaining the true end of man; not an ephemeral pleasure, but a permanent beatitude—not a good for a day, but for all time.  The impression derived from reading this one work on alchemy induced me to look further, and without much effort I obtained a considerable number of volumes, over three hundred, of a strange character, on the philosopher's stone and hermetic philosophy; some of which are of course worthless, but all of which show, beyond the possibility of doubt, that the philosopher's stone was a mere symbol for human perfection, or for something supposed to be essential to that perfection.  There is not a single volume in my possession that could have been written by any one in pursuit of actual gold, though many of the works show that their authors had but very crude opinions as to the real object of the philosophers.

It is not my purpose now to comment at length upon this subject.  Referring the reader to my *Remarks*, I will simply say, that after much study, I came to the opinion that, while MAN was the subject of alchemy, and his perfection was the object of the art, that object required for its attainment certain *means*, which were, however, as carefully wrapped up in symbolism as the end itself. At length, I became convinced that those means were as clearly stated in Scripture as the use of human language will allow. In short, all of my studies drew my attention to the declaration of the Lord in the Sermon on the Mount;—" Blessed are the pure in heart, for they shall see God : "—for it appeared very clear that the philosophers had in some way connected the perfection of man with a knowledge of God, the former leading to the latter, yet the latter being as a sign of the former. But this knowledge of God was not a mere outward belief in the existence of a great but undefined power over nature, which even the most ignorant savages acknowledge, but an inward experience or spiritual sight, by which the subject of the experience was brought into some sort of communion with the Spirit of God, so as to realize the knowledge as a possessiou.

When the object was thus far recognized, as I considered, my attention was gradually carried upon the means of attaining it, as obscurely indicated by these writers, and I could not fail to see them chiefly in the text just recited.

I found in alchemic and hermetic books one pervading doctrine, common to all of them, though expressed very obscurely; and it was this—that, while every writer made use of a word of his own choosing to designate the undescribed *matter* of which the philosopher's stone was to be made, they all prescribed as a first step in the work of making the stone, a process of purification. Whatever other directions are given, they all tell us to *wash* the *matter*, to *purify* the *matter*, &c., and they have much to say of what they call the *philosopher's soap*, the *soap of the wise*, or *the vinegar of the wise*, &c.

After comparing many books together, and weighing carefully the circumstances obscurely hinted at, I became convinced that the *matter* of the philosophers was man, and that the *soap* referred to, the *vinegar*, the *oil*, &c., was no other than the conscience; but the conscience, acting freely and not under external and violent influences. While the conscience is one thing itself, it takes a great variety of names according to the condition of the subject upon which or in which it acts. To one it is a messenger of peace and of joy inexpressible, while to another it whispers woe unutterable, and pours out vials of wrath upon the terrified and doomed soul; and this it does, independently of the power of man, who has no control whatever over this all-pervading and ubiquitous spirit. This is the spirit that is "in the midst" when two or three are gathered together in the name of God, and which can neither be kept out nor in, by "shut doors" ever so strongly bolted.

At first, indeed, it seemed a very simple thing, altogether insufficient, as a basis, for so many books and for such results as appeared to be claimed for it; but I observed that the philosophers, as they call each other, speak of their art as both simple and difficult:—like all other arts perhaps, easy to those who are skilled in their practice, but difficult to the uninstructed; or like the yoke of Christ, easy in one sense, to the willing and obedient,—but a fearful labor to the selfish and the obdurate.

Be this as it may, I kept my attention upon it, and, continuing to read Hermetic books, I found that the *unenforced* and *natural* office of the conscience served as a key for the explanation of many otherwise inexplicable passages in Hermetic writings; and I finally rested in the conviction, that whatever the truth might be in itself, the Hermetic writers intended to indicate that a pure heart, or what the Psalmist calls a "right spirit," is the way to the philosopher's stone, if it is not the stone itself,—the pearl of great price ; for this pearl is not a mere hope, no, not even the hope of heaven, but it is heaven itself.

I had long seen, as I thought, that the knowledge of God is essential to the peace of man, and that this knowledge must be something different, as I have said, from the mere recognition of an unknown powerful being over nature, which "the strong seeks to conquer, and the weak to avoid ; " and seeing, as I thought I did, that the object of the Hermetic philosophers was the perfection of man, and that this perfection was to be found in some knowledge of God in a peculiar sense, and that the way to this knowledge lay through the purification of the heart, I was carried, I say, to the text of Scripture just recited, yet in such a manner as to see the operation in something like a *circle ;* for it appeared that while the pure in heart are said to see God, this condition itself is not attained but by the agency or power of the Spirit of God.  This " circular " operation is especially referred to by the alchemist, or Hermetic philosopher, *Artephias*, as stated, page 90 of my *Remarks*. It is, as I consider, the very same point in philosophy which is so much insisted upon in religion, where we are told that, while faith is essential to salvation, it is not attainable by the "natural man," unassisted by the grace of God. There is much injudicious preaching on this subject, however well intended, by which many honest minds are greatly perplexed and severely tried without benefit; and, still worse, many hasty and bold wits are driven to take refuge in a sort of logical infidelity, out of which it is extremely difficult to extricate themselves.

I will not now dwell upon this point further than to say, that the difference between the desire of happiness and the desire of being worthy of happiness, or the difference between the love of God's blessings and the love of God, &c., may show the difference between the *conditions* of different men, so as to indicate who may and who may not feel that they are tending to that state to which the Lord referred in the text I have re-cited.

If now I should say that the blessing and the condition necessary for its attainment, were believed to be the gifts of God, not attainable by the unassisted efforts of man, without urging metaphysical reasons for it, I should undoubtedly state one of the reasons why a certain class of men, appearing in all ages, have drawn a veil over what they have to say on this subject. They have felt that all the instruction man is able to give to man, on the subject of God and of God's blessings, must terminate in referring man to God, as the author and finisher of a faith which is said to partake of his very nature.

In popular estimation religion and philosophy seem to stand opposed to each other; but this results chiefly from regarding the forms and ceremonies of religion as its substance, on the one side, and considering mere learning, or memory knowledge, as philosophy on the other. But if philosophy be defined as wisdom, and philosophers be regarded as lovers of wisdom, we may see a channel through which the philosopher may come into harmony with one in whom religion is not a ceremony but a sentiment. But this is not the place for an essay on this subject.

In my volume of *Remarks* upon alchemy I undertook to show, by citations from the writings of alchemists and Hermetic philosophers, as I have already said, that the *subject* of the Hermetic art is MAN, and that the *object* of the art is the perfection of man. I demonstrated that the Hermetic writers communicated with each other by means of a conventional language, writing of salt, sulphur, and mercury ; of Mercury, Sol, and Luna, &c., &c., through an endless variety of expressions, instead of man, or of body, soul, and spirit; and that by the transmutation of metals, the genuine alchemists meant the transformation of man from a state of nature to a state of grace. I made it appear, by abundant extracts with easy interpretations, that the Hermetic writers had, in fact, but one subject; and that it was, or shall I say it is, MAN,—including his relation to nature on the one side, and to God on the other, an inseparable trinity :—that, though their science or art is obscure in itself, and is disclosed, or rather hidden, in exceedingly dark, metaphorical, and figurative language, they nevertheless all treat of MAN ;—of his mind as a spirit, and of his body as an earth ;—that they used a multitude of expressions, seemingly pointing to other things, especially to chemistry, but in reality explicable by a due knowledge of man, as the image of God, and the central and most important being of God's creation.

I endeavored to point out some of the reasons why those writers concealed themselves from general observation by their enigmatic modes of writing, of which there were many, and expressed the opinion that no reason now exists for not making them known in their true character,—that of religious philosophers ; somewhat, it may perhaps be justly thought, too much given to mysticism, especially if measured by what are called the practical tendencies of our age.

I admitted that there were pretenders to the Hermetic art, who brought disrepute upon the art itself, by practising their impostures upon the simple, easily deceived, and upon the avaricious, whose cupidity drew them to a study, the first principle of which excludes every thing selfish, base, and mean.

I also admitted that many, with no evil design, assumed the garb or outward dress of the Hermetic writers, who were not masters of the art, and that these also contributed to bring the proper subject or object of the writers into disrepute, by attempting to carry a purely moral design into the field of physical science, vainly striving to make the Hermetic key supply the absence of patience and study in the pursuit of the natural sciences, into which no short road of entrance is likely ever to be discovered, so as to dispense with the necessity of industry and continuous application.

I pointed to the conscience as the true natural instrument, provided by God, for a healthy renovation of man, to the exclusion of the passions, especially the degrading passion of fear, which ought only to be used when gentle means fail,—as we read that stones were resorted to when tufts of grass failed to bring the "rude boy" from the forbidden fruit.

In admitting, as I did, that mistakes were made by some who imagined themselves in possession of the Hermetic secret, my mind did not fully and clearly rest, at the moment, upon Emanuel Swedenborg, a man of immense learning and unexceptionable personal character, who has risen in this age to be the head of a considerable body of Christians who believe that the New Jerusalem has recently descended upon earth, or is about to come down from heaven to bless the world.

As I desire to guard against being misunderstood on a subject which I am sure is important, and wish above all things not to mislead any one, I must explain that, by referring to the conscience as the natural instrument of the purification of man, I do not mean to be understood as saying that this is the peculiar secret of hermetic philosophy ; but that it is the way to it.   The secret itself, we are told, has never been discovered, and never will be discovered by any one until, by a suitable moral and spiritual discipline, the seeker shall feel in a condition to stand unabashed in the presence of God under the simple but momentous text of Scripture, " Blessed are the pure in heart, for they shall see God ; "—not that the wicked do not see God also, but they see him as another personage.

I suppose I must attribute the opinion I have recently adopted with respect to Swedenborg, in part, at least, to a habit of looking beyond the letter, in the interpretation of obscure and mystical writings, acquired or *practised* in the preparation of my *Remarks on Alchemy and the Alchemists*. Whatever the cause may have been, I was surprised, a few weeks since, on looking into Swedenborg's *Heavenly Arcana*, at being reminded of the use made by many of the hermetic philosophers (the alchemists of the middle ages) of the first verses of Genesis, and I was thereupon induced to look a little further into the resemblances to be found between the writings of Swedenborg and those of the hermetic philosophers. The result has been—without denying the genius and knowledge of Swedenborg—a decided opinion that he was a follower of the hermetic class of writers, and that his writings are to be judged and interpreted from the standpoint of hermetic philosophy, however difficult it may be to acquire the right position for that purpose; for it is no easy matter.

A mere isolated coincidence of expression or thought on a particular point, between the writings of Swedenborg and those of the alchemists, would be of little or no importance; but if it shall appear that, besides many remarkable points of identity between Swedenborg and the mystic class of writers to which I refer, the *principle* of interpretation employed by Swedenborg upon the first books of Moses, and especially upon the first verses of Genesis, can be substantially pointed out in the writings of the alchemists, though not applied precisely as Swedenborg applied it, it cannot fail to surprise many, and must be of importance in estimating the claims of Swedenborg to special illumination,—whether those claims be made by himself, or by his admirers or followers in his behalf.

If there was a hermetic secret, or something passing under that name, as the philosopher's stone, for example, and no one doubts this, it is exceedingly improbable, that the secret should not, in some form or other, come to the surface.

That it did exhibit itself in many forms during the middle ages, and even very lately, can be easily shown; so that there is no natural presumption against the position I take, that Swedenborg's mystical writings are modelled after those of the hermetic writers, and may be interpreted from the standpoint of hermetic philosophy; and this, too, without assuming that Swedenborg was what was called an *adept* in the fullest sense. According to my understanding of hermetic books, the true secret of the hermetic art cannot be written—it can only be written about; and the attempt to write about it *directly*, is a very sure method of losing one's self in a cloud of words conveying to the judicious no genuine instruction. It amounts to this, and I say it with all possible reverence, that when God speaks in man, the man (in man) must be silent; and not only this, the man must be silent that God may speak,—which we may suppose the true ground of the much talked of Pythagorean *silence.*

We have an immense field of natural inquiry open before us, in which all of our natural faculties may be employed usefully, both in learning and in teaching; but it is said that there is one subject which God reserves to himself, and teaches only to a "select few of the simple and

true," who may not at all be acquainted with the
sciences commonly so called ; not that ignorance
of any kind can be an advantage to us, but that
no kind of natural science or knowledge can
supersede the conditions necessary for the attainment of what is called the knowledge of God.
It may be said that there is no mystery or secret
in this; that every one admits it; yet the more
considerate may see in it the very mystery of
godliness, the profoundest secret of life,—the
secret about which the hermetic writers employed
themselves, and in view of which, as I intend to
show, Swedenborg wrote his mystical books,
dropping the terms of *salt, sulphur*, and *mercury*,
in favor of *ens, cause*, and *effect*, yet substantially
writing in the vein of the hermetic art, treating
of man as a spirit; or, as man on the one side a
*spirit*, and on the other an *earth;* of man as, by
nature, an "inchoate" production, tending to
perfection, but needing the help of a divine art
to advance him thereto.

We have now a large class of Christians,
generally, as I believe, of more than ordinary intelligence, and, as I also think, usually distinguished for gentleness and amiability, who are
known as Swedenborgians, though I believe they
prefer to be called members of the New Church,

or members of the New-Jerusalem Church.  They have grown in numbers and importance very gradually; unlike many sects, in this respect, that have sprung into being from the local preaching of some enthusiastic fanatic, whose appeals to the passions have overborne the reason, and through the imagination and the feelings, have effected organizations of great extent, and even considerable duration.  Swedenborg was not a preacher, nor do we know historically that he was an oral teacher to any great extent. He was a writer, and a very voluminous one. In his early years he was employed in practical life, and in the acquisition of knowledge, especially scientific knowledge, and was, without doubt, one of the most learned men of his age.

Swedenborg was born at Upsal, or, as some accounts say, at Stockholm, in 1688, and died at London, at the age of 84, or 85—for there is a question as to the precise year of his birth. Somewhere near the middle period of his life his thoughts and labors took a decidedly religious turn.  In referring to the occasion of it, he speaks of *the opening of his internal sight*, as if something like a supernatural influence had been exerted upon him, which he attributed to the

Lord, a name of vast importance in Swedenborg's writings.

After the opening of his internal sight, as Swedenborg called it, he wrote almost exclusively upon the subject of religion, and left behind him a library of volumes of his own works, containing his opinions upon religion, and his interpretations of Scripture—not according to the letter, but according to the spirit, that is, according to his own spirit, as many may say; or, as some believe, according to the teaching of the Lord, by means of the opening of his internal sight.

The sect of Swedenborgians, as I will call them, has grown up, as I have said, gradually; and the members are generally well-informed and sincere; for the most part, reading and thinking people; as, indeed, they are measurably obliged to be, because the doctrines of the sect, next to the Scriptures, are to be found in books written with a vast deal of thought, and without the slightest appeal to the passions.

Among the many works left us by Swedenborg, throughout which his principles are scattered without much order, and repeated in every variety of form, it is difficult to name any one in particular in which his doctrines are comprised as a whole; but I should refer to the work entitled *Angelic Wisdom concerning Divine Love and Divine Wisdom*, as likely to give a student an insight into his most abstruse principles.

His work concerning Heaven and Hell, "from things heard and seen," is perhaps the most characteristic application of the doctrines.

As a systematic last thought, perhaps his work entitled the *True Christian Religion* might be first read with advantage, by one desiring a general understanding of Swedenborg's opinions. It was the last, or one of the last works he published.

2

# CHAPTER II.

I OUGHT in candor to express my opinion that there is an underlying principle throughout Swedenborg's writings, which a mere reading of his works will hardly give.

I would indicate the direction in which it is to be sought, in some degree, by desiring his reader to consider that Swedenborg, in his interpretation of Scripture, professes to have looked beyond the letter to the Spirit by which the letter was dictated. He, of all men, appropriated and applied the declaration of St. Paul, or at least the first part of it, that the letter killeth, but the Spirit giveth life; and the reader of Swedenborg's interpretations must not suppose that he is exempt from that necessity which lay upon Swedenborg himself, of finding the *Spirit of Truth*, as essential in the comprehension of mystical and symbolical writings.

We too must use the Spirit; and surely it is an undeniable right to mete out to Swedenborg

the measure he applied to others. He would
have us do so, if I understand his writings ; and
his friends must not deny us a license in reading
his works, which he dared to take with the Holy
Scriptures. But by what spirit shall he be
judged ?  Here lies the only difficulty in the
case.

This difficulty will be measurably overcome,
when the student receives into his mind the *idea*
which, in Swedenborg's mind, bore the name of
the *Lord;* for words are the names of ideas and
images in the mind, and can only be intelligibly
used when apprehended with precision for the
ideas and images they express.  To what purpose
can any one speak of the *Lord*, and yet have in
his mind no idea represented by that word ? or
how can any one read of the Lord, and understand what he reads, without having in his mind
the idea expressed by that word ?  We see the
importance of this principle in mathematics and
in other subjects, and why not in theology ?  The
mathematician affirms the principles of a triangle
with the idea of a triangle in his mind, and not
the idea of a circle ; and the student of mathematics apprehends the properties of a triangle
with the idea of a triangle in his mind, and not
the idea of a circle.

With Swedenborg, the reception of the idea of the LORD was the opening of his internal sight. That idea working in the mind of Swedenborg produced or *educed* that spirit, or was the seal to it, which represented the spirit of truth, and which became for him the measure by which he judged of all things. It gave him what was to him a knowledge of the *substance* of all things, or in other words the knowledge of God.

It might be expected from any one proposing to give any account of Swedenborg, that some effort would be made to explain the sense in which he understood the expression, the LORD, so freely used in his writings; but it is extremely difficult to do so.

I advertise the reader that this word, the LORD, or Swedenborg's understanding of it, is the key-note to his whole philosophy,—so far as one word can express it.

It is not enough to say, popularly, that by this word he meant Jesus Christ; for although he so used the word as to be applicable to the Son of God, he understood it in a sense not often met with in the ordinary preaching of the day;— nor is it sufficient to refer to the WORD, as used by St. John, for the same reason ;—nor do we reach a complete idea of it by a mere verbal declaration that he meant the second person of the Trinity ;—neither do we learn his meaning by saying that by the Lord Swedenborg meant the Divine-human, the God-man.

We might as well at once, yea better adopt his own expressions, and study the meaning through the synonyms he uses and the application he makes of them.

We should bear in mind, however, that the truth precedes the expression of it, and must underlie and interpret it, while the expression, at the same time, should carry us to the truth expressed.

He says, then, that the Lord is [a] man ; also, that the Lord is God, and that the Lord is Life, the Life of all things.

The student will hardly see this as Swedenborg seems to have done, until he sees in the idea of the Lord, that is, of Life, the death of death ; for death, in Swedenborg's sense, is not the end of life, but an event in life : man being, in the Lord, not in himself, ever-living.

It will be difficult to find in Swedenborg's writings any elucidation of the opening words of John :—In the beginning was the Word, and the Word was with God, and the Word was God.

The same was in the beginning with God. All things were made by Him, and without Him was not any thing made that was made.

And the Word was made flesh.

How did Swedenborg understand this important doctrine? Are we to suppose that he looked first to God and then to the Word as the Lord? or did he look to the Lord and then to God? Did he look to the Lord and then to man; and then by a reflex idea, return from man to the Lord, and thence to God, with the amazing inference that God is **a** man, or dropping the article—that, God is man?

Can we consider that man is the nearest being to man, and thence the starting-point of study? Can we say that man is a *natural* being, and then invert the terms, and say that he is a *being* of nature; and finally, under the notion that every *particular* expresses the *universal*, can we proceed further and say that *man*, not as an individual, but as a universal, is *the* being of nature; and then, can we say, that life is the being of nature, and that life is the Lord, and the Lord is God, and, thence, that God is *man?*

Can we say that man is an *intellectual* being, and thence, by a similar process, affirm that man, not individually but universally, is the being of intellect or of intelligence; and thus posit intelligence in the Lord as a spiritual world of which the Lord is God, and so again affirm that God is man?

Or yet further, can we say that man is a *spiritual* being, or individually a being of spirit; and, universally, the being of spirit; and then say that the spirit is life, that life is the Lord, and the Lord is God, and thus again reiterate that God is man?

Or, can we say that man is a *living* being, a *being* of Life, living not in himself but in the Lord and thence in God, and that, as the image declares the pattern, therefore God is [a] man?

Can we say that man is a being in existence, *individually*, and that *universally* he is *the Being* of existence; or, in other words, that he is the substance of all things; and, when regarded in God, the self-existent substance; and that God is the Lord, and the Lord is Life, the Life of man, who is nothing of himself; and thus, do we touch the essence of the doctrine, that man must *deny* himself individually to live universally, that is, before he can realize in himself the life of God: and can this doctrine be so presented to man as that he may attain to it through his rational nature, or must he receive it, if he receives it at all, as the gift of God, the gift of the Lord, the gift of Life, the Life of God in the soul ; and does this reception constitute what is called regeneration,—and does it carry with it the idea or sense of a secret inaccessible to the natural man ?

Can it assist us in seeing into this important subject, to consider a few texts of Scripture where the truth lies hid in the letter ?

The WORD which was with God and was God, was made flesh, and was seen of men. The WORD spake and said, I and my Father are one.

And the WORD prayed : "Sanctify them, through thy truth : Thy WORD is truth."

And the WORD prayed : "That they all may be one ; as thou, Father, art in me, and I in thee, that they also may be one in us : that the world may believe that thou hast sent me."

"And the glory which thou gavest me have I given them ; that they may be one, even as we are one : "

"I in them, and thou in me, that they may be made perfect in one ; and that the world may know that thou hast sent me, and hast loved them, as thou hast loved me."

"And the Word said : " It is expedient for you that I go away : for if I go not away, the

Comforter will not come unto you; but if I depart, I will send him unto you."

"But when the Comforter is come, whom I will send unto you from the Father, *even* the Spirit of Truth, which proceedeth from the Father, he shall testify of me."

"Howbeit, when the Spirit of Truth is come, he will guide you into all truth."

And St. Paul says: "I am crucified with Christ: nevertheless I live; yet not I, but Christ liveth in me."

From these few texts I will, with the leave of the reader, make a transition to an alchemic work by an Arabian, *Alipili.* "I admonish thee, whosoever thou art, that desirest to dive into the inmost parts of nature, if that thou seekest thou findest not within thee, *thou wilt never find it without thee.* If thou knowest not the excellency of thine own house, why dost thou seek and search after the excellency of other things? The universal orb of the world contains not so great mysteries and excellencies as *a little man, formed by God to his own image.* And he who desires the primacy amongst the students of nature, will nowhere find a greater or better field of study than himself. Therefore will I follow the example of the *Egyptians,* and from my whole heart, and certain true experience proved by me, speak to my neighbor in the words of the *Egyptians*, and with a loud voice do now proclaim: O MAN, KNOW THYSELF; *in thee is hid the treasure of treasures.*"

What is this treasure? Perhaps it is the knowledge of the WORD; the knowledge of the Lord; the knowledge of God; and its possessor may possibly be able to say with St. Paul,—"Henceforth know we no man after the flesh: yea, though we have known Christ after the flesh, yet now henceforth know we him no more."

It may possibly assist the reader to form some idea of Swedenborg's understanding of the expression *the Lord*, as life, and as one thing, to read an extract from the alchemic tract, De Manna Benedicto, to wit:

"My intent is, for certain reasons, not to prate too much of the matter, which yet is but *one only thing*, already too plainly described; nor of the preparation, which is the second and greatest secret: But I have constituted these lines for the good of him that shall make *the Stone* [shall find the Word that was made flesh?] if it shall fall into the hands of such a one; for to him it shall show and set down in plain terms, as plain as possibly my pen can write to the very letter, such magical and natural uses of it, as many that have had it never knew nor heard of; and such as when I beheld them, *made my knees to tremble, and my heart to shake, and I to stand amazed at the sight of them.*"

I have many reasons for believing that Swedenborg's knees had also trembled, that his heart had quaked, and that he had stood amazed, when he discovered, or thought he discovered, in himself the " secret of the Lord," which then became for him an open secret, called by him the opening of his internal sight.

This gave to him, as I suppose, what was *for him* a miniature representation of all things under one idea, which he called the Lord.

Many efforts have been made to describe or express this idea, but without conveying the idea itself.

It has been said by one writer to contain the ideas of all things, almost like so many seeds.

Another has compared the mind, in possession of this idea, to the most exquisitely polished corner of a diamond, placed in light, giving an image of all things against it.  Others have compared the mind to a mirror,—though few can " hold it up to nature," because the images returned are af-

fected by the condition of the mirror, as Plotinus
has said, and Lord Bacon after him.

Whatever view be taken of this, there is no
reason to doubt that Swedenborg had what
seemed to him a clear opinion upon this subject,
as an underlying principle, from which his
thoughts all flowed, as a river from a fountain,
and unless this idea can be mastered, it will not
be an easy matter to judge of Swedenborg's writings.

The reader cannot be too careful in keeping
distinct from each other things or questions that
differ from each other.  It is one thing to determine or ascertain the principle of a man's thought,
—his love, as Swedenborg would say ;—it is another and a very different question, to determine
the value of that principle.  Swedenborg called
his principle,—the principle from which he wrote,
—*the opening of his internal sight;* and I must
urge upon his student that in this he presents us
a problem, calling for solution before his writings
can be read with intelligence ; for it seems very
plain, that if we accept his simple declaration on
this point, and fall short of a comprehension of
it, we must necessarily subordinate our principle
of life to that of another man ; and then we must

determine upon some other ground why we accept Swedenborg's declarations or revelations of truth, and reject those of other men,—those of Jacob Behmen for example,—who have claimed an authority as high as Swedenborg could have pretended to; for there are many competitors in this field, vast numbers of men having lived, written and died in the belief of their being the subjects of special illumination.

I will now proceed to show wherein Swedenborg appears to have drawn some of his doctrines, seemingly by *inference* from the alchemic and Hermetic writings, occupying most of my space with extracts, for I wish the reader to judge for himself.

# CHAPTER III.

The first point of similitude to which I shall refer, between Swedenborg and the Hermetic writers, may assist the reader in forming some idea of what the Swedish Philosopher understood by the expression *the Lord*, already, though imperfectly, examined.  I refer to it with some timidity, being fully aware of the delicacy of the questions connected with it.  It touches upon what may be regarded as *the Secret* of the Hermetic writers, and while I am of the opinion that Swedenborg drew his doctrine of the Lord, in part at least, from those writers, I feel disposed to protest against its being supposed that what the alchemists, or Hermetic philosophers, considered their *Secret*, has been openly declared in any part of Swedenborg's writings.  I desire to express the opinion that Swedenborg did not precisely apprehend the Secret of Alchemy, while yet, as I must believe, he thought he had entered upon its possession, and a large part of his philosophy rests upon that supposed possession. That he appropriated the idea in part from the Hermetic writers I cannot doubt, but I feel very sure that he misapprehended a point in connection with it which has led him astray in some important particulars. I do not say this in a presumptuous spirit, as if I knew the *Secret* of Hermetic philosophy, and had it in my power to improve the representations of so great a man as Swedenborg. It is possible I presume for a very humble man to perceive some mistakes even of a very great man.

I do not wish to appear as assuming to know the Hermetic Secret, nor do I intend it to be understood, by a pretence of modesty, that I could reveal the secret if I would. I plainly declare, without pretence, that I have some idea of what lies at the root of the Hermetic Art, but I do not feel at liberty to attempt to state it. If I am right in my supposition about it, the art will take care of itself without the help of man; and, moreover, it will remain in the world though all the books about it should be destroyed.

In referring now, as I intend to do, to what Swedenborg, as I believe, thought was the Hermetic Secret, I wish it to be understood that I do not endorse his representation of it, while I re-

peat nevertheless that he was a follower of the
Hermetic class.  No Hermetic writer has written
the hundredth part of what Swedenborg wrote,
and this alone might lead any one to suspect that
he did not precisely touch upon the veritable secret, which seems everywhere to have closed the
lips of the adepts.  His friends may suppose that
this is surrendering the point I am endeavoring
to establish, and thus affirm that his position is
an independent one, in no manner connected
with the Hermetic philosophers; but it should
be remembered that Calvin and Arminius both
took their doctrines from the Scriptures, and yet
differed from each other on a vital point.

But to come now to the parallel.

Paragraph 3483, *Heavenly Arcana.*  " Whatsoever anywhere appears in the universe, is
representative of the Lord's Kingdom, insomuch
that there is not any thing contained in the universal atmospheric region of the stars, or in the
earth, and its three kingdoms, but what in its
manner and measure is representative; for all
and singular the things in nature are ultimate
images, inasmuch as from the Divine proceed the
celestial things appertaining to good, and from
these celestial things the spiritual things appertaining to truth, and from both the former and

the latter proceed natural things.  Hence it may appear how gross, yea, how terrestrial, and also inverted, human intelligence is, which ascribes all and singular things to nature separate or exempt from influx prior to itself, or from the efficient cause.  They also who so think and speak, seem to themselves to be wiser than others, when yet angelic wisdom consists in ascribing nothing to nature, but all and singular things to the Lord, thus to a principle of Life, and not to any thing dead.  The learned know that subsistence is perpetual existence, but still it is contrary to the affection of what is false, and thereby contrary to the reputation of learning, to say that nature continually subsists, as it originally had existence, from the Lord.  Inasmuch now as all and singular things subsist from the Divine, that is, continually exist, and all and singular things thence derived must needs be representative of those things whereby they had existence, it follows, that the visible universe is nothing else but a theatre representative of the Lord's Kingdom, and that this latter is a theatre representative of the Lord himself."

"3484. From very much experience I am instructed, that there is but one single source of life, which is that of the Lord, and that this Life flows in and causes man to live, yea, causes both the good and the wicked to live ; to this life correspond forms which are substances, and which by continual divine influx are so vivified, that they appear to themselves to live by or from themselves. This correspondence is that of the recipient organs with the life received ; but *such as the recipient organs are, such is the life which they live.* Those men who are principled in love and charity are in correspondence, for the life itself is received by them adequately ; but they who are principled in things contrary to love and charity are not in correspondence, because the life itself is not received adequately ; hence they have a life existing with them according to their quality. This may be illustrated by the case of natural forms into which the light of the sun is influent ; such as the recipient forms are, such are the modifications of that light ; in the spiritual world the modifications are spiritual ; therefore in that world such as the recipient forms are, such is the intelligence and such the wisdom of the inhabitants."

In this last paragraph Swedenborg sets forth life, the life of the Lord, as the *one* thing in all ; and, as I must believe, he thought *that life* to be the *one thing* to which the alchemists have referred in so many ways, as the one only thing required in their work,—the work of making the philosopher's stone ;—the one thing, as Swedenborg evidently thought, essentially to be known in the acquisition of wisdom or the celestial life.

The allusions to the *one thing*, without describing it, may be found in any Hermetic work whatever, for I think there is not one Hermetic writer who does not refer to the " one thing needful ;" but I would not recommend any student to be hasty in concluding that he knows precisely what this is, nor need he be forward in determining the wonders it works in the world.

I will cite now a few passages from alchemic or Hermetic books, in which reference is made to the *one thing*, and I must leave the reader to form his own opinion as to whether Swedenborg thought he had " laid hold of it," in his notion of the one life in all, the life of the Lord, as he calls it.  But I must ask the reader to excuse me for suggesting his taking the matter into his own thought, under an appeal to God for protection against error ; for the opinion of no man living or that ever has lived can stand him in stead on such vital questions, in the day of trial.

"There is no road but one to find the *quick* sulphur,"—quoted in *Zoroaster's Cave.*

I must beg the reader to believe that this language was not invented and used by thoughtless people, much less by triflers who were careless of the honor of God. It must be attributed to reverence for what were regarded as sacred mysteries, especially the mystery of godliness. By quick sulphur was symbolized the spirit of God, or the life of God, to find which is salvation to man.

In the following passage the same thing is called *water :*

" Thou needest but one thing, namely water, and one operation, to wit, decoction, to white and red, in one vessel,—understand, of one nature." —*Zoroaster's Cave.*

Again : " Although the wise men (meaning Hermetic writers) have varied their names, and perplexed their sayings, yet they would always have us think of but one thing, one disposition, one way. The wise men know this one thing; and that it is one they have often proved."—*Ibid.*

Again: " In the multiplicity of things our art is not perfected. For it is one *stone*, one *medicine*, in which consists the whole *magistery ;* to which we add nothing extraneous, nor take away any thing, but only, in our preparation, that which is superfluous."—*Ibid.*

Again : "White and red proceed from the same root, without any other nature intervenient. For it dissolves and conjoins itself, makes itself black and citrine, white and red; espouses itself, conceives, brings forth, and does all to the perfect end."—*Rhasis.*

Again: "Our *water*, gilded with *solar sulphur*, is the secret of the Egyptians, Chaldeans, Arabians, Persians, and Greeks."—*Anonymous.*

In the above passage, by *our water*, may be understood *our spirit;* and by *solar sulphur*, that which in a preceding extract is called *quick-sulphur;* indicating that man is perfected by the spirit of God; the *one thing*, which Swedenborg called the life of the Lord.

Again: "Mercury alone perfects the work. In it we find all that we need: to it we add nothing extraneous."—*Thos. Aquinas.*

Again: "The *stone* is one: yet this one is not one in number, but in nature."—*Zoroaster's Cave.*

Again: "This mystery is wont to be made of one only thing: therefore put this in thy mind, for thou needest not many things, but one only thing."—*Morien.*

When Morien is represented to have said

this, he at the same time told his pupil, who was an eastern king, that the *one thing* was in himself.

The Hermetic writers call it by an endless variety of names, constantly warning us, however, that it is but one only thing.

If the reader has seen the volume of "Remarks upon Alchemy," he may the more easily perhaps understand these extracts, to which I will add several more without further explanation, my purpose being simply to show that Swedenborg thought the *one* thing (in all) is the life of the Lord; and to show also, that he adopted his form of writing most likely from Hermetic books.

Again: "And know for certain, that the philosophers cared not for the names, but one name, and one action; to wit, to seethe the stone, and bring forth his soul; because their stone is always one."—*Avicen.*

Again: "The matter of this work, according to all authentic philosophers, is one only thing, containing in itself all necessaries for the accomplishment of its own perfection."—*Ripley.*

Again: "And know that the philosophers declare, that the permanent water is taken out of light; but the light maketh fire, and the light

shining and transparent, becometh like one stray-
ing seeking lodging: but when light is conjoined
unto light, it rejoiceth; because it came out of
it, and is converted into it."—*Mireris.*

The author of *the Revelation of the Secret
Spirit* has a succession of extracts, with remarks
on this point, of which the following is an example:

"One saith, ' our stone is no other but salt;
who worketh in this art without salt, is like unto
him who would shoot a bow without a string.
If the omnipotent God had created no salt, the
art of alchemy had not been. Salt is coprose,
and coprose is salt; all lesser and greater miner-
als truly are nothing else but salt: nothing is
more fluxible than salt: nothing more piercing
than salt, and his nature: nothing cleaner, purer,
more spiritual, and more subtle, than salt and his
nature. Nothing stronger than salt and his nature; nothing more incombustible than salt and his
nature; nothing more volatile than salt and his
nature; nothing sweeter than salt and his nature;
nothing more sour than salt and his nature!'

"These passages, (says the author,) seem to
be repugnant to each other—sweet and sour;—
but they are to be understood, *sour* before preparation, and *sweet* after."   [Said of man.]

"And following it is said, 'nothing is nearer to the fire than salt and his nature; nothing more lasting and fit to preserve things from putrefaction than salt and his nature.'

"Then, seeing that salt, even as *he* is, without other preparation, is of such virtue that it preserveth things from putrefaction, as we see by experience, what will it do, when the elements are separated from it, and it shall be reduced into a fifth essence? I think with myself that it shall be that, which our philosopher understandeth to be the *secret spirit*.

"But the philosopher saith, 'Salt is the *life of all things:*' and Morien saith, 'But this stone is not a vulgar stone, because it is more precious —without which nature worketh nothing at any time, and its name is One.'

"Therefore, whoso knoweth salt and his dissolution, knoweth the secret of the ancient wise men. Therefore set thy mind upon SALT. Think not upon other things. For in it only is hid the science, and the chief mystery, and the greatest secret of all the ancient philosophers."

*Thomas Norton* (1477) in his *Ordinal of Alchemy*, speaks of the *one thing* under the name of *magnesia*, and describes it by what he calls its *colors*, which, he tells us, may assist in enabling us to discover the "principal agent" (in the work of making the stone). He concludes what he says of colors by comparing *magnesia* to a *crystal*, which *appears* to have the color of any and every object over which it is placed ;—meaning to indicate that it is one thing seen seemingly under the varieties of all things. This is an illustration taken from the sense of sight. Norton goes through all of the senses in the same way, smelling, hearing, &c., as if they gave us notice of some *one thing* in fact, under infinite forms.

This one thing Swedenborg calls life, the life of the Lord.

*Sandivogius* describes the One thing under the name of nature, but takes care to tell us that the nature to which he refers is *invisible*, though she works, he says, visibly. He describes it as *one thing*, taking the form or character of the "place" where it is, and he illustrates it by saying: "Let there be set a vessel of water upon a smooth, even table, and be placed in the middle thereof; and round about it let there be laid divers things, and divers colors, also salt, and every one apart: then let the water be poured forth into the middle, and you shall see that water to run abroad here and there ; and when one stream is come to the red color, it is made red by it; if

to the salt, it takes from it the taste of the salt,
and so of the rest. For the water doth not
change the place, but the diversity of the place
changeth the water."

He says that "Nature is one, true, plain, perfect, and entire in its own being, which God
made from the beginning, placing his spirit in it:
but know (he continues) that the bounds of nature
is God himself, who is also the original of nature.
For it is certain, that every thing that is begun
ends nowhere but in that in which it begins.  I
say it is that only alone, by which God works all
things : not that God cannot work without it (for
truly he himself made nature, and is omnipotent),
but so it pleaseth him to do.  All things proceed
from this very nature alone; neither is there any
thing in the world without nature."

" *  *  *  Moreover, nature is not visible,
although she acts visibly : for it is a volatile
spirit, which executes its office in bodies, and is
placed and seated in the will and mind of God.
Nature in *this place* serves us for no other purpose but to understand her *places*, that is, to understand how to join one thing to another, according to nature.  *  *  The *place* of *nature*
is no other than, as I said before, what is in the
will of God," &c.

That which *Sandivogius* calls nature, expressly taking the word from under its common signification, saying, among other things, that it is invisible, is what Swedenborg intends by the word Life; but what I desire to say is that, either he did not precisely apprehend the sense of the alchemists, or his readers are in precisely that predicament with respect to himself; for who knows, from reading Swedenborg, what *life* is? If he had himself an idea of it, he has not been able to communicate it to others.

To show still further a probable source of Swedenborg's idea of *life*, and of its submitting, as it were, to the character of the *subject* in which it acts, or what he calls its *recipient*, I will recite an additional passage from the alchemist *Norton*, where he treats of what he calls the *concords*, which, as he says, are necessary in the *work* (of making the *stone*.)   But I will go so far as to say that the *places* referred to by Norton are different sorts of men, some of whom are adapted to the work, and others not,—no great mystery surely, when openly stated; for who does not know that men differ from each other in their capacity for goodness, truth, piety, &c. ?

" The Fourth Concord is full notable
Between this Arte and PLACES *convenable*,"

[For *places convenable*, let the reader understand *men suitable* for the work.]

> "Some places must needs be evermore dry,
> Close from air, no ways windy;"

[i. e. free from passions.]

> "Some must be dark and dim of sight,
> In which sun-beams none may light;"

[i. e. by sun-beams we may understand Reason, which scarcely finds entrance at all in some men whose " affections are dark as Erebus,—the motions of whose spirit are dull as night."]

> "But for some *Places*, the truth so is,
> They cannot have too much brightness:
> Some *Places* must needs be moist and cold
> For some works, as authors told;
> But in our Works in every place,
> Wind [passion] will hurt in every case:
> Therefore for every work in season,
> Ye must ordain *Places* by Reason.
> Philosophers said by their engine, [ingenuity, genius,]
> How it [the Stone] should be wrought within locks
>      nine:

[This *nine* refers to an old notion of the five senses and four virtues in man, (see Philo,) in whom the philosopher's work is perfected.]

> " *Astrologers* said it was a grace,
>     To find a chosen working Place ; "

[i. e. a *grace*, to find a man so perfect in body and mind, as to be a suitable subject to be carried forward into what the philosophers called a *plusquam* perfection.]

> " For many things will wonders do
>     In some Places and elsewhere not so,
>     But contrary wonders be of one thing
>     In contrary countries wrought without leasing ;
>         [lying,]
>     Whereof no other cause may appear,
>     But only contrary *Places* of the sphere :
>         *        *        *        *
>     Wherefore wise men which for this Art sought,
>     Found some Places [some men] concordant, some
>         Places nought ;
>     Truly such *Places* where Lechery is used
>     Must for this Art be utterly refused."

In *Ashmole's* Theatrum Chemicum Britannicum there are many passages which *seem* just enough to point to life as the *one thing*—to delude a hasty reader. The language is very antiquated, and would not be quoted for its beauty ; but a lover of truth does not rest upon mere words.

"Our Stone is made of one simple thing,
   That in Him hath both Soul and Life ;
   He is Two and One in kinde [*in nature,*]
   Married together as man and wife :
   Our Sulphur is our Masculine,
   Our Mercury is our Feminine,
   Our Earth is our Water clear ;
   Our Sulphur also is our Fire,
   And as Earth is in our Water clear,
   So is Air in our Fire.
   Now have ye elements four of might,
   And yet there appeareth but two of sight ;
   Water and Earth ye well may see,
   Fire and Air be in them as quality :
   This Science may not be taught to every one,
   He were accurst that should so done."   Page 352.

At page 381, in a conversation between Father and Son, the Father tells the Son, who asks where the "one thing doth grow"—

"In every place (Son) you shall him well find ;
By Taste and by Color thou shalt him well know ;
Fowls in the air with it do fly,
And Fishes do swim therewith in the sea :
With *Reason of Angels* you may it discern," &c.

In this passage I consider that the allusion to angels—the *Reason* of Angels—is precisely in Swedenborg's sense, to be explained hereafter.

The reader shall also see that the Hermetic writers had a secret language called *Lingua Angelorum.*

The following passage seems to set out with *verbal* accuracy Swedenborg's doctrine of the Lord, yet let the reader beware of supposing that mere words can teach this "selcouth thing."

"My beloved *Son* I command thee,
As thou wilt have my love and blessing,
That thou to God kneel on thy knee,
And to Him give laud and thanking,
For these gifts of grace given unto thee,
To have true knowledge of this worthy science,
That many men seek by land and sea,
Yet cannot find it for any expense:
I shall shew thee my *Son* here a hid secret,
Because thou art virtuous in thy living,
Of me else shouldst thou never it weet [*know*],
And for thou art wise in thy council keeping,
And therefore I charge thee on my blessing,
Not to shew it to any man living,
For it is the first principle of our blessed *stone,*
Through which our noble work is relieved;
Note well that I shew to thee my *Son,*
If *sulphur* be absent our work is deprived [*dead*];
Our *Sulphur,* my *Son,* is Water and Fire,
Constraineth the Body till it be dead;
Of them thou hast never thy desire,
Till *he* be blue as any Lead;

After all this he doth revive,
That in his Vessel before was dead;
I can no better in my reason contrive,
Than to figure him to the great God-head.
For as there died no more than one,
Howbeit that there be Persons Three,
The Father, the Son by might is One:
The Holy Ghost make our full Trinity:
A similitude like unto our *Stone*,
In Him are things Three which are concluded all in One;
Our *Sulphur* is likened to the Holy Ghost,
For He is Quick [living] called the Spirit of Life,
In His working of might he is most.
He raiseth onr Body from death to Life,
Many, my *Son*, with Him do rise,
The Holy gospel therein is expert,
The number my reason cannot contrive."    Page 383.

In *Salmon's* commentary on *Hermes* the *one* thing is affirmed in many ways, of which the following is an example:—

The matter of our *Stone* is but *one;* and therefore nothing can be more alien from the Art than to seek for it in many things; Nature is not mended or made better, but by a nature of its own kind.   As vinegar makes vinegar,—so our Art begins with mercury, and with the same mercury it is finished.   [Swedenborg's "Life."] It is a kind of *Proteus*, which, creeping upon the earth, assumes the nature of a serpent; but being immersed in water, it represents a fish; presently taking to itself wings, it ascends aloft, and flies like a bird; yet notwithstanding it is but one and the same *Mercury.*   *   *   *   Till you have pu-trified the matter [i. e. brought about a true hu-mility], you have not made one step in the true way; but that being done, you have accom-plished the first sign of the Art, as Hermes testifies.

The following additional passage from Swe-denborg will show the similarity of *idea* to which I refer—yet with a difference, for I am unwilling to allow that Swedenborg attained the *veritable* idea:—

"In regard to the *Life* of every one, whether man, or spirit, or angel, it flows in solely from the Lord, who is essential Life, and diffuses him-self through the universal heaven, and even through hell, consequently into every individual therein, and this in an incomprehensible order and series; but the Life which flows in is re-ceived by every one according to his prevailing principle; good and truth is received as good and truth by the good; whereas good and truth is received as evil and the false by the wicked,

and is even changed into evil and the false in
them. This is comparatively as the light of the
sun, which diffuses itself into all objects on the
face of the earth, but is received according to
the quality of each object, and becomes a beautiful color in beautiful forms, and of an ugly color
in ugly forms." Par. 2888, *Heavenly Arcana.*

Any number of passages like the above might
be recited from Swedenborg, *unifying* the whole
of life, so to say, and in that, as I believe, Swedenborg thought he saw the truth as the Hermetic writers saw it; but it is certain that he but
partially saw it; and making his partial vision a
ground of reasoning and philosophy, it was unavoidable that he should expand himself, as it
were, into inconsistencies, as he certainly has
done, notwithstanding his vast knowledge and
genius. He is at fault as to the nature of what
he calls the *recipient*, the *proprium*, and the *will*,
and conveys no clear knowledge of them, or of
what he calls Life either.

Swedenborg is not perfectly consistent with
himself,—not *absolutely* consequential. He says
at times that the *soul* makes its own *organ ;* and
then in other places, he speaks of the *organ* as the
recipient of life, as if it was something of itself;

then, again, he will refer all things to God, including the recipient : but, a page or so afterwards we come again perhaps upon the notion that the recipient in man is something itself, and while theoretically denying all independent reality to it, he calls it the *proprium*, the root of *self*, and, so far, he calls it altogether evil.  In short, Swedenborg does not appear to have clearly conceived the precise *unity*, so as to merge the *duality* ; and in this, as I suppose, he did not reach the Hermetic point of view of the *Stone*, the *one thing*.  He often speaks of the Lord as the One, the one life in all, and says he is in Heaven and in Hell also.  Then he says something similar of the *Grand-Man*, as a comprehensive word including all men, good and bad, that is, Humanity ; then he tells us, in other places, that those only are in the *Grand-Man* who are in love to the Lord and in charity towards the neighbor, these being in Heaven ; while those who are in the love of self and the love of the world, &c., are out of the Grand-Man, and are in Hell.  He tells us that Hell is from man, as is also Heaven ; that evil men are in Hell, and constitute it, and yet that evil comes from hell; and he so buries this *circle* of reasoning in words, that a hasty reader does not perceive that he is learning

nothing on the subject. He is even more wide
of all rational representation on the subject of
the *will*. Swedenborg sets forth the doctrine of
the omnipotence of the Lord as extending to all
things, including the human will, and yet contends strongly for the freedom of will in man.
On this subject the Swedish philosopher gives us
no light whatever, but is on a footing with the
most ordinary pretenders to philosophy among
us. God is all in all, and yet man has a free-
will; but how this is to be understood, Swedenborg does not explain. He tells us that man
must act "as if" he was free, but must *know* that
he can do nothing without God. In plain words,
he must endeavor to put something like a decep-
tion upon himself, and cheat himself into the belief of his freedom, knowing all the time that he
is nothing of himself, and must refer all power
to God.

The reader will find nowhere, as I believe, so
close an examination of the question of Being
and non-being—God and man—as in Plato's
Sophist, a model of a Hermetic work, where
Plato indicates *the Supreme* as the one true and
genuine *Sophist*, all others being imitations, some
nearer and others more remote, the nearest being
what he calls the " *scientific imitator ;* "—imita-

tor of what?—of the true invisible Sophist, who sometimes, as Plato says, " exhibits himself as the instrument of the thing" exhibited.

This opinion may strike most readers of Plato with surprise; but that I cannot help.

Plato, in the Sophist, beyond all question, has intimated his opinion that God may *appear in man;* and he was perhaps better prepared by his studies and contemplations, to acknowledge God in Christ, than any other man that ever lived, except the Apostles themselves.

# CHAPTER IV.

Swedenborg was not mad, nor was he under any peculiar hallucination. His doctrines are everywhere disclosed with the calmness of science, and there is no sign of enthusiasm in any part of them except in the form of earnestness in behalf of truth, or of what he considered as such. There is very little that can be regarded as controversial in his writings, and nothing of asperity, unless occasionally a word may show something of it, when referring to the Roman Catholic High-Priest, or to the particular tenet of the Athanasian creed which asserts a trinity of persons in the divine nature, Swedenborg contending for the unity of God, of one person, but of three essences, or three somethings which I will not undertake to define.

Among the many volumes written by Swedenborg, we have one work in English, entitled

*Heavenly Arcana,* extending to twelve volumes octavo, one object of which is to give the spiritual or internal sense of the books of Moses,—or of Genesis and Exodus, for the interpretation extends no farther.  He has written five large volumes upon the Apocalypse, and many other works in exposition of his doctrines and opinions.

The *principle* upon which the Heavenly Arcana, and many of Swedenborg's other works were written, is usually called that of *correspondence.*  It is stated, repeated, and enforced in many places throughout his writings;—most briefly perhaps, yet most formally, in the *True Christian Religion,* page 267, thus : *There is not any thing in the mind to which something in the body does not correspond : and this which corresponds may be called the embodying of that.*

It might require a volume to expound this principle,—to do it justice,—to show its foundation and explain its application : and then it might call for another volume to refute the doctrine, or show that, if true even, it is beyond the power of man to apply it to any use : and, when thus refuted, it would not stay refuted, but would again come to the surface in some form or other, and remain, as it will, a subject of controversy in the world to all time ;—the reason of which lies in the nature of man, as a compound being of *thought* and *body.*

I do not understand, myself, that a knowledge of this principle of correspondence was claimed by Swedenborg as a revelation in any special sense, but that the application of it, that is, the power to use it, grew up out of or under the influence of some special light from the "Lord," Swedenborg calling this influence *the opening of his internal sight.*

The *principle* of correspondence itself is supposed by many to be in Plato. The *spiritual world*, in Swedenborg's sense, seems very similar to what is understood by Plato's *intelligible world*, or world of *ideas*, as being the *types* or *patterns* of all material things in the universe, common articles of furniture included, " beds," &c.

This doctrine has had its advocates and its opposers ever since the days of Plato, and was no doubt the ground of the controversy which preceded Plato, and was characterized by him as a *giants' war.* In the middle ages the war was carried on under the names of realism and nominalism. It will be definitively settled when the nature of man shall be known, and it shall be understood in what sense he is a spiritual being, and in what sense he is a material being, and not before.

Professor Butler, late of the Dublin University, has left some lectures expounding the Platonic doctrine very fully, and with as much clearness perhaps as the subject admits.

The professor's namesake, the immortal author of Hudibras, has ridiculed the doctrine in the person of one of his types of man, of whom he says :—

> " Th' intelligible world he knew,
> And all men dream on't to be true,
> That in this world there's not a wart
> That has not there a counterpart ;
> Nor can there, on the face of ground,
> An individual beard be found
> That has not, in that foreign nation,
> A fellow of the self-same fashion ;
> So cut, so color'd, and so curl'd,
> As those are in the inferior world."

Ridicule is a powerful weapon, well calculated to drive away shallow pretenders to an art not understood, 'tis said, by one in a million ; whose truth nevertheless is affirmed and evidenced by all the tokens of sincerity that man can give, including the renunciation of fame and of wealth, and even by the sacrifice of life itself ;—though all this, it is admitted, can prove nothing but sincerity.   But to return to Swedenborg.

He refers to the doctrine of correspondence, distinctly, in his work on the Animal Kingdom (vol. i., p. 451), written before he came into the spiritual light; and if I mistake not, his Hieroglyphic Key, exhibiting many examples of the doctrine, was also among his earlier works.

In the application of the doctrine, I understand that Swedenborg's friends claim for him something like a special illumination, using this word as a sort of compromise expression, implying something very extraordinary and uncommon, but not precisely supernatural in the sense of the miraculous.

He tells us himself in the first pages of the Heavenly Arcana, that he will disclose something never before published.

But I expect to show that the *principle* of this doctrine of correspondence was known, and, to some extent applied, at least by implication, to the interpretation of the first part of Genesis, by the Alchemists or Hermetic Philosophers, before Swedenborg was born.

Without going into minute details with regard to the interpretations themselves, I will simply say that his principle declares, that the letter of the Mosaic record encloses a spiritual sense, which can by no means be gathered by a literal reading of those records; and, particularly, that the opening verses of Genesis are not to be understood as referring to the creation of the natural world, but to the re-creation, that is, to the regeneration of man.

The *process* of the regeneration of man, Swedenborg affirms, is signified in the first verses of the book of Genesis.

Those who wish to satisfy themselves, as to details or particulars, may consult the first pages of the Heavenly Arcana, where the doctrine of correspondence is stated and applied.

It is my purpose to show that the alchemists, the mystic seekers after the philosopher's stone, who were in fact spiritual philosophers chiefly busy about the new birth or the regeneration of man, virtually put the identical interpretation upon the opening verses of Genesis that Swedenborg did, though not with the direct purpose of interpreting the book of Genesis.

I desire to say, however, before proceeding any farther, that I do not undertake to decide upon the validity or the value of the interpretation. It is my vocation to bring to light a curious question, which I am sure is worthy the examination of considerate men, but every one must make a decision upon the question for himself.

*Thomas Vaughan,** under the name of *Eugenius Philalethe*, about the middle of the seventeenth century, published a number of works on Alchemy or Hermetic Philosophy, in nearly every one of which the author has something to say of the interpretation of Genesis, referring the reader to the spirit and not to the letter; that is, calling his attention away from the letter to the spirit. I find it difficult to select among many passages, those which may indicate in the least compass the principle to which I have referred as the basis of the doctrine of correspondence, but I will commence with a work entitled *Magia Adamica*, published in 1650. In this work there is a long discussion, the object of which is to prove that Moses was a natural *Magician*, by

---

* *Dean Swift* pronounced one work by Vaughan—*Anthroposophia Theomagica*—to be 'most intolerable fustian;' but this judgment is of little value, coming from a professed wit, whose disappointments in life, working on a selfish nature, drove him to ridicule, not the follies of men, but the very race itself; insomuch that, in most cases, whoever laughs at the Dean's wit is unconsciously laughing at himself. Swift had no idea of the class of writers to which *Vaughan* belonged, and from the very nature of his life, if we can rely upon the history we have of him, was necessarily shut out, "by a wonderful providence," from all knowledge of the Hermetic Art. Vaughan, however, is not classed among the *adepts*, and was set down as not having reached "the greater pyrotechny."

which was meant that he was by nature a *wise* man ;—a proper derivation from the ancient use of the word *magi;* and, further, to prove that he wrote of magic [wisdom] under a *veil;* and by magic *Vaughan* understood Alchemy or Hermetic Philosophy; that is, the Philosopher's Stone; the *Stone* being man, the object of the art being the perfection of man, as I have set forth in my Remarks on Alchemy and the Alchemists.

Philalethe affirms that in Genesis *Moses* "hath discovered many particulars [beyond what appears in the letter] and especially those secrets that have most relation to this [Hermetic or Alchemic] art. For instance, he hath discovered [that is, made known] the *Minera* of man, or that *substance* out of which *man,* and all his *fellow creatures* were made. This is the *First Matter* of the *Philosopher's Stone.* Moses sometimes calls it *water,* sometimes *earth;* for, in a certain place I read thus : And God said, *Let the waters bring forth abundantly the moving creature that hath life, and fowl that may fly above the earth in the open firmament.* But elsewhere we read otherwise, thus : *And out of the ground the Lord God formed every beast of the field, and every fowl of the air.* In this latter text we read that God made every *fowl* of the *air* out of the *ground;* but in the former it is written, that he made them out of the *water.* Certainly *Aristotle* and his syllogism can never reconcile these two places; but a little skill in magic [wisdom] will make them kiss, and be friends without a charm. This *substance* then (continues Philalethe) is both *earth* and *water,* yet neither of them in their common characteristics, but it is a *thick water* and a *subtle earth.* * * * The Philosophers call it *water* and *no water, earth* and *no earth:* and why may not Moses speak as they do? or why may they not write as Moses did? This is the true *Damascen earth,* out of which God made man." * * * * * "But this is not all that Moses hath written to this purpose; I could cite many more *magical* and *mystical* places; *but in so doing I should be too open;* wherefore I must forbear."

The author then undertakes to show something of what he calls the *practice* (of Moses) corresponding to the *art* of the philosophers in making what the Hermetic writers called *aurum potabile;* and then makes this important declaration :—

"If I should insist in this place on the *Mosaical Ceremonial Law,* with its several reverend *shadows,* and their *significations,* I might lose myself in a wilderness of mysteries, both divine and natural; for, verily, *that whole system is but one vast* SKREEN, *or a certain majestic umbrage drawn over two worlds visible and invisible.* But these are things of a higher speculation than the scope of our present discourse will admit of. I only inform the reader that the *Law* hath both a *shell* and a *kernel;* it is the *letter* that speaks, but the *spirit* interprets."

It must be recollected that the author was a Hermetic philosopher, and will tell us nothing openly. He, too, speaks through the letter, and leaves the reader to gather his meaning as he best can by the exercise of patience, judgment, candor, and ingenuity; or, it may be, with those who are blessed with it, by the help of the Spirit.

He proceeds next to show that the "manifest" part, that is, the *letter*, was intended for the general mass of men, "whose thoughts (says he) were fixed here below, [in the senses and upon sensuous blessings,] but the *hidden*, for the few only, whose minds aspired upwards to heavenly things."

It might fatigue the reader, or I could cite a dozen pages or more to show that the alchemists regarded the books of Moses as a *screen*, needing the *spirit* for an understanding of the "internal sense," as Swedenborg calls it; and that the opening verses do not refer to the natural or material world, but to the regeneration of man.

The reader has seen that *Vaughan* distinctly speaks of the writings of Moses as a *screen*.  Let us now see if we can discover what the Hermetic Philosophers thought was behind it.  But we must remember that we are dealing with Hermetic writers, who write "before and behind," "within and without."  They *suggest*, but rarely tell us any thing openly.  Their writings are full of obscurity, because it was thought that the common people could not endure the truth, or would misuse and abuse it.  But the common people of this age would have been uncommon people when Hermetic books were written.  The subject, I warn the reader, is of more real importance than any other one thing that can enter the mind of man.  But to proceed.

*Sandivogius* was an alchemist of perhaps as high repute as any of the seekers of the *mystic stone*, with a new name written upon it, "which no man knoweth saving he that receiveth it."  I cannot give the date of his works in Latin; but, a part of them appeared in English in 1650, and a second edition in 1674, with the title:—"A New Light on Alchemy, taken out of the Fountain of Nature and Manuel Experience: To which is added a Treatise on Sulphur."

In the "Address to the Reader," the translator takes the ground that Philosophy and Divinity are one and the same; in proof of which he says:—

"Can any deny that Hermes, Plato, and Aristotle, though pure naturalists, were not most deep divines? Do not all grant, that the two first chapters of Genesis are true divinity? I dare affirm that they are the most deep and the truest philosophy. Yes, they are the ground and sum of all divinity and philosophy: and if *rightly understood*, will teach thee more knowledge of God, and of thyself, than all the books in the world besides."

This particular writer says no more on this point; but we shall soon see to what that *understanding rightly* of Genesis refers, and that it is the regeneration of man, which is consummated when the fiat of the Eternal sends "light" into the soul of man. The reader will please observe and remember the vast importance attached by the alchemist to the two first chapters of Genesis, when *rightly understood*.

The next work on alchemy to which I will refer, has so remarkable a title that I will copy it entire, desiring the reader to notice the claim to *inspiration* therein set up, by the publisher, not by the writer, by which it may be seen that Swedenborg had a forerunner on this point. The Swedish mystic (?) had predecessors in his own peculiar walk. The title runs :—

"*Secrets Revealed : Or, an Open Entrance to the Shut Palace of the King. Containing the greatest Treasure in Chymistry* [Alchemy] *never yet so plainly discovered* [made known]. *Composed by a most famous Englishman, styling himself* Anonymus, *or Eyræneus Philaletha Cosmopolita : who, by* Inspiration *and Reading, attained to the Philosopher's Stone at the age of twenty-three years*, Anno Domini, 1645."

This work was published in 1659; and the 5th chapter opens as follows :—

"Let the Son of the Philosophers hearken to the *Sophi* unanimously concluding, that this *Work* [that is, the work of making the Philosopher's Stone] is to be likened to the creation of the universe. Therefore, *In the beginning God created the Heaven and the Earth, and the Earth was void and empty, and darkness was upon the face of the deep ; and the Spirit of the Lord was carried upon the face of the waters, and God said, Let there be Light, and there was Light.*

"These words (says this author) are sufficient for a Son of Art, for the Heaven ought to be conjoined with the Earth upon a bed of friendship and love," &c.  In the conclusion of the chapter the author exclaims, in the language of Holy writ, "Good God!  How wonderful are thy works!  'Tis thy doing, and it seems miraculous in our eyes.  Father, I thank thee, that thou hast hidden these things from the wise, and revealed them to babes."

What can the reader understand by this language, but that the writer had been the subject of some extraordinary experience; and to what can it be referred with so much probability as to that known in Scripture usually under the name of the new birth; that is, the regeneration of man?  And yet the *work* is illustrated by a direct reference to the first verses of Genesis, which another alchemist tells us will teach us, *if rightly understood*, more than all the books in the world besides.  Let the language of Eyræneus be considered also in connection with the declaration of Vaughan, that the books of Moses have both a shell and a kernel, and that the *letter* of the Pentateuch is one vast screen drawn over two worlds, visible and invisible:—what must then be inferred?  To answer this truly, one may perhaps need to find, first, the Philosopher's Stone.

Here is another passage, and I take it from Espagnet's "*Arcanum, or, the grand Secret of Hermetic Philosophy, wherein the Secrets of Nature and Art, concerning the matter and manner of making the Philosopher's composition, are orderly and methodically manifested.*" (1650.)

"The generation of our Stone (says this writer) is made after the pattern of the creation of the world; [let the reader consider that it is *man*, passing through the process of regeneration :— from a chaotic state of darkness, ignorance, and passion, to a state of light, knowledge, and freedom, under the teaching and guidance of nature and God,] for it is necessary (says *Espagnet*) that it have its chaos and first matter, wherein the confused elements do fluctuate, until they be separated by the fiery spirit : they being separated, the light elements are carried upwards, and the heavy downwards.  The Light [knowledge] arising, the Darkness [ignorance] recedes. The waters are gathered into one, and the dry land appears.  At length the two great luminaries arise, and mineral virtues, vegetable and animal, are produced in the Philosopher's Earth." That is, in the Man, who is the subject of this regeneration, for this is the "earth which is no earth, and water which is no water,"—the most wonderful product of the universe.

The above passage, it is true, simply compares the *work* to that of Genesis; but this mode of writing is very common with the Hermetic philosophers. They often *compare* the *Stone* to *man*, saying that, like man, their *Stone* has a body, a soul, and a spirit; meaning thereby that the attentive reader shall understand that the *subject* of the *work* is man. Occasionally some of the writers express themselves quite openly, but in such a manner that they appear to be indulging in a digression, leaving the subject of the Stone aside.

They attribute a trinity to man, and in this also Swedenborg is in harmony with them, for he describes man as having a natural, a spiritual, and a celestial nature,—sometimes called outward, inward, and inmost,—which, he says, are successively " opened " in man, under certain conditions. To have the *inmost* " opened " is to be in the celestial state, where *principles* and eternal truths are contemplated, and facts are seen in their principles, out of relation to either time or place. This places a man in what Swedenborg calls the third heaven, and constitutes him an angel. Here he disputes with no one [see paragraph 270, Heaven and Hell]: all is light and truth, and the individual in this state constitutes "a heaven in its least form."  A society of such men is heaven in a larger form, while the whole race, or mankind, if it could come into this state, would constitute the universal heaven, where all would "appear as one man before the LORD," who is the Divine Humanity of God, the WORD, the Eternal Truth, the Life.

I am speaking only of what I understand to be the theory of Swedenborg, and in the most general manner.  His principal works may be easily had by those who desire to become acquainted with his system more in detail.

I find still another reference to the books of Moses in Espagnet, on this point, which I will copy.  The writer brings into requisition for Hermetic illustration, in addition to Genesis, a few verses from Deuteronomy, and I will not curtail the passage, though a part of it is a repetition of what has been already recited.

"Some have sought (says Espagnet) for the latent philosophical *earth* by calcination, others by sublimation; many among glazed vessels, and some few in vitriol and salt, even as among their natural vessels: others enjoin that it be sublimed out of lime and glass.

"*But we have learned of the Prophet that:—* ' *In the beginning God created the heaven and the earth; and the earth was without form and void, and darkness was upon the face of the deep: and the Spirit of God moved upon the waters; and God said, Let there be light, and there was light; and God saw the light, that it was good, and he divided the light from the darkness,*' &c.

"And Joseph's blessing, spoken of by the same prophet, will be sufficient for a wise man (Deut. 33):—

"' *Blessed of the Lord be his* LAND, *for the* APPLES *of heaven, for the* DEW, *and for the* DEEP *that lieth beneath; for the apples of fruit both of* SUN *and* MOON; *for the top of the ancient mountains; for the* APPLES *of the everlasting hills,*'" &c.

Upon which Espagnet says: "Pray the Lord from the bottom of thy soul, my son, that he would bestow upon thee a portion of this blessed *Land.*"

By *land*, here spoken of, Espagnet evidently supposes was meant what in the sixth chapter of Secrets Revealed is called—"the waters enclosed within, which do shun our sight, and yet really and truly are. These are those waters (says Espagnet) that the author of the *New Light* speaks of, to wit, which are, and do not appear until the

*Artist* pleaseth." This ARTIST (of man) is again referred to in the same chapter, in which the work of regeneration is still spoken of figuratively. Thus :—" Let *Diana* be propitious unto thee, who knows how to tame the wild beasts [the wild passions] ; whose two doves [the so-called two luminaries] shall temperate the malignity of the air with their feathers ; then the youth [the philosophical child] enters easily in through the pores, presently shaking the waters above, and stirs up a ruddy and rubish cloud :—Do thou bring in the water over him even to the brightness of the moon, and so the darkness which was upon the face of the abyss [the unregenerate man] will be discussed by the spirit which moves itself in the waters [the same man] : thus by the command of God [the sole ARTIST in this spiritual work] light shall appear : separate the light from the darkness the seventh time, and then this sophic [wise] creating of thy Mercury [thyself] shall be complete, and the seventh day shall be to thee a Sabbath of rest."

This may all appear very mystical, and, taken literally, no doubt it is so : but to the considerate reader it may indicate the point I am endeavoring to establish ;—that the Hermetic philosophers interpreted the writings of Moses, I mean, the opening verses of Genesis, as symbolical of the regeneration of man, which Swedenborg, in violation of the Hermetic law of secrecy, has openly asserted as his own understanding of those writings.

# CHAPTER V.

To show that I do not speak at random in comparing Swedenborg's doctrines to those of the Alchemists, with respect to the three natures in man, I will refer here to a work by Philalethe, entitled *Anthroposophia Theomagica* (published in 1650), page 38, where the author says :—

" As the great world consists of three parts, the *elemental*, the *cœlestial*, and the *spiritual*, above all which God himself is seated in that infinite inaccessible *light*, which streams from his own nature ; even so Man hath in him his *earthly* elemental parts, together with the *cœlestial* and *angelical natures*, in the centre of which moves and shines the *Divine Spirit*."

No one need look far into Swedenborg's writings without finding the above doctrine, only slightly varied perhaps in the phraseology used in stating it.   For example :—

"There are three principles in man, which

concur and unite together,—the natural, the spiritual, and the celestial. The natural principle never receives any life except from the spiritual, nor the spiritual but from the celestial, nor the celestial unless from the Lord alone, who is Life itself."—*Heavenly Arcana, par.* 880.

This is sufficiently clear for my purpose, and perhaps I ought not to oppress the reader with long extracts in further illustration of this doctrine and its application. Swedenborg changes, indeed, the terms employed and the order of them, but the meaning is changed with them, maintaining the same sense, or nonsense, if the reader chooses, though there appears to be some sense in this view of a very abstruse and mysterious subject. I would have the reader notice the use of the word *angelical* by the alchemist, corresponding to Swedenborg's use of the word *celestial*, as the third state or nature of man ; because Swedenborg himself, as I have already stated, speaks of man as an *angel* when in this third state, or when his "interior sense" is "opened to the third degree." This can hardly be called an accidental coincidence.

Hermetic writers constantly refer to the doctrine of the Trinity in unity, while treating of their STONE, but they wrote so obscurely that they overshot themselves; for while intending by this obscurity only to withdraw their books from the merely ignorant and from the profane, they have for the most part closed them from the learned and from the well disposed also. They never speak of the *Stone* as MAN, directly; but they often compare it to man, meaning that the attentive reader shall understand that man is the real subject. The following passage from " Ripley Revived " (1678) will show what I here refer to :--

" Our STONE is likened to MAN, who although he have a wife different from him in sex, yet she is one with him in nature; and in this sense man is called the *microcosm*, or less-world : for indeed, next to man, who is the image of God, the Stone is the true little system of the great world. * *

" This STONE is also called *Trine*, or *Trinity in unity*, from the homogeneity of the matter :—as Trevison saith: Our STONE is made of one root, that is, of two Mercurial Substances, &c. This *Trinity* is discerned in the components; for first there is the Body, which is *Sol;* and the water of *Mercury ;* in which, besides its mercuriality, there is a spiritual seed of *Sulphur*, which is the *Secret Fire*. This is the *Trinity*, and these

are called the *Body*, the *Soul*, and the *Spirit:*
the Body is the dead Earth, which increaseth not
without the celestial virtue; the Spirit is the
Soul of our Air or Chamelion, which is also of a
two-fold composure, yet made one inseparably;
the Soul is the Bond of *Mercury*, without which
our *Fire* never appears, nor can appear, for it is
naked."   *   *   *   *   "Thus is the *Trinity*
proportionable, to wit, three natures in the first
mixture.   The Work is carried to perfection according to the virtue of a Body, Soul, and Spirit:
for the *Body* would never be penetrable, were it
not for the *Spirit*, nor would the *Spirit* be permanent in its super-perfect *Tincture*, were it not
for the Body; nor could these two act one upon
another without the Soul, for the *Spirit* is an *invisible thing*, nor doth it ever appear without
another GARMENT, which garment is the SOUL."

I might insist here, and illustrate at length,
that this GARMENT (in alchemy) is what is understood in Swedenborg to be the *Spiritual Body*
of MAN, the true MAN.   In the natural man, so
called, this soul is supposed to be chaotic, and it
needs to be touched by the *Spirit;* which nevertheless it bears within itself, as yet unknown to
itself, and it remains unknown until the " Artist,"

God, pleaseth. And here the text is often repeated, the wind bloweth as it listeth, &c.

With respect to this *garment*, I will adduce another passage in which it is still more plainly indicated—from the same writer,—remarking, by the way, that it was the notion of the *Spiritual Body* as represented by Swedenborg, that first attracted the attention of a learned professor in New York, who published a volume on the subject announcing himself a Swedenborgian.

"Thus (says *Cosmopolita*), thy Work is brought to the true Touch-stone, and that is Trinity in Unity; for in this *pondus* of your *Mercury* [yourself, reader,—for the subject is man] you have a potential Body [Swedenborg's Spiritual Body], which is one part of three of the *Mercury* [of the man] which may by Art be made to appear. [This Art they call divine.] This potential Body is to be reckoned to your actual Body, and that makes with it two ; and so, *in potentia*, you have two of the Body to one of the Spirit, which is three to three, and one to one. And this potential Body is at first spiritual and volatile, *in manifesto*, for the unity sake ; for without it there could be no unity. Thus then a potential Body but an actual Spirit, is joined with an actual Body, by which means the actual Body, when it is actually dissolved and made no Body, but a Spirit or Spiritual Body, this potential Spiritual Body, which was in the water before, receives this potentialized Body, and both unite and congeal together, and is endowed with a double nature and virtue, that is, Spiritual and Corporeal, Heavenly and Earthly. And thus is made an union of which the proportion of the water in its first preparation, and its due mixing with its Body, was the moving cause, really though hiddenly enforcing the compound by the necessity of its end, which it could not have done had it not been so proportioned."

The reader may decry this subject as much as he pleases, and may ridicule the idea that the alchemists were religious philosophers; but whoever will take the pains to look into their mystical writings may easily see their true subject, and with some patient study may learn something of their arcane opinions; and then he cannot fail to see, if acquainted with Swedenborg's writings, that the Swedish Philosopher trod in the footsteps of *Philaletha Cosmopolita*, and others of the mystic Stone seekers.

Swedenborg says that the end (object, aim, or

purpose) of the Lord, is a universal heaven *through* man; that the angels of heaven were all once men; that Heaven is constituted or composed of men in the angelic or celestial state.

This doctrine is abundantly found in Hermetic books, though, as the writers express themselves obscurely, it requires some acquaintance with their manner of writing to perceive their purpose; but I may possibly make it appear to the attentive reader.

There is scarcely any one principle or dogma more frequently referred to in Hermetic works than one to be found in what is called the *Smaragdine Table*, attributed to HERMES,—a work comprised in about a page of ordinary printing, written by nobody knows who, and nobody knows when, to wit:

" *That which is above is as that which is beneath, and that which is beneath is as that which is above, to work the miracles of one thing.*"

This principle is, in truth, the very root of Swedenborg's doctrine of *correspondence*, and shows also its connection with his doctrine of the LORD; for the "above" and the "beneath," are the spiritual and natural worlds of Swedenborg; and the "one thing" is the LORD, the Life of the two worlds.   In Swedenborg's language the

*Lord* is the *End*, the *spiritual* world the *Cause*, and the *natural* world is the *Effect;* yet the *Effect* contains the *Cause*, and both express the Life. Call these *Salt*, *Sulphur*, and *Mercury*, and we shall express the same thing in alchemic language. The natural world, so called, meaning the visible, is a world of effects, and symbolizes or "corresponds" to the spiritual world, and would be nothing without it, as the spiritual, in its turn, would be nothing without the Life, the "one thing" in all.

It is common in the world, as I know very well, that a doctrine obscurely stated is for that very reason imagined to enclose extraordinary *arcana* of undefined and inexpressible importance,—a remark I think proper to make that the reader, if necessary, may be put on his guard against trusting his imagination in the interpretation of mysteries.

I would have no one accept any interpretation that shall not appear rational. It is much better to forbear making an interpretation altogether than to devise a merely fanciful and fictitious one, under a vague notion that we are obliged to understand every thing, for there are many things that we cannot understand at all. No temporary convenience or imaginary satisfaction can compensate for adopting an error as the substantial truth.

This doctrine or dogma of Hermes appears in many forms in the Hermetic writings. In one form it reads, translated from the Coptic, as alleged :

> "Heaven above, Heaven beneath ;
> Stars above, Stars beneath ;
> All that is above is also beneath :
> Understand this and be happy."

In commenting upon these dark hints, Philalethe says :—

"To speak plainly, Heaven itself was originally extracted from *Inferiors* [out of man, says Swedenborg], yet not so entirely, but that some portion of the Heavenly natures remained still below and are the very same in essence and substance with the separated stars and skies. Heaven here below differs not from that above but in her captivity, and that above differs not from this below but in her liberty. The one is imprisoned in matter, the other is freed from the grossness and impurities of it ; but they are both of one and the same nature, so that they easily unite ; and hence it is that the Superior descends to the Inferior to visit and comfort her in this sickly infectious habitation."

This descent of the superior to the inferior, the reader can hardly fail to perceive, does not refer to the physical stars, visible in the heavens. He will come nearer to the true design of the writer by considering Swedenborg's point of view, by which man is placed, as it were, in the *middle*, between two extremes of nature and spirit, communicating with both :—with the natural world by or through his sensuous nature (the " outward "), and with the celestial world by his " inmost " nature.  By *stars* is simply figured the *principles* of the superior, that is, the spiritual world.  The Hermetic writers often refer to the lovers of their art, as seekers after *stellar* secrets, —meaning heavenly secrets;—simply the more unseen and divine portions of the nature of man.

The correspondence of superiors with inferiors is referred to, precisely in Swedenborg's sense, by Philalethe in *Lumen de Lumine* in these words : " There is not an herb here below, but he hath a star [that is, a *spiritual* principle] in Heaven above."  But, by *above*, is meant *inward*.

In the so called spiritual world, *inward* and *outward* answers to what is called, in the natural world, above and below.  And as the inward world has its central principle, it is called a sun, by ' similitude ' to the visible sun as the principal object of control in the natural world. Yet the student would make a great mistake in imagining that this is any thing but a similitude; for these writers, I mean Hermetic writers, Swedenborg included, are any thing but materialists.

In Swedenborg's view, man, as he is sensuous, or according to his sensitive nature, is the natural man in St. Paul's sense, and is in the lower or outer world: as he is intellectual, he is in the second heaven; as he is celestial (*angelical*, as the alchemist would say), he is in the third heaven, that is, the superior or inmost world,—even here in the body;—for this is the doctrine; but in every case, according to the Divine Laws of "order," which under no circumstances are ever violated, as they have their existence in the unchangeable nature of God.

I state this as my understanding of Swedenborg's theory, and so far as words can express any thing upon so difficult a subject, the theory may be substantially found in the Hermetic writings: the difference being that Swedenborg undertook to develop the doctrine more fully and to write more openly than any genuine Hermetic philosopher has ever felt at liberty to do, though Swedenborg himself has exhibited his opinions under a veil.

Notwithstanding the obscurity of these mystic writers, they contrive to suggest indirectly their subject.    They discuss at large the properties of the *magnet,* and then show what they intend by comparing the magnet to man.    Thus says one :

"I may well presume to compare the *loadstone* in disposition with MAN, considering the admirable virtues and dignity of the one in the animal kingdom ; and the miraculous operations and mystical properties of the other in the mineral region.    As for MAN, there is such a supereminent and wonderful treasure hidden in him, that wise men have esteemed that the perfect wisdom of this world consisteth in the knowledge of a man's self, namely, to find out that secret mystery which doth lurk within him."    [Let this *treasure* and this *mystery* be supposed to be the "one thing" referred to by *Hermes* in the *Smaragdine Table,* or the life of the Lord, as expressed by Swedenborg, as something really in, but yet to be discovered by the so-called natural man, and the importance of the subject will be sufficiently appreciated.    But to resume.]    "For *man* (says my author) is said to be the centre of every creature, and for that cause he is called *microcosmus,* or the little world ; *centrum et miraculum mundi, the centre or miracle of the world*, containing in himself the properties of all creatures, as well celestial as terrestrial, and consequently of the *load-stone.*"   [This is the author's mode of telling his readers that what he says of the load-stone is to be applied to MAN.]   " Man is (continues this writer) *Templum Dei, the Temple of God; Corpus Christi, the Body of Christ; Habitaculum Spiritus Sancti, the Habitation of the Holy Ghost*, as the apostle hath taught us. Neither verily may it be imagined, that God would make choice of an unworthy dwelling-place.   And therefore, in the consideration thereof, and our inquiry after so great a mystery, we have need to proceed with our exactest discretion and judgment, from the visible things of man to the invisible, that is, to penetrate with the sharpest edge of our wit by demonstration, *à posteriori ;* or from the external man, into the bowels of his secret, mystical and internal being; wherefore we proceed thus: Seeing that MAN is rightly reported by *Hermes* to be the son of the world, as the world is the Son of God, being that it is framed after the image of the Archetype, for which cause he is termed the Little World, it will be requisite to understand that he is in like manner *divided into a heaven and earth*, as the great world was, and consequently containeth in itself no otherwise his heavens, circles, poles, and stars, than the great world doth. And also, as we find that the spiritual image of the heavens, with their circles and poles, are delineated also in the earth, and every particular thereof, as it appeareth in the *load-stone and iron*, so the character of the inward man is deciphered and portrayed out in the outward man, no otherwise than we may judge of the fashion of the kernel by the shell."

This writer then proceeds to place the true *pole* of man in the *east*, where Swedenborg also placed the *true north* in what he called the spiritual world. This *pole* of man is the " one thing," the *Lord*, the *life*,—the discovery of which in himself Swedenborg called *the opening of his internal sight*, and thence, in Hermetic language, he wrote of *heaven* and of *earth* in the sense of the above writer, without going out of himself, and his writings will never be properly understood except from this point of view.

This same writer expresses the very principle of Swedenborg, as follows: " There is nothing in the lower world, but hath his like in the starry world [meaning the spiritual world], whose beams and influences it receiveth."

I must now be so candid as to say that this writer is no other than the much-abused *Robert*

*Fludd,* the *too open* Hermetic author of a work, the express aim of which was to prove that the Mosaical History was "*grounded upon the Essential Truth or Eternal Sapience,*" published in 1659. The people of his day were not satisfied that he should believe in Moses, but required him to believe in Moses as they did, and upon their grounds, and would not allow him to point out what he deemed much higher and surer grounds, such as might allow a man, "while giving honor, to retain his own honor." Swedenborg is still more *open,* but he addressed what he considered more enlightened times ; but he too is a Hermetic philosopher nevertheless.

No genuine Hermetic writer has ever hoped to make that clear to the ordinary and unassisted understanding of man, which is, as they assert, the express work of the Spirit of God upon the heart of man, by which (as the phrase is) he becomes a "new creature." They have the authority of St. Paul for this ; but I may as well state at once that *conversion,* in the sense of the Hermetic philosophers, is a rare spectacle in the world, and is not usually a product of camp-meeting excitements ; but I should be too bold if I undertook to define it. The nature of the operation carries with it what the Hermetic writers call the *Secretum Artis*, the incommunicable secret: on which point I will cite one or two passages from Hermetic books.

These writers say that there are three principal stages or steps in the progress of man towards the perfection of his nature. In the *two* first, man works or may work co-ordinately with nature; that is, in the development of his sensuous and of his intellectual nature: but "in the third God works alone," and man can only be a recipient observer. The third and last step man is not supposed to take by any known natural power proper to him as an individual; but he is a passive recipient from a power above him, when in a proper state for "reception." This state or condition, suitable for reception, does not exist so long as man is devoted to things of time, and in love, not with God, but with the created things of God. "The world does not know me," says the personified *principle* in one of the Hermetic books, "because it loves not *me*, but *mine*."

It is a common doctrine: it is preached every sabbath throughout christendom, to numberless inattentive and heedless hearers, who are said to be heedless because they are of the world, and love the things of time before the things of eternity. One main difference between the ordinary teaching and that of the Hermetic philosophers is, that the latter make no direct attempt to exercise the prerogative of God. They say that the "third state" cannot be taught, as ordinary knowledge is taught; and, acting consistently with this doctrine, they do not aim directly to teach it; neither do they allow that that *state* itself is subject to the ordinary reason of man, who, without the *Light* they speak of, is wanting in the very grounds of an argument on the subject.

" Certainly (says Philalethe) I cannot yet conceive how reason may judge those principles, *quorum veritas pendet à sola revelantis authoritate*, whose certainty wholly depend on God, and by consequence is indemonstrable without the Spirit of God. But if I should grant that, which I will ever deny, verily, I shall still say, that a *true faith* consists not in reason, but in *love ;* for I receive my principles, and believe them being received, *sola erga Revelantem amore,* only out of my affection to Him that reveals them. Thus, our Saviour would have the Jews to believe him first *for his own sake,* and, when that failed, for his works' sake ; but some divines believe, only for Aristotle's sake: if logic renders the tenet probable, then it is creed ; if not, 'tis Alcoran." *

* For celestial angels do not know what faith is except it be

By *reason*, in this passage, I understand, the *process* of reasoning, which, simply, cannot create its own *data*.  Reasoning may be ever so accurate, considered as a *process*, yet if its basis or foundation be not firm,—and this the *process* of reasoning cannot give—the reasoning itself is but a castle in the air.  The point is, that there is something in man, truly, the divine in man—which nevertheless needs development—which is not *reasoning*, but the principle of Reason itself; most commonly called *faith*, yet something quite different from belief.

Now this *faith*, which is so necessary to man, which translates him into the so-called celestial (or angelical state), which *transmutes* his soul and transports him out of the lower world into a higher region, as the doctrine alleges, and which cannot be attained by the unassisted will of the natural man, is the *incommunicable secret* to which Philalethe refers in the following passage, to wit ;—after indicating darkly and obscurely the external and internal means deemed to be necessary for placing a man in the right position for receiving a blessing from above, he proceeds :

of love ; and the universal heaven is of love, no other life being existent in heaven but the life of love.—Heavenly Arcana, § 32.

"There is nothing now behind but that which the Philosophers call *Secretum Artis:* a thing that was never *published*, and without which you will *never perform*, though you know both *Fire* and *Matter*."

Speaking of the failures of Flammel and others, for the want of this *secret*, the author brings in an adept as saying of his own labors and studies, that, "after the sixth year, I was entrusted with the *Key of Power* by secret *Revelation* from the Almighty God. This *Key of Power* was never put to paper by any Philosopher whatever."

The object of the Hermetic writers in these obscure allusions and insinuations is to throw the reader off from a dependence upon mere outward teaching for a knowledge which is only acquired through, as they say, the alone Spirit of God, touching, as by a divine fire, the heart of man. Hence the designation of some of these writers as "Philosophers by Fire," as others are said to have been "baptized by Fire."

The same thing is referred to in the following passage :

"But that we may come at last to the scope proposed : God the Father is the metaphysical, supercelestial *Sun :* The Second Person is the

*Light;* and the *Third* is *Amor Igneus,* or a *Divine Heat* proceeding from both.  Now, without the presence of this *Heat,* there is no *reception* of the *Light,* and by consequence no influx from the *Father of Light.*"

This sounds so much like Swedenborg, who has so much to say of a *Sun* of the spiritual world, and of light, heat, influx and reception, that I think it necessary to say that I am reciting this passage from the Alchemist Philalethe, and not from the Swedish Philosopher: and will proceed with the extract:

" For this *Amor* (says Philalethe) is the *medium* which *unites* the *Lover* to that which is *beloved,* and probably 'tis the Platonic's *Dæmon Magnus, qui conjungit nos spiritum præfecturis.* I could speak much more of the offices of this *Loving Spirit* [Does not John say that God is Love?], but these are *Magnalia Dei, et Naturæ,* and require not our discussion, so much as our reverence.  Here also I might speak of that *Supernatural generation,* whereof Trismegistus : *Monas gignit Monaden, et in se suum reflectit Ardorem.* But I leave this to the Almighty God as his own essential mystery."

Surely these mystic Philosophical Stone seekers have been strangely ignored or misunderstood in the world; but sure I am also that, in their day, they were despised and condemned only by the "younger sort," or by the worldly minded who needed a caution, to be found in the 10th Book of Plato's Laws.

That which the Hermetic Philosophers call the *Secretum Artis*, or the incommunicable secret,—the essential mystery of God, Swedenborg called *the opening of his internal sight*, but without the smallest attempt at explanation.

If what is thus far adduced fails to indicate the class to which the Swede belonged, I should be much disposed to say, that none are so blind as those who will not see. Yet I by no means intend to say that Swedenborg drew his doctrines entirely from the Hermetic Philosophers. Every student, to some extent, depends necessarily upon the labors and studies of his predecessors, and is in some degree bound to consult them and profit by them; but the labors of fallible men do not carry their own key with them. That must be found elsewhere, or we read blindfolded.

There is a coincidence between Swedenborg and the Alchemists, which many may think merely accidental and unimportant; but I will point it out, since I am upon the subject.

Swedenborg wrote a work entitled, " Outlines

of a Philosophical Argument on the Infinite," in which he speaks of the *infinite* and the *finite* as so opposed to each other in their nature, that they can by no possibility unite, but by means of a third something, which he calls a "*Nexus.*"   By this theory he thus prepares himself to receive the doctrine of the Divine-human, the God-man, that is, Jesus Christ, as that *nexus*, or means, in short, of uniting God and man.

It is unnecessary to state this more in detail, as the work of Swedenborg may easily be had and consulted by those who choose.

In a Hermetic volume by *Cambachius*, entitled *Sal, Lumen et Spiritus Mundi Philosophici: or, the Dawning of the Day*, &c., published in English in 1657, the author commences the second chapter thus :

"The body of the world lies open to our senses, but its spirit lies hid ; and in the spirit its soul, which cannot be united to its body, but by the mediation of its spirit ; for the body is gross, but the soul is subtle, far removed from all corporeal qualities.   For the union of these two, we must find some *third*, participating in both natures, which must be, as it were, a corporeal spirit, because the extremes cannot be conjoined without an intervenient ligament, that hath affinity with both. The heaven, we see, is high, the earth low ; the one pure, the other corrupt : how then shall we exalt this impure corruption, and conjoin it with that active purity without a mean? God, we know, is infinitely pure and clean ; man extremely impure, and defiled with sins. Now these could never have been conjoined and reconciled, but by the mediation of Christ Jesus God-man, that true attractive glue of both na·tures," &c.

In the statement of the doctrine, the alchemist may seem to have the advantage, by avoiding the express use of the word *finite* in reference to man ; and Swedenborg might be asked how, upon his theory, his *Nexus*, if either infinite or finite, can instrumentally unite the two extremes, absolutely opposed to each other in their natures, by supposition. For if the Nexus be finite, it cannot unite with the infinite, and if infinite, it cannot unite with the finite, and would thus fail to answer the demand of the theory.

With the terms Spirit and Body, the difficulty does not appear to be so great, while we have, in fact, a palpable instance of their union as we suppose in *Man*, bespeaking therefore the theoretic possibility of a god-man,—called the Lord throughout Swedenborg's writings.

I will here add one or two minor points, to establish a connection between Swedenborg and the alchemists, drawn, I admit, from bare allusions, which however are to my mind very decided, to wit:

In Swedenborg's Angelic Wisdom concerning Divine Providence, I find the following paragraph:

"36. The wisdom which comes to perception, is the perception of truth from the love of it, especially the love of spiritual truth; for there is civil truth, moral truth, and spiritual truth: those who are in the perception of spiritual truth from the love of it, are also in the perception of moral and civil truth; for the love of spiritual truth is the soul of the latter. I have sometimes spoken with the angels concerning wisdom, who said that wisdom is conjunction with the Lord, because the Lord is wisdom itself; and that he comes into that conjunction who rejects hell from himself, and so far into it as he rejects: they said that they represent wisdom to themselves as a magnificent and most highly furnished *Palace*, into which one ascends by *Twelve Steps;* and that no one comes to the first step, except from the Lord by conjunction with Him; and that every one ascends according to conjunction;

5*

and that as he ascends he perceives that no one is wise from himself, but from the Lord; also that the things upon which he is wise, compared with the things upon which he is not wise, are as a few drops to a great lake. By the *twelve steps* to the *Palace of Wisdom* are signified goods conjoined to truths, and truths conjoined to goods."

Before pointing out to what the allusions in the above paragraph refer, I think it necessary to say, that Swedenborg considered man, as to his internal nature or spirit, as in the spiritual world, his outward nature or form being in the natural world, and hence man is said to be in the spiritual world, not figuratively but literally. In keeping with this, I read in Philalethe:

"I look upon this life as the progress of an *Essence Royal:* The soul but quits her court to see the country. *Heaven hath in it a scene of Earth;* and had she been contented with ideas, she had not travelled beyond the *map.* But *excellent patterns* commend their *mimes. Nature* that was *so fair* in the *type,* could not be a *slut* in the *anaglyph.* This makes her *ramble* hither to examine the *medal* by the *flask,* but while she *scans* their *symmetry,* she *forms* it. [The reader is requested to remember here, that Swedenborg speaks of the body as an organ of and *formed by* the soul.]  Thus (continues Philalethe) her descent speaks her *original :*  God in love with His own beauty frames a *glass* to view it by *reflection ;* but the *frailty* of the matter excluding *eternity*, the *composure* was subject to *dissolution*.  Ignorance gave this release the name of *death*, but properly it is the *soul's birth*, and a charter that makes for her *liberty :*  She hath several ways to break up house, but her best is without a disease.  This is her *mystical walk*, an *exit* only to return."

Upon this view it is, that man is said to be, by Swedenborg, or according to his doctrine, in Heaven or in Hell, or between these as two extremes, *as to his spirit*, and according to the state of his spirit.  Heaven and Hell, in Swedenborg's sense, are not places but states; that is, states of the spirit of the man who is the *subject*, of whom Heaven and Hell are predicated; Heaven and Hell, in fact, having no existence but in relation to man.

Now, all the *ideas* a man may have are said to be in the spiritual world; or, it may be said, that he who understands the truth of his own nature, knows that *by*, or *through*, or *in* his ideas he is in communication with, or rather is in, the spiritual world, and so far as he has ideas he sees into the spiritual world.

When these ideas bring into his presence the members of a certain "society," referred to by Swedenborg in many places,—meaning perfected men, or, in other words, regenerate men,—the man, if a (mystical) member of that society himself, is said to be in communication with angels; and whatever is *thought* in the view of such men is called a conversation in the spiritual world.

This is the precise ground of Swedenborg's *memorable relations*, which are nothing in the world but his individual opinions of men and things under a slight veil, and this is entirely in accordance with the spirit (?) of Swedenborg's own statements, made apparently to guide his reader in understanding him.

To return now to the paragraph cited from Swedenborg:—he tells us that he has spoken with angels concerning *Wisdom*,—of their speaking of it as a *Palace*,—and, finally, of *twelve steps* leading to it.

If Swedenborg had explained his own meaning, we should have been bound to accept, so far as he is concerned, his own explanations, but he has merely told us that the first step is taken by man "from the Lord," and that all of the other steps are taken by "conjunction with the Lord." The mysticism would have been removed, by the way, if he had said, that the steps are taken by a strict adherence to the truth, which he does indeed, substantially say in the same paragraph.

But to what did he refer in this allusion to *angels*, to a *Palace*, and to *twelve steps* leading to it?

I answer, without the slightest suspicion of error, that the *angel* who spoke to him of a *Palace* was no other than the alchemist *Cosmopolita*, who left a work behind him entitled, "An open entrance to the shut PALACE of the KING;" or, in other words, to a knowledge of the wisdom of God.   He *spoke* to Swedenborg through his book.

And the *twelve steps* is an allusion to one or both of two of the most noted Alchemic or Hermetic books extant; one by the Monk George Ripley, and the other by a monk also, Basil Valentine.   Ripley's work is entitled, "*The compound of Alchemy, or the ancient hidden Art of Alchemy : containing the right and most perfect means to make the Philosopher's Stone, and Aurum Potabile, with other excellent experiments. Divided into* TWELVE GATES."   This work was written in the reign of King Edward the Fourth, and was dedicated to him.

Basil Valentine's work was published in English in 1670. I know not when it was written. It is entitled, "*A Practical Treatise, together with the* Twelve Keys *and Appendix, of the Great Stone of the Ancient Philosophers.*"

These *Twelve Gates*, and *Twelve Keys*, are the Twelve Steps to the Palace; that is, to a knowledge of the wisdom of God;—to that wisdom, be it remembered, which is whispered by the Spirit of God to the loving soul that approaches his infinite presence in humility.

The sharpest eye will detect nothing in the writings of Swedenborg, voluminous as they are, in contradiction to any thing here advanced, in explanation of his mystical mode of writing.

One of the properties—one of the boasted or pretended properties, it may be,—of the Philosopher's Stone, is to confer youth upon the aged: it not only gives inexhaustible wealth, but insures perpetual youth. Here I find another and a decided point of connection between Swedenborg and the Alchemists; and, as the Hermetic writers say that " one book openeth another," the readers of Swedenborg's writings may possibly be in the best position, if they understand his writings, for interpreting the paradoxes of the still more obscure writers.

In paragraph 414 of the work on Heaven and Hell, Swedenborg says, that "to grow old in Heaven is to grow young." The angels of Swedenborg, then, must be considered as in possession of the Philosopher's Stone.

Throwing aside all studied obscurity, what is the meaning of this? Swedenborg says that the *love* of man is his very *life ;* and, as is the *love*, so is the *life*. Now man is in the midst between, as it were, God and the world, the one eternal, the other perishable. If we consider this theoretically, we may suppose that the love which is directed to the eternal may share its perennial nature, that is, a man in this love enjoys perpetual youth,—not in his body indeed, for this is of the world and must perish, but in his spiritual nature. But to love the perishable, or in other words the world, is to live in a succession of disappointments, since the objects of love are perpetually perishing, and to live in this state is to grow old indeed, not merely in years, but in cares.

Are we then to abandon the world, in order to attain this state? Not so: this is a long-since exploded doctrine, and we know now that God is not to be loved and served by withdrawing from the world and living as hermits, but by living in the world and attaining that middle point, so difficult to see and understand,—of "loving the world as not loving it," or of using the world as not abusing it, 1 Cor. vii. 30, 31. The difficulty of the discovery may be great; but, when made, it may be the finding of the Philosopher's Stone, and prove that Swedenborg thought himself in possession of it, under the sense of the opening of his internal sight, which was to him the *secretum artis* of the Alchemists.

I do not regard the opinion of Hermetic writers on the subject of creation as belonging to their peculiar doctrines, but on this point also Swedenborg and the Hermetic philosophers occupy the same ground. Swedenborg says that God created the world "out of [a] substance which is substance in itself;" but as he says that substance in itself is God, his doctrine is plain from this alone, and there is no question that his opinion was that God created or made the world, not from nothing, but from Himself. His followers contend strongly for this opinion, and earnestly defend it against the charge of Pantheism.

On this point the younger Van Helmont

expresses himself as follows, in the form of a *Query*:

"Seeing then that Man, the Little World, being created by God, must come to such a state, wherein continually without ceasing he may be melioriated, and raised from one degree of glory to another, and so become still more and more God-like, (if I may so speak,) or be incessantly advanced;—because, by this continual revolution and glorification, he still comes nearer to God, and yet can never come to an end of his approaches, (forasmuch as in God there is neither beginning nor end,) but this melioration and glorification must continue without end :

" Will it not follow from hence, that Man, as being a compendium of all the creatures of God, hath had no absolute, though a respective beginning;—because, if otherwise, they must also have an end: and because also, that, if they have a beginning, before the same, they were not, and consequently that they sprang and came of nothing?  Now, seeing this cannot be, because by this means, a NOTHING must be conceived to be in God; whereas indeed He is the Eternal Being of all beings, blessed for ever!

" They indeed, (continues Van Helmont, speaking openly on this point,) who imagine to themselves a creaturely God, and according to their gross conceptions, or their outward senses, shut up God in a determinate place or circumference, consistently with this their imagination, must suppose that a Nothing (which neither is, nor can be conceived of, or comprehended by themselves or others) before the creation of the world, did exist together with God. For whatsoever is beyond the bound which they have set themselves, that they call a Nothing. Or else they must assert that God made a Nothing out of which he afterwards created all things; which is a contradiction, because a Nothing cannot be made, for whatsoever is made or is, must be something. Moreover, according to this assertion God must have made himself to a Nothing (because there was nothing then but God) which is very absurd."

I will just remark, in passing, that Plato endeavors to show, in the Sophist, that we cannot conceive of Nothing, the idea of which is formed (he says) by first necessarily conceiving something, and then mentally negating or denying it; so that in the idea of Nothing there is always the idea of something.

I cannot suppose that the opinions I have

thus far expressed of Swedenborg will be favorably received by those who, upon full consideration, as they believe, have adopted an opinion of him and his writings implying a special illumination in his case, inaccessible to other men; but these views will not offend the class of men referred to by Swedenborg himself, in a letter of the 15th of July, 1771, to the Landgrave of Hesse-Darmstadt, to whom he sent a copy of his *True Christian Religion*, requesting that those only might be selected to judge of it, " who love the truth, and who love it only because it is truth." " If you take others (says he) they will see in this work no light but only darkness."

Everywhere in Swedenborg's writings appeal is made to a love of the truth, for the sake of the truth alone, as the proper pre-requisite in him who would sit in judgment upon the truth. He makes no appeal to the passions and denies that there were any miraculous interpositions in his day.

For my own part I find no insuperable difficulty in understanding Swedenborg's writings, at least to as great an extent as can be to any use or benefit in life. For this purpose I need but one liberty, a liberty to which he could take no exception were he living, and to which his followers have no right to take any exception. *One single liberty alone is required*, and Swedenborg's writings will be brought within the field of natural comprehension, and they will be found full of truth and wisdom,—of love to God and charity to all mankind;—so full of wisdom as to place their author among the foremost lights of the world, though shining in darkness. And what is that liberty? It is simply the privilege of employing the rule of interpretation upon his writings which he employed upon the sacred Scripture;—the privilege of measurably disregarding the letter and looking to the spirit for the sense of what he wrote.

I say that Swedenborg was a Hermetic Philosopher, and purposely wrote obscurely; and that he was not in a dream, but in a state of perfect "wakefulness,"—to use his own language.

# CHAPTER VI.

THE zealous friends of the Swedish philosopher, without much judgment as it appears to
me, have collected a considerable body of traditions, called " documents concerning Swedenborg,"—published in New York in 1847,—calculated, if to be relied upon, to take him out of the
pale of humanity ; but among all those stories I
see nothing to impress me through my *marvel*
faculty, while some of his acknowledged letters
and declarations explicitly deny all miraculous
intervention in his case, the opening of his internal sight not being a special miracle in his favor,
but an experience possible for other men,—no
doubt of an extraordinary character.

In a letter to Dr. Oetinger (Nov. 11, 1766),
he gives reasons why no miracles need be expected in his day, to wit, that miracles only " convince an outward belief," which, according to
Swedenborg's theory, is not efficacious in salva-

tion.   He might have urged that there is no necessary connection between the exercise of power and the truth of a doctrine.

He further tells Dr. Oetinger, in the same letter, that he had been chosen from a *philosopher* to the office of *a teacher*, "*to the end*, that the spiritual knowledge," revealed in his day, "might be reasonably learned and rationally understood," —a plain declaration, surely, that he appealed only to our natural faculties, and laid no tax upon our mere credulity.

Yet he uses some strange language in this same letter:   He says, for example, in answer to a question proposed by Dr. Oetinger, as to whether he had "spoken with the Apostles," that he had "spoken one whole year with Paul, and also of what is mentioned in the Epistle to the Romans, 3. 28.  I have spoken (he continues) three times with John, once with Moses, and I suppose a hundred times with Luther, who owned to me that, contrary to the warning of an angel, he had received the doctrine of salvation by faith alone, merely with the intent that he might make an entire separation from Popery.  But with angels (he goes on to say) I have conversed these twenty-two years, and daily continue to do so."

How are we to understand these declarations?

Certainly, for this purpose, we cannot adopt a more ready or secure plan than to follow the example of Swedenborg himself, and seek him in the spiritual world, and obtain satisfaction from himself.

That this may be done without much difficulty, I have it fortunately in my power to show, in the clearest manner, having conversed with Swedenborg myself in the spiritual world, and it is only necessary for me to " relate " the particulars of what passed between us.  I have in fact had not merely one conversation with him, but have met him many times, and have questioned him very closely ; and although there are some few points on which he has shown very little disposition to be communicative, yet, on the whole, I have much reason to be thankful for full explanations on other points.

I was chiefly induced to make the acquaintance of Swedenborg by certain encomiums upon him by his friend *Mr. Wilkinson*, whom I met in the spiritual world also, some twelve or thirteen years ago, and who, in fact, introduced Swedenborg to me.  The philosopher had a veil over his face, and it was some time before I could obtain a clear view of his features.  At length, however, I could see that this veil became less and less opaque, until finally it was almost transparent, which he explained to me by saying that he was not in the habit of allowing every one to see his face, but only those who sought his acquaintance from a pure regard for the truth, and not from idle curiosity. He tells me that he never makes himself known to those who seek his acquaintance with any sinister purpose, and not even to those whose chief desire is to get to heaven; for he assures me that the way to truth is not through heaven, but contrarily the way to heaven is through the love of truth. He says this is the only thing valued in heaven, and that no one is admitted there who is without it. I have spoken with him several times with regard to his letter to Dr. Oetinger, and he has "owned" to me that, in what he says in that letter of having spoken with Paul, he merely meant that he had studied Paul's epistles for a whole year: that, in what he says of Luther, he only intended to express an *opinion*, derived from the study of Luther's works, and from a consideration of the relations he held to the church of Rome, and to the time in which he lived.

As to what he says in that letter of talking with angels, he assures me that, when in the world, he belonged to a " Society *wherein things relating to heaven and to the soul were the only subjects of discourse and entertainment*" [see Swedenborg's own account of himself, 1769]; that he referred to the members of that society as angels, because of the innocency, simplicity, and truthfulness of their lives. He further assures me, that in all of his writings he has endeavored to set forth *the love of truth, for the sake of the truth*, as the true test of knowledge; and he seemed very confident that those who have that love of truth will understand his writings without serious difficulty.—[*Concluding paragraph of Heaven and Hell.*]

He referred me to many declarations in the course of his work on Heaven and Hell, and elsewhere, to prove that by Angels he merely meant regenerate men, who have forsaken, not their duties in the world, which are never to be neglected, but the love of the world, and who have vowed a life of perfect innocency before God and man. He has told me—and this may surprise some of his followers—that he had some difficulty with himself in selecting the title for his work on Heaven and Hell; that he thought of calling it a work on the Happiness and Misery of Man; but as he reflected that such ordinary expressions would not be likely to arrest attention, he adopted the other, which means the same thing.

He has explained to me, that his *memorable relations*, to be found in two or three of his works, were only introduced because he thought that such " remarkable particulars " might " probably excite the reader to their first perusal."   [Letter to the Swedish Ambassador, without date, page 166 of the *Documents*.]

I told him that a great many stories had been put in circulation about him, supposed to show that he had miraculous powers ; but he assured me that nearly all of them are " fictions " invented by " foolish novelists," [Letter to the Landgrave of Hesse Darmstadt, July 1577], and, as to those that are true, they should " not be regarded as miracles."  [Same Letter, and also Letter to M. Venator, July 13, 1771.]

I asked him in one of our conversations, how he came to use so strange a mode of writing,— by which, said I, many people have been deceived ;—he answered by saying,—that they are not deceived as to doctrine, which every man must receive upon his own conscience, and not upon the conscience of another : and that such a mode of writing has been in use among wise men from the earliest period of time, of which fact he said he had taken especial care to warn his readers again and again in his writings, on purpose to guard against being understood literally.

I told him I thought it doubtful whether he would be held excusable for adopting the form of writing he had used :—upon which he looked very grave, and said that he hoped no one would be injured by any thing he left behind him in the world ; that his purpose was always to serve and benefit mankind ; that, as he himself had not depended upon a literal reading, even of the Scriptures, he could not imagine that any one would lean upon the literal sense of his writings, and forego the practice of charity, which he had taken so much pains to inculcate.  He referred me to the concluding paragraph of his Letter to M. Venator, where I find he says that—" Every truth in the word shines in Heaven ; and comes down from thence into this world, *to those who love truth because it is truth;* " and he said that by the use of the word *those* he intended to include all men who love truth for the sake of truth, and not from the hope of reward ;—adding that truth is its own evidence in the same sense as that virtue is its own reward ; and that neither the one nor the other can be possessed but by a life of truth and charity.

He then came close to me, and whispered something into my ear;—upon which I told him that I thought he was right, or, at all events, that as he thought himself so, it was sufficient for me.

In one of our last conversations, I asked him how he came to write that little work which he called *Earths in the Universe*. He asked me if what he said there of different kinds of men, calling them *Earths*, having certain predominant characteristics, was not true; and whether it was not as easy to locate a representation of human character in Mars or Jupiter—in Venus or Mercury, as in London or Paris, in Amsterdam or Stockholm? He reminded me that man, as to life, is a spirit, but, as to body, an earth. I then remembered that the Alchemists designated different sorts of men sometimes by metals, as gold, silver, lead, &c., and sometimes by planets, as by the Sun, Moon, Mercury, Venus, Saturn, &c., and I desisted from asking any further questions at that time.*

* The compiler of a *Compendium of the Theological and Spiritual Writings of Emanuel Swedenborg*, published by Crosby & Nichols and Otis Clap & Co., 1854, calls attention in a note, page 68, to what appeared a remarkable fact; that, as a *scientific* writer, Swedenborg knew there were more than seven planets; but when, afterwards, his spiritual sight was opened, he speaks of only seven. The explanation of this is the fact, that the Al-

It may be observed that Plato speaks of two sorts of men, hard to be discerned by the generality of mankind, because they occupy extremes, one living in darkness and the other in light; meaning simply that the generality of men are of a mixed nature, not very good and not very

chemists used the planets as symbols only; they did not use them astronomically. They placed the sun in the *midst*, with an equal number of planets on each side, to exhibit, for their purpose, a certain *equilibrium;* which Swedenborg also speaks of, especially at the close of his Treatise on *Heaven and Hell*. If the reader has a perfect copy of Sir George Ripley's *Compound of Alchemy*, he may observe at the end a *plate* or *diagram* of the Alchemic scheme, such as was without doubt iu the mind of Swedenborg. He was not writing of *science*. Most of the Alchemic writers refer to these seven planets, the author of the *New Light of Alchemy* (9th Treatise), somewhat minutely, arranging them first in the following order, to wit; *Saturn, Jupiter, Mars*, the Sun, *Venus, Mercury*, and the *Moon*. The author then proceeds to arrange them in *triplets*, by bringing the extremes together, with the *Sun* between each couple; thus, Saturn, the Sun, and the Moon; then Jupiter, the Sun, and Mercury; and finally Mars, the Sun, and Venus;—each exterior couple representing conditions of what these writers call the Two Luminaries (active and passive), with the Sun in the middle, their real sun in this scheme, however, being invisible.

Whatever may have been their real purpose, they have used but seven, and Swedenborg, in his theological or Alchemic writings, limited himself to the same number, though, as a man of science, he knew there were more. They were merely used as symbols.

bad, and from the lack of experience, or observation, or both, they do not readily conceive of natures much above or much below themselves. Hence the worst of men are below ordinary conception, while the best of men are above it.

The best of men Swedenborg describes as angels, and speaks of them as of another *earth* than ours; but he is speaking of men nevertheless, in our midst, yet men who live to the spirit and not to the flesh;—men who love the truth, and whose chief delight is in it;—who love to think of God and of eternal things; who are in the habit of realizing in themselves God's eternal presence, and thence acquire or enter into a *sense* of their own eternity, in the very centre of which they find themselves as if waking from a dream, in such a manner that what had seemed most real becomes shadowy and imaginary, while that which had been regarded as mystical and visionary becomes the only real. Yet all this in the body and in a state of perfect " wakefulness;" and such men know that they are no longer in a dream, though they feel that to talk of such experiences must seem like dreaming to those who are in the sleep of nature.

It is very plain that no one while in the body

can ever, in any strict sense, be said to be out of the body, though it is easily conceivable that a man may be in such a state, through the energy and action of his inner life, as scarcely, if at all, to feel the pressure of his body, and may hardly know he has a body :—and this is as possible in the purely intellectual life as through the affectional or passional nature, where it often occurs. It has been well said, that we may and do *perceive* those ideas and inner actions of life which we *conceive* by the intellect, and know them to be far more real, though unseen outwardly, than the so-called outward realities, which are often known to be shadows while we observe them.

In every point of view, it seems certain that no man, while in the body, will ever see beyond his nature considered in its double existence as inward and outward, and hence no man will ever travel, we may be sure, to another world, while in the body, and bring back thence any thing but what he carries with him, or may find here before he sets out upon his journey.

That God, nevertheless, should enlighten the minds of some men according to their capacity for reception, ought not to surprise any one in whom the doctrine of God's omnipresence and omnipotence is a living truth, and not merely a verbal creed practically alien to the life, and capable of being roused only by "storms and earthquakes" of the inner or outer world. "To see God only in what seems to disturb the peace of nature is to see him only in his terrors, and is scarcely to see him at all."

Swedenborg's memorable relations, as he calls them, for he does not call them revelations, are nothing but intellectual exercises, conducted under the idea of God's eternal presence, and thinly veiled with a phraseology selected and adopted for no other purpose in the world but to remove them or show *their* removal from the sensuous world. The natural man knoweth not the things of the Spirit; they are foolishness to him; and therefore he will not listen to them as in this world, spiritually observed, or, in Swedenborg's own language, as seen in a "celestial idea;" but he will listen to one who tells him that he has seen such things, in the spirit, in another *earth*, or in some *star* beyond the sun! But this is a fiction, and whoever thinks otherwise is greatly deceived, and misses the purest benefit of Swedenborg's writings.

It is but fair and just to interpret Swedenborg according to the *spirit* of these remarks, and the more so as, by paragraph 50 of *Angelic Wisdom concerning Divine Providence,*—and in number-less other places,—he seems to tell us in open plain language how to understand what he says of *angels.*

"No one (says he) thinks from space and time when he thinks concerning those who are in the spiritual world." He says that, "angels and spirits are *affections* which are of *love,* and *thoughts* thence," and that, "when any one [*any one,* not himself only] thinks about another from affection, with the intention that he wishes to see him, or to speak with him, he is set forthwith present."

" * * * * Space and time make nothing towards presence, for the reason that affection, and thought thence, are not in space and time ; and spirits and angels are affections and thence thoughts."

I find a remarkable coincidence with the idea or principle here expressed, in a very singular Hermetic volume, published in English (trans-lated from the French) in 1650, with the title *Unheard of Curiosities concerning the Talis-manical Sculpture of the Persians, the Horoscope of the Patriarches ; and the Reading of the Stars.*

This is purely a Hermetic book, and though absolute nonsense to the general reader, it is *in-*

6*

*terlarded* with the main doctrines of Swedenborg enigmatically expressed, especially the doctrine that *God is Man.**  The book had passed through two editions in French before it appeared in English, which may assure us that it had *readers,*

---

* The reader may find a great deal of Swedenborgianism anticipated in the writings of the elder *Van Helmont.*  Van H. in his *Vision of the Soul* expressly says that, inasmuch as God "hath vouchsafed to adopt only the soul of man to the image of Himself, it appears also a genuine consequence, that the *immense and ineffable God is also of human figure;* and that, by an argument drawn *à posteriori*, if arguments be of any validity in this incomprehensible subject."

It will be recollected that Swedenborg says again and again, that God always appears before the angels *as a man.*

The doctrine of the *grand-man* pervades a volume by the younger *Van Helmont,*—the father and son were both Hermetic philosophers,—entitled, *Paradoxal Discourses of F. M. Van Helmont, concerning the Macrocosm and Microcosm, or the Greater and the Lesser World, and their Union,* published in English in 1685.   In this work, Hermetic throughout, ch. iii., sec. 1., treats of *Matter* and *Spirit* under the symbolic expressions, *Water* and *Quick-sand.*  When the author says that *diggers for metals* everywhere, even under the highest mountains, are sure to come to *Quick-sand,* he means that searchers for truth, in pursuing their inquiries through nature, always reach a *Spiritual* limit, "beyond which there is no farther digging."

At page 65, of the *Microcosm,* the *thoughts* of man are called *Spirits,* and are classified into good and bad *Angels* of man.

Swedenborg calls the affections and thoughts thence, *Spirits* and *Angels.*

whether fools or not. The book is full of learning,
Latin, Greek, and Hebrew, and may demonstrate to the curious reader that there was a class
of men altogether out of, if not above the common
order, who cultivated a science or art entirely
unknown to the " common sort." This *art* was
Hermetic philosophy, which has been cultivated
in all ages though under various names, including
*astrology.*

But, for the *coincidence*, which it is my object
to bring out:

" Those then (says this author) that are well
skilled in the Secrets [Hermetic Secrets] of the
Theology of the ancients, assure us, that those
that first set up images in their temples, resem-
bling the shapes of angels that have appeared
upon earth, had no other design in so doing, save
only the more easily to invite down those blessed
spirits, by the force of the resemblance. And I
know not whether or no, by the very same virtue
of resemblance, which is found betwixt God and
men; (*Faciamus hominem ad imaginem, et simi-
litudinem nostrum:*) it hath not rightly been
affirmed by some Divines, that the Son of God
would nevertheless have become man (yet without suffering death), though *Adam* had never
fallen. But speaking of things, as they are now

at present, we know, that *Jesus Christ* is found in the midst of those, that speak, with *Faith*, of his name : because that *when we speak with affection of any one, we represent him to ourselves in our imagination.* When, therefore, speaking of *Jesus Chist* we fancy him as he is, *he is instantly present with us, appearing to our hearts at the very instant that we there frame his image by our imagination.* So true it is, that resemblance hath the power to work wonders, even upon him that hath dependence upon no other, and is not under any power or law. But such conceptions as these are to be entertained with all piety and humility; and proposed with such sanctity, as becomes those that speak of so adorable a subject."

I will note, in passing, that the identical doctrine of Swedenborg, as expressed in paragraph 50, *Divine Providence*, is in the 10th book of the *Pymander* of *Hermes*, whose very name has been given to the philosophy cultivated by Swedenborg. See, especially, paragraphs 117 to 124 inclusive. But, upon reflection, as the *Pymander* is out of print and scarcely known, I will copy these few paragraphs, which the reader may at his leisure compare with the doctrine of Swedenborg.

117. " All things are in God, not as lying in a

place ; for place is with a body, and immoveable, and these things that are there placed, have no motion.

118. "But they lie otherwise in that which is unbodily, than in the fantasy, or to appearance.

119. "Consider Him that contains all things, and understand that nothing is more capacious than that which is incorporeal, nothing more swift, nothing more powerful : but it is most capacious, most swift, and most strong.

120. "And judge of this by thyself; command thy *soul* to go to INDIA, and sooner than thou canst bid it, it will be there.

121. "Bid it likewise pass over the *ocean*, and suddenly it will be there; not as passing from place to place, but suddenly it will be there.

122. "Command it to fly into Heaven, and it will need no wings, neither shall any thing hinder it ; not the *fire* of the *Sun*, not the *ether*, nor the turning of the spheres ; not the bodies of any of the other stars ;—but, cutting through all, it will fly up to the last and furtherest body.

123. "And if thou wilt even break the *whole*, and see those things that are without the world (if there be any thing without), thou mayest.

124. "Behold how great power, how great

swiftness, thou hast! Canst thou do all these things, and cannot God?"

Let these passages be compared with Swedenborg's doctrine of *space* and *presence*, and with the power of resemblance, &c., and they will be seen to be the same.

If we will take Swedenborg's own description or designation of what he understood by *angels* and spirits, and not *imagine* full-faced little cherubs with wings, there need be no difficulty.

According to Swedenborg, man is inwardly, or as to his spiritual nature, in the spiritual world; but externally, or as to his sensuous nature, he is in the natural world.

Here is a passage from *Divine Love and Wisdom*, which assuredly ought to tell us how the author would be understood, when speaking of *angels*.

"All that is here said of the angels, and of their turning to the Lord as a sun, is also to be understood of man, *as to his spirit*; for man, as to his mind, is a spirit, and if he be in love and wisdom, he is an angel; wherefore also after death, when he puts off his externals, which he has derived from the natural world, he becomes a spirit or an angel: and since the angels constantly turn their faces eastward to the sun, consequently to the Lord, it is also said of the man who is in love and wisdom from the Lord, that he sees God, that he looks to God, and that he has God before his eyes; *by which is* MEANT [I italicise this] *that he leads the life of an angel.* Such things are said in the world, as well because they actually exist in Heaven, as because they actually exist in man's spirit. In prayer, who does not look before him up to God, to whatever quarter his face is turned.

" The angels constantly turn their faces to the Lord as a Sun, because *they are in the Lord and the Lord in them,* and the Lord interiorly leads their affections and thoughts, and constantly turns them to Himself; consequently, they cannot look any otherwise than to the East, where the Lord appears as a Sun : [I beg the reader, for his own sake, not to take this in a physical sense ; but rather think it symbolic of the star which appeared in the east.] Hence it is evident (the passage proceeds), that the angels do not turn themselves to the Lord, but that the Lord turns them to himself. For when the angels [I repeat, that Swedenborg is speaking of man, but under certain conditions rarely met with ; and therefore the sense is, that when men] think interiorly of the Lord, they do not think of him otherwise *than in themselves.* Interior thought itself, does not cause distance; but exterior thought, which acts as one with the light of the eyes, does make distance; the reason is, because exterior thought is in space, but not interior thought, and when it is not in space as in the spiritual world, still it is in the appearance of space.

"The turning of the angels to the Lord is such, that at every turn of their bodies, they look to the Lord, as a Sun before them: an angel [a man, when in the right state for it,—for it is not true of the sensuous man] can turn himself round and round, and thereby see various things which are about him, but still the Lord constantly appears before his face as a Sun. This may seem wonderful, but nevertheless it is the truth."

What is this but a mode of speaking of a man who lives in the idea of God's omnipresence? Such a man is said to see from a *celestial idea,* and though he looks upon the very same things externally that are visible to the natural man, they are, by virtue of the "celestial idea," so to speak, transformed into the spirit; while yet, they remain the same externally. Hence Swedenborg often reiterates that things in the spiritual world, as to external appearance, are the same as in the natural world.

The distinction lies in the nature of man, or in the different conditions of different men.

But I may be told that in a letter to Dr. Oetinger, of the 8th of Nov., 1768, Swedenborg "sacredly and solemnly declares that the Lord himself had been seen of him," and that he sent him to do what he did, and that for that purpose he had "opened and enlightened the interior part of his soul," so that he could "see what is in the spiritual world and those that are therein," and that, "that privilege had been continued to him for twenty-two years."

The question arises with many,—how can Swedenborg's veracity be maintained, and any other than a literal interpretation be put upon such explicit declarations?

I would answer, that as large a latitude of interpretation of Swedenborg's declarations must be allowed as he himself took with the equally explicit statements in the Scriptures. Whatever others might say of this license, neither he, if living, nor his friends have any right to complain. How then does the case stand?

We read expressly that God spake to Moses

out of the burning bush, and that the bush though burning was not consumed. Millions and millions of the human race, putting faith in the Scriptures, receive these statements as literally true ; but Swedenborg does not hesitate to interpret this burning bush as a symbol of the *Law*, in the letter of which was contained the Spirit of God, like the fire which burned in the bush but did not consume it, and he apparently placed no value upon the literal reading of the text.

But how is Swedenborg to be understood, in the letter to Dr. Oetinger?

I would gather an answer by an easy inference from part of a discourse by a celebrated divine of the last century on Micah, 6. 8. *He hath shewed thee, O man, what is good ; and what doth the Lord require of thee, but to do justly, and to love mercy, and to walk humbly with thy God.*

The author, the Rev. John Heylyn, 1770, prefers the marginal translation, which reads— "To humble thyself to walk with God ;"—upon which he proceeds to show that pride separates us from God; that, by pride, men are always thinking of themselves, so as "to leave no room for God in their souls;" that "self usurps his altar there;" but that Humility dethrones the idol, self, which profaned God's temple, and leaves "Him his proper place in our affections;" that God cannot be known to the soul until *humility has cast down all imaginations and every high thought that exalteth itself against the knowledge of God;* that, God can only be known as the sovereign good of the soul; that, not to know him as infinitely desirable, is to be ignorant of him; for that, he is our supreme good, and the soul cannot be said to know him, who does not apprehend him as such :—but that, the soul cannot apprehend him as her supreme good while any created good has the preference in her esteem.  The author then proceeds to show, that, when humility has prepared the heart for the knowledge of God, "He graciously vouchsafes to MANIFEST himself to our souls, causing there a lively SENSE of his PRESENCE;"—the author citing God's promises, *Is.* 57. 15, and *John* 14. 21, 23, to encourage us in humility and the practice of virtue, affirming that, upon these conditions, "God will MANIFEST himself unto us;" that Jesus Christ and his Father "will come unto us, and make their abode with us," &c.

I see no need of supposing that Swedenborg meant any thing more, in affirming that the "Lord" had been "seen of him," than that, with respect to himself, the promises of Scripture to the truly humble had been fulfilled. The *secretum artis* had, as he thought, been given to him, and his sense of the magnitude of this "gift of God" may, in some degree, be estimated by its consequences, as shown in his life and labors.

That the "Lord" had commanded him "to do what he did," merely signifies, that under the consciousness of possessing a great truth, he felt an impulse to work for the good of mankind; and, acknowledging this impulse to have proceeded from the author of all good, he did not hesitate to speak of it as the command of the "Lord," and feeling it as such he religiously obeyed it.

The assumption, if it was one, that the Lord had commanded him to "do what he did," was common with Hermetic writers during the middle ages. They refer to their knowledge as supernaturally acquired,—as acquired by *inspiration*,—and although they often declare that they are not permitted by God to *reveal* or make known the truth beyond a certain limit, yet up to that limit they claim to speak by express authority, or by the "command" of the Lord. One or two examples of this will suffice. *Basil Val-*

*entine*, after treating of what he calls *natural and supernatural things*, says :

" What I have done, has not been done from a desire of vain and transitory glory ; but I have been induced thereunto by the command of Christ the Lord, that his glory and goodness in eternal and temporal matters, should not be concealed from any man, but to the praise, honor, and glory of his holy everlasting name,—that it might be exalted, acknowledged, and revealed in his Majesty by reason of his Highness and Almightiness, through the confirmation of his wonderful deeds.   And secondly, I have been led thereunto by Love and Charity towards my neighbor,—for his good as for my own ;  *  *  * and likewise that the Supremest mystery may not quite be suffocated in darkness nor be drowned in overflowing waters, [i. e. suffocated by *ignorance*, or drowned by animal *passions*,] but be delivered out of the deep and filthy mire of the *Idiotish Crew* by the right appearance of the true Light—" &c.

Here is enough to show that others besides Swedenborg claimed to publish their sense of truth by the *command* of the Lord.

In the above passage Basil Valentine, an alchemist be it remembered, refers to the " command" of the Lord as his authority for what he taught.

The anonymous *Cosmopolita*, another alchemist, and one of the most ingenious among them, in *Ripley Revived* (1678), refers to both a *commission* and a *permission*, the latter word being very frequently used by Swedenborg, as his readers will remember; for example,—as (Something) *has been unknown to this day, it is* PERMITTED *to relate, &c. :*—this language is frequently met in the writings of Swedenborg.

*Cosmopolita* writes;—" It is to be understood that the most wise God hath a ruling hand herein, and all the *Sons of Art* have their *commission* as it were given them; they write and teach according to that *permission* which the Creator of all things hath given them." But, nevertheless, as they taught in figures, parables and allegories, he continues, as follows :

" And truly it is not our intent to make the Art common to all kinds of men; we write to the deserving only; intending our books to be but as way-marks to those who may travel in these paths of nature, and we do what we can to shut out the unworthy: yet we write so plainly [so openly] that as many as God hath appointed to this Mastery shall certainly understand us, and have cause to be thankful for our faithfulness herein. This gratitude we shall receive from the Sons of this Science, whatever we have from others: Our books, therefore, are intended for the former; but we do not write a word to the latter. Moreover, we write not our books for the information of the illiterate, as though every vulgar *mechanical* distiller, alchemist, or sophister, should readily carry away the Golden Fleece; nor do we intend that any covetous man, who makes gain his utmost ends, shall readily gather the Apples of the *Hesperides*; nor yet, that any, though *learned*, should by once or twice careless and slight reading of our books be straightway made a philosopher: Nay verily, the Majesty of this Science [call it the true knowledge of God] forbids so great impiety; it is the gift of God, and not of men: our books are for those who have been or intend to be employed in the search of nature; we hint the way; prayer to God and patient persistence in the use of means, must open these doors. Let, therefore, profound MEDITATION, accompanied with the blessing of God, Furnaces, Coals, Glasses, and indefatigable pains, be thy interpreters, and let them serve for commentaries upon our writings. So I did; so I advise thee:

and may the blessing of God attend all studious, virtuous searchers in this art."

Swedenborg, about a century later than Cosmopolita, wrote much more openly than his predecessors in the *Art;*—and why? Because he thought that the world had so advanced in knowledge as to receive without injury the strong " meat,"—that God is [a] man, and has actually been "seen " in the world in his humanity;—that God is the Lord; that the Lord is Heaven; that Heaven is in man ; that men are the stars of Heaven, differing indeed in " glory " (St. Paul), but that in every *metal* (as the alchemists express it) there is a little " gold ; "—and that this gold, " this stone, this wealth, this treasure, though it be but like to a grain of mustard seed, yet it grows to be the greatest of all trees, in whose branches the birds of the air make their nests, and under whose shadow the beasts of the field dwell." *Salmon's* Commentary upon *Hermes.*

The absence of *quotations*, or references to authorities, in Swedenborg's theological writings, has been observed, and the reason assigned for it by his admirers is, that as he derived his knowledge directly from the teaching of the Lord (through the opening of his internal sight) he had no occasion to fortify his communications by any such references.

This also was a pretence of the alchemists.

Thus, in " *Secrets Revealed* (1669), the author says,—" I could cite all of the philosophers that write of this thing, but I need no witnesses ; because, being myself an *Adept*, I do write more plainly than any heretofore."

In another place he says :—" As I write these things for the good of my neighbor, let it be enough, that I profess there is none that ever writ in this art so clearly; and that many a time in writing I laid aside my pen, because I was rather willing to have concealed the truth under a mask ; but God *compelled* me to write, whom I could not resist, who alone knows the heart, to whom only be glory forever."

In another place, still, he says :—" He that hath this [the Stone] needs no information from another ; himself now standing in the centre, he may easily view the circumference, and then experience will be, next to the Spirit of God, his best guide."

*Sandivogius*, in *A New Light of Alchemy*, writes in a similar manner. Indeed,—if the reader has access to the writings of *Basil*, *Valentine*, *Sandivogius*, *Cosmopolita*, and—I had almost said

7

*or*—Espagnet, all of them Alchemists, he may derive great assistance from them in understanding Swedenborg ; and, on the other hand, the study of the Swedish philosopher will throw great light upon their obscure writings.

Whether Swedenborg was or was not mistaken, either in regard to his doctrines, or in his opinion of the intelligence of the age in which he wrote, in comparison with that of an earlier period—see on this subject one of his letters to *Dr. Oetinger*—is not for me to determine. It is certain that he was a Hermetic philosopher, writing, not so *very* obscurely, under the idea that the *Alpha* and *Omega* are ONE, and intimating that these *two* are God and man, and yet but ONE NATURE.

I have often suggested the importance of separating in our minds the idea of the truth from the representations of it by those who profess to teach it ; and on this subject, more than on all others, it is necessary to have regard to this principle. Those who are curious in their inquiries into the nature of Hermetic Philosophy, under its various names in the world, for it is a very *Proteus*, should first seek to learn what its adepts taught, and then propose to themselves an altogether different question, as to the verity of their teaching; and they cannot be too careful as to what they receive as the truth of God.

As to Swedenborg, he was a man, and no more; human, and therefore fallible; and the light he speaks of, though always clear in itself, is never so in what Swedenborg himself calls its ultimate, especially when this ultimate is a con-catenation of ink-marks called human writing or printing. Here the light must always shine *darkly*. And this induces me to say that possibly,—though I have no wish to judge him,—possibly, I say, he made a mistake in so far overstepping the law of Hermetic silence, as to expose himself and his writings to be misunderstood as they have been.

Yet there is no need of misunderstanding him, if due attention be paid to his own declarations, adjusted, according to the Hermetic rule, to " the possibility of nature." It is not contrary to this possibility, that the " Lord " should MANIFEST himself to man, though this be the work of *the* " Artist " of man, and not of man, *an* artist. It is is only an exaltation of nature in or through man, by which the man is, as it were, taken out of himself, as an isolated and selfish being, and elevated into the universal, where he works for the good of the whole, finding his own happiness in his labor.

I have already cited a few passages from Swedenborg to assist in determining how his language in reference to angels and spirits is to be understood. By angels he meant *men*, but men perfected in their nature,—perfected in the spirit, if the reader pleases,—and men too, *living* or *dead*, if he had any *idea* of them, as I will show presently. They must be or must have been without guile,—turned inside outwards, as John Isaac Hollanders expresses it in his Alchemic work *Of Saturn*,—to be classed with Angels.

As to the *extent* or *reach* of the so-called internal sight or view of the spiritual world, we have some remarkable testimony from General Tuxen. Let it be considered.

If the account may be relied upon, it appears that on one occasion Swedenborg was presented to the Queen of Sweden, who, says General *Tuxen*, expressed her satisfaction at seeing him, and asked him, "Whether it was true that he could converse with the deceased? He answered, Yes. She inquired further, Whether it was a science that could be communicated to and by others? No. What is it, then? A gift of the Lord. Can you, then, speak with every one deceased, or only with certain persons? He answered [and the reader should attend to this answer], I can not converse with all, but with such as I have known in this world; with all royal and princely persons, with all renowned heroes, or great and learned men, *whom I have known either personally or from their actions or writings;* consequently, with all, *of whom I could form an* IDEA; for it may be supposed that a person whom I never knew, nor of whom I could form any IDEA, I neither could, nor would wish to speak with."

It would appear, then, that Swedenborg's knowledge of *facts* was not increased by his sight of or into the spiritual world. His original *ideas* remained the same, while his sight into the spiritual world continued. What then took place? Plainly nothing more than that his *ideas* underwent an examination from a spiritual point of view, and inferences and results were derived from them, which were themselves considered spiritual;—but only in the sense that the original ideas were, and Swedenborg's theory places all of the *ideas* of man in the spiritual world; for man, as to his "interior" spirit (or nature), says he, "is in the spiritual world."

It was the pretence to greater infusions of *light*, the mistakes of excited imaginations, or the daring impostures of corrupt and wicked men,

that brought out the following eulogy upon
Ralpho :

> " His knowledge was not far behind
> The knight's, but of another kind,
> And he another way came by 't;
> Some call it Gifts, and some New Light.
> A lib'ral art that cost no pains
> Of study, industry, or brains.
>     *     *     *     *
>
> But as he got it freely, so
> He spent it frankly and freely too.
> For saints themselves will sometimes be,
> Of gifts that cost them nothing, free.
>     *     *     *     *
>
> He could deep mysteries unriddle,
> As easily as thread a needle
> For as of vagabonds we say,
> That they are ne'er beside their way :
> Whate'er men speak by this new light,
> Still they are sure to be i' the right.
> 'Tis a dark-lanthorn of the spirit,
> Which none see by but those that bear it ;
> A light that falls down from on high,
> For spiritual trades to cozen by :
> An ignis fatuus, that bewitches,
> And leads men into pools and ditches
> To make them dip themselves, and sound
> For Christendom, in dirty pond ;
> To dive like wild-fowl, for salvation,
> And fish to catch regeneration.
>     *     *     *     *

> But what bigot durst ever draw,
> By inward light, a deed in law ?
> Or could hold forth by revelation
> An answer to a declaration ?
> For those that meddle with their tools,
> Will cut their fingers, if they're fools."

There is nothing in any of Swedenborg's writings, justly interpreted by rules to be found in the writings themselves, to give occasion for such severity.

In what respect, then, was Swedenborg's knowledge advanced, by his sight into the spiritual world ?

His friends might say that it was purified from *image* or *sensuous* elements, and clarified; and in proportion as this was done, his knowledge, from being special, became universalized, living upon principles, and not merely upon *image* facts; so that, as he says himself, he was not solicitous about his memory of *things*, but depended more upon an intellectual life, where one principle holds, as it were, a multitude of facts, and is the test of the truth of all facts having relation to the principle.

With Swedenborg the ordinary tenet, asserting God's omnipresence—which with most men is merely a form of words, a mere verbal confession of faith without influencing the heart and life—became a living truth. As the Divine is in all things, as all men say by habit, Swedenborg, by contemplation, came practically into such a state as to see all things in the Divine; but—and it is important to observe this—he saw nothing in the Divine but what he saw, inwardly or outwardly, in the world, the two worlds, natural and spiritual, being, in fact, but one world united, as he called it, by correspondence; which correspondence is so exact, that all things in the spiritual world *appear* as in the natural world; "so similar (says he), that as to external aspect there is no difference."—(*Heaven and Hell*, par. 582.)

Those who fall into, or reach this state of vision, are usually called mystics, though upon what just ground this is considered a reproach, I confess, I do not understand, seeing that such men do but practically live in the doctrine of God's omnipresence, which others assert, but practically deny; but those who assert the principle, and yet deride the mystic, do but confess their ignorance or their hypocrisy, or, if they prefer the term, their infidelity. He is the infidel, whose life and practice denies his confession of faith, not he in whom the faith and practice are united.

# CHAPTER VII.

I HAVE incidentally shown in what manner many passages in Swedenborg's writings are to be interpreted, and have indicated some principles by which most of his writings may be understood. I will now interpret a few more passages, but the reader must bear in mind that the Swede was a Hermetic philosopher writing under a *veil*, often writing of man as man in a natural sense, and then of man as a *spirit*, and again as a regenerate man (calling him an angel); and, besides these different modes of speaking of him, he is sometimes called a *house*, a *world*, an *earth*, a *temple*, a *tabernacle*, a *palace*, the palace of a king, not made with hands, for nothing is more certain than that Swedenborg might have cautioned his readers in the language of Cambachius, the Alchemist:

"Let me entreat you (addressing the reader) to take notice, by the way, that when you find any mention made of *heaven, earth, soul, spirits;*

7*

or *our heaven*, &c., these are not meant the *celestial Heaven*, or *natural earth;* but terms used by the philosophers to hide their sayings from the wicked: spoken with all due reverence to the *Divine Majesty;* of whose glorious attributes the true philosophers and astrologers are as tender as *Classical John;* yet this I thought good to *mention*, being cautious lest any spark of my flint should touch the *wild-fire* of his *beacons;* but that my SALT may rather preserve the hopes of the intelligent reader, to dive through his studies to his crowned *haven*."—(*Sal, Lumen, Spiritus Mundi Philosophici*, 1657.)

I will just remark, in passing, that the *Astrologers*, the *true* astrologers here referred to, were not ignorant and pretentious predicting impostors, but were students of "astral" secrets, meaning the heavenly principles, or the spiritual nature of man, wherein the philosopher sought his *cœlum*, a place of heavenly peace, to be enjoyed in silence, and not in the noise of the world, where there is always danger of bringing its possession into jeopardy.

The reader is now invited to consider a few passages from Swedenborg's writings.

Paragraph 174, *Heaven and Hell:* " When

it has been given me to be in company with *angels*, the things which were there have been seen by me altogether as those which are in the world; and so perceptibly, that I knew no otherwise than that I was in the world, and there in the palace of a king: I also spoke with them as man with man."

In this paragraph, the *World* is the universe; the *Palace* is man; the *King* is the king of kings, and the *Angels* are men perfected in the spiritual or celestial sense, men who lived, like Swedenborg, in a constant sense of God's presence, expecting a continuance of that state beyond this "transitory and educational scene." I state this as the theory; let the worth of it be examined by every man for himself.

Par. 177, same work: "Because *angels* are men and live with one another as the men of the earth do, therefore they have garments, habitations, and other like things, yet with the difference that they have all things more perfect, because in a more perfect state."

Why more perfect? Simply because they are supposed to live to the spirit, and not to the body, but the angels spoken of are men, nevertheless, living in the world, though not of the world.—*John* xvii. 16.

The habitation of the soul, and the soul itself the habitation of the spirit, is sometimes spoken of as a garden, a paradisiacal garden, where there are flowers and fruits, such as are " nowhere to be seen in the world," and these fruits are said to be gathered, " according to the good of Love in which the intelligent are."

The *angels* are said to " see such things, because a garden and paradise, and also fruit-trees and flowers, correspond to *intelligence and wisdom*." " That such things (he continues) are in the heavens, is also known in the earth, but only to those who are in good, and who have not extinguished in themselves the light of Heaven by natural light and its fallacies ; for they say, when speaking of Heaven, that such things are there as *the ear hath not heard nor the eye seen*."

Any one may see, at least when it has been pointed out, that Swedenborg here simply distinguishes two classes of men *in the world*, and not out of it—one living to the Spirit, and the other to nature in a subordinate sense ; and that the *fruits* spoken of are the fruits of the Spirit, as love, joy, peace, long-suffering, gentleness, goodness, faith, meekness, temperance—against which there is no law.—*Gal.* v. 22, 23. He says that those who have extinguished in themselves the light of heaven, still testify their belief in heaven by saying that such things are in heaven as "eye hath not seen," &c., and he might have added, as a recent writer* has done, that " the Heaven of God is not only that which eye hath not seen, but that which eye shall never see."

This is the true interpretation, the *internal* sense of Swedenborg's reference to the flowers and fruits of paradise.

Why is it that most men are so willing to defer the joys of paradise to another world, as if they were unattainable here ?  Is it because, as we commonly hear or read, they prefer the sensuous to the spiritual fruits, and do not understand how they may possess both, by " using the world without abusing it ? "  Is it because they prefer the present to the future, while yet it is certain that the future is contained in the present ?

In paragraph 190, *Heaven and Hell*, we read—

" The houses in which angels dwell are not built like the houses in the world, but are given them *gratis* by the Lord, to every one according to their reception of good and truth."

Let this be interpreted by the following pas-

* F. W. Robertson, Third Series, Sermons.

sage from PHILO, simply understanding that Philo's theoretic man of *virtue* is Swedenborg's *angel :*

"God has thought fit to give as a reward to the *virtuous* a *house* thoroughly well built and well put together from the foundations to the roof; and the most natural house for the soul is the body, inasmuch as it does many things necessary and useful for life, and especially on account of the mind which has been purified by perfect purifications ; and which, having been initiated in the divine mysteries [has had its internal sight opened, as Swedenborg would say], and having learnt to dwell only among the motions and periodical revolutions of the heavenly bodies, God has honored with tranquillity, wishing it to be completely undisturbed and exempt from any contact of those passions which the necessities of the body engender." * * * "This is the mind (continues Philo) in which the prophet [referring to Moses] says that God walks as in his palace; for the mind of the wise man [Swedenborg's angel] is in truth the palace and the house of God." * * * * "But all these statements are uttered in a metaphorical form, and contain an allegorical meaning."

I consider Swedenborg a strict rationalist,

when rightly understood, and not mystical at all except in the form of his writings.

The concluding passage of the work on *Heaven and Hell* was no doubt expressly designed as a caution to the reader, that the whole subject of the book is to be " reasonably learned and naturally understood," as Swedenborg expresses himself in a letter to Dr. Oetinger.

Par. 603 : " What has been said in this work concerning heaven, the world of spirits, and hell, will be obscure to those who are not in the delight [affection or love] of knowing spiritual truths, but clear to those who are in that delight, especially to those who are in the love of truth, for the sake of truth, that is, *who love truth because it is truth;* for, whatever is loved enters with light into the idea of the mind, especially truth, when it is loved, because all truth is in light."

Swedenborg might well have concluded his work in the language of a great man who flourished a century before him, whose works he must necessarily have studied, for " he read every thing," but whom he never alludes to.

" If the way that leads to this [spiritual state] seem arduous, still, it may be trod : and arduous it must be, since it is so rarely found.  For, if

our supreme good were at hand, and could be
easily attained, how should it be neglected by
almost all?   But all excellent things are as difficult as rare."

Books of alchemy and Hermetic philosophy
are filled with references to two certain things,
very uncertainly known, called the sun and moon,
which are also called active and passive, agent
and patient, and hundreds of other names; and
great care is taken to set forth their mystical
unity as an origin, or originating principle, whence
proceed innumerable effects.   Thus, also, Swedenborg has much to say of the marriage of the good
and true and of its happy fruits.   The two things
are supposed to be attributes of one thing, in an
indissoluble trinity, holding the whole world in
a nut-shell, no larger than the alchemist's egg,
whatever that is.

I cannot positively say that Swedenborg had
reference to the *sun* and *moon* of the alchemists
in paragraph 1529, Heavenly Arcana; but in
that paragraph he says,—" It is perfectly known
in Heaven [meaning to men in the angelic state],
but not so in the world of spirits, whence so great
a Light [as he had just been treating of] comes,

viz., that it is from the Lord; and what is surprising, the Lord appears in the third Heaven, to the celestial angels as a *Sun*, and to the spiritual angels as a *Moon*." In the succeeding paragraph he adds, that "the *Sun* signifies the celestial principle [which he calls good], and the moon, the spiritual principle" [which he calls truth]. He then adds, that, "By virtue of the Lord's Light in Heaven there appear wonderful things, which cannot be expressed, being so innumerable."

To understand these expressions, the reader must study Swedenborg's view of the *three* natures in man, the natural, spiritual, and celestial, the last being in fact a state of grace, when the soul is, as it were, lifted out of the body, and death disappears, or so far loses its character that if it is not entirely lost sight of it becomes a mere transition event, a " mystical passage," from an apparent to a real life, from a life in time to eternal life, the entrance into which involves the negation of the apparent, or, in other words, self-denial in accordance with the Scriptures. But there is a true and a false self-denial. Renounce *and* realize, says the true doctrine; whereas the false says, renounce *to* realize, this latter being no renunciation at all, but a mere prudential calculatiou of profits. The essence of the distinction lies in the import of the two words, *and* and *to*, as above used, the difference having the power of a differential in the calculus.

Let the student see the sun through the fixed assymptote, and the moon through the changeable hyperbola, and seize their dependence, one upon the other, or their connection, one with the other *in the cone,*—of course, regarding this as a figure.

If the readers of Swedenborg imagine they have a clearer idea of Swedenborg's *sun* and *moon*, than the Hermetic writers had, or supposed they had, of their *sun* and *moon*, I must think they are mistaken.

Swedenborg should not be taken literally. Those who understand him literally must be absolutely stultified. The reader must find the spirit by which he wrote. If he fails in this he will read to no purpose, except, indeed, that Swedenborg's external sense (to use his own language) is good ; that is, he everywhere recommends truth and goodness, charity and love. No one can be injured by reading him literally, but his real sense is as little on the surface as he thought that of Genesis itself. A general reader would suppose that Swedenborg meant by the expression, *the other life,* some life *other* than a life in this world, a life in another world than this in which we live. But he means the higher life in this world and not out of it; a life of reason and conscience, of truth and virtue, of "good and charity," in contradistinction to a life in the lower affections and passions.

At the hazard of repetition I must desire the reader to consider attentively Swedenborg's notion of there being three natures in man, and explain what he says by his own theory. The whole may be rejected if the reader sees fit; but still, Swedenborg ought to be judged by his own rules. Speaking of the three natures, or three degrees of life, as he sometimes calls them, he says, par. 3747, Heavenly Arcana:

"I have been instructed concerning these three degrees of life in man,—that it is the last degree of life which is called the external or natural man, by which degree man is like the animals as to concupiscencies and phantasies. And that the next degree of life is what is called the internal and rational man, by which man is superior to the animals, for by virtue thereof he can think and will what is good and true, and have dominion over the natural man, by restraining and also rejecting its concupiscencies, and the phan-

tasies thence derived; and, moreover, by reflecting within himself concerning heaven, yea, concerning the Divine Being, which the brute
animals are altogether incapable of doing. And
that the third degree of life *is what is most unknown to man*, although it is that through which
the Lord flows into the rational mind, thus giving
man a faculty of thinking as a *man*, and also
conscience, and perception of what is good and
true, and elevation from the Lord towards himself."

In *The True Christian Religion*, page 37,
Swedenborg says, on this same subject:

" The perfection of life consists not in thought,
but in the perception of truth from the light of
truth. The differences of the life with men may
be thence ascertained; for there are some who,
as soon as they hear the truth perceive that it is
truth. [These are in the highest life, or what
Swedenborg calls the celestial life, and they are
his angels, when doctrine and life are united.]
There are others (says he) who do not perceive
truth, but conclude it from confirmations by appearances. [This is what he calls the middle or rational state, in which men reason about truth and
become skilful in the sciences, where they stand
as it were upon the threshold of the celestial state,

but do not, in virtue of mere science, enter into that state, into which the simple and true may enter even without science.  In the celestial state men do not reason about the truth they see, because it is a *possession*.  The student may find the idea in Plato's Theætetus.  A sense of this possession constitutes the heavenly or celestial state, that is, the angelic state.  The reader may dispute the fact of there being such a state, if he pleases : I am only stating the theory by which Swedenborg ought to be interpreted.  The lowest state of man, in this same connection, Swedenborg says, is with those " who believe a thing to be true because it was asserted by a man of authority."

A writer of vast penetration and power of reasoning had set forth these identical distinctions in 1677, a century prior to Swedenborg's day, in the following words :

'We perceive many things, and form universal notions from single things represented to us through the *senses*, mutilated, confused, and without relation to the intellect; and also (we form them) from signs ; for example, by reading or hearing certain words, we call things to mind, and form certain ideas of them like those by which we *imagine* things.  These I will in future call knowledge of the first kind. [This, I will remark, is Swedenborg's lowest kind of knowledge, accessible to all men, but full of error.] Secondly (says this ingenious author), we form them from our having universal notions and adequate ideas of the properties of things, and this I call reason and knowledge of the second kind. [This is Swedenborg' middle state, where men of science are found. The author proceeds :] Besides these two kinds of knowledges, there is a *third*, which I will call intuitive knowledge. And this kind of knowing proceeds (or descends) from the adequate idea of the formal essence of certain attributes of God, to an adequate knowledge of the essence of things."

This last kind of knowledge is what Swedenborg calls celestial: its possession is realized as heavenly, and it elevates a man from the natural and rational state into the celestial, while yet in the body. Thus he says, speaking of this state, par. 3884, Heavenly Arcana :

" Let it be noted that, although I was in Heaven, still I was not out of myself, *but in the body*, for Heaven is in man, in whatsoever place he be ; and thus, when it pleases the Lord, a man may be in Heaven, and yet not be withdrawn from the body."

Here is an explicit statement of fact, as founded upon an equally explicit statement of doctrine, addressed to our experience and faculty for discovering or verifying truth.

Swedenborg's readers may fancy, while perusing his pages, that they are reading of another world than this we live in (I do not say *on*), but they are mistaken.

In the same way, when Swedenborg speaks of man in contradistinction to angels, he means man, not in the highest sense, for in this sense the Lord is man ; but in the lowest sense, that is, he means the natural man, as yet unawakened to the infinite depth of his spiritual nature.

In like manner, when Swedenborg speaks of what takes place after death, in by far the majority of cases, he refers to the transition from a natural to a spiritual life, when "old things pass away, and all things become new."

Angels in this sense die to the world, that is, they have taken leave of the love of the world, as opposed to the love of God. In this sense the Alchemists speak of the *Stone*, as "the cut-throat of covetousness, ambition," &c. To the "natural man" this may be "foolishness." But if we would understand Swedenborg, we must take into view his actual opinions of the nature of man, and especially have regard to its higher or *inner* developments, and not merely man in his lower and sensuous character, groping *upon* the surface of the earth, looking outwardly for that which can only be found within.

"There appertain (says Swedenborg, par. 1893, Heavenly Arcana) to every man an internal man, a rational man, which is intermediate, and an external man, which is properly called the natural man." Death is regarded as a birth: thus the lower life is supposed to die as the higher life is developed. The expression, *spirits from the world*, so often used in Swedenborg's writings, means men who have passed from the natural to the spiritual life.

In what Swedenborg says of *infants in the spiritual world*, and of their education and growth into "intelligence and wisdom," he is but commenting upon the doctrine that the kingdom of Heaven must be entered as a little child. He is not treating of another world, but of a *changed state* in this world. His reference in such cases to the "former life in the body," is to the natural life as distinguished from the spiritual life.

I would have the students of Swedenborg consider, while reading his writings, that he was a man, writing to men of man; of that man, if the

reader chooses, whom he called the Lord, or some
times the *grand-man;* and if he asks specifially
as to his meaning in the use of this expression,
the grand-man, I feel disposed to suggest, in addition to what I have already said, that, in Swedenborg's view, all the men in the world, all that
have been and all that shall be, are modifications
of one man, invisible in essence, but visible nevertheless in every human being; for, we have
the highest authority for it, the Lord is not far
from any one of us,—in Him we live, and move,
and have our being. We do not live in ourselves. When we think otherwise, we virtually
separate ourselves from the true life,—we virtually deny the Lord,—and to that extent are truly
dead while living. This I understand to be Swedenborg's doctrine. To know the Lord is to be
alive indeed. To be ignorant of the true life is a
species of death, to which we must die in order
to live.

The readers of Swedenborg may remember
his description of what he calls the punishment
of the *veil,* in the spiritual world—paragraphs
963 and 964, Heavenly Arcana;—to understand
which we must consider that, according to Swedenborg, to be in Heaven is to be in the presence
of the Lord—that is, of God; and hence the great-

est misery is to be shut out from this presence,—and this misery is even the greater when man is unconscious of it. Now this ignorance of the Lord takes place in every man, passing by the reasons for it, in whom the love of self prevails over the love of God, and especially in every man who lives in sin, it being the property of every delusion of the phantasy, to draw a " veil," as it were, over the inner eye of the sinner who, thence, is shut out from the sight of the Lord; and this is the punishment, as Swedenborg calls it, of the veil. In this state men are described as being sensible of their being under a veil, and as making efforts to rid themselves of it by " running hither and thither," and struggling, sometimes with mighty efforts, to retain the *veil*, yet see through it, which is impossible. This merely means that men are sometimes in love with something which they know is of the forbidden tree; but as it is but a little, a *very small matter*, as they fancy, they hope to reach Heaven with it, when the nature of Heaven excludes all sin, and thus excludes those who adhere to any darling " phantasy " not admitted there.

The doctrine is simple, and well known; and all that Swedenborg says of it is adapted to the comprehension of a child, only he has thrown an air of mystery over it, as if he saw beyond this world and was treating of another. But *this world*, in Swedenborg sense, is the world of nature, while the " other " is the world of *grace*, yet in this world also. The difference is that between a " man of the world," and a *holy* man, the former being willing to secure the supposed advantages of external fortune by condescensions compromising his spiritual life, while the latter lives in the fear of God even more than in the hope of Heaven, though Heaven is a fruit of this very fear.

To enter into wisdom is to enter into innocence, and innocence is represented by childhood; but Swedenborg distinguishes very sharply between the children of nature and the children of grace ;—I use this word for convenience, but not in any fantastical or fanatical sense. To be truly in grace is to be a true man.

Swedenborg utters, indeed, some very strange notions about seeing people in the " other life," that is, after death; saying, that they do not know otherwise than that they are still living in the world. This may refer to the condition of some men after a solemn *initiation* into some society. I admit also that he seems to give very positive statements of the condition of the good and the bad in a life beyond the grave literally understood ; but these must be regarded as his mere opinions, on a level with the opinions of Plato at the close of the Republic, or with the dream of Scipio. It is highly interesting to know the opinions of thoughtful men upon such a topic, but we enter into a voluntary vassalage when we accept any such representations as substantial irrefragable truth.

In paragraphs 2308 and 2309, Swedenborg, as everywhere else in his writings on such points, merely expresses his own opinions, formed, indeed, under a sense of the presence of the Lord. "No one," says he, "ever suffers punishment in another life on account of hereditary evil, because it is not his ; consequently he is not blamable for it," &c., &c. And then he speaks of "the nature of the education of infants in Heaven, viz., that by the intelligence of truth, and the wisdom of good, they are introduced into the angelic life, which is Love to the Lord, and mutual Love, in which is innocence ; but how contrary to this the education of infants on earth is, may appear from the following example amongst many others which might be mentioned : On a time I was in the street of a great city, and saw little children fighting together ; a crowd of people immediately gathered round them, and beheld the sight with much satisfaction, and I was informed that parents themselves sometimes excite their children to such combats; the good spirits and angels, who saw these things through my eyes [that is, his own *feelings* and *thoughts*, which he nevertheless attributed to the Lord], held them in such aversion that I was made [that is, he *felt*] sensible of the horror they expressed, especially at this circumstance, that parents should incite their children to such things; they [the spirits and angels, that is, his feelings and thoughts] declared that, by so doing, parents extinguish in the young bosoms of their children all mutual love, and all innocence."

This I suppose to be the way to read and understand Swedenborg. He called his feelings and thoughts, attributing them to the Lord, angels and spirits, and these told him thus and so; and by the same rule we must interpret Swedenborg, for he was one of us, and saw nothing in the universe but what we may see if we will lay off the veils which shut the truth from us. It is the simplest thing in the world; but, simple as it is, let the reader be sure it is sufficiently vast in its consequences.

# CHAPTER VIII.

THE followers of Swedenborg of the present day, or many of them, ask how certain portions of his writings, exhibiting deep truths of life beyond the reach, as they think, of ordinary men, are to be explained, except on the supposition that he was especially illuminated from heaven; and they ask also, how we can account for many of the stories connected with his name, which they think well authenticated and out of the ordinary course of events, except on the supposition of supernatural aid.

In the first place, no one is obliged to *explain* every thing that takes place in the world, or suppose a miraculous interposition. There are many things—an infinity of things—of which men can give little or no account to themselves or to others. In the next place, nothing is explained in a philosophical sense by referring it to supernatural power. This is a pious feeling—a religious explanation—but it extends equally to all things, and for this reason to nothing in particular. When we say that all things are providentially under the government of God, we include equally the things we know, and the things we do not know;—the things which we say, philosophically, we understand, and those which we do not understand. All philosophical knowledge, strictly speaking, refers to second or intermediate causes, more properly called *conditions*, under which phenomena are observed to take place. The knowledge of such conditions, or second causes, does not take our knowledge from under the veil of mystery involved in the idea of the one cause which is all in all, both Alpha and Omega. Nothing is more fallacious, therefore, than the idea that we are attaining philosophical knowledge by referring *particular* things to God, since all things must be referred to God, both what we know philosophically, that is, by second causes, and what we do not know. This may be easily understood by considering any one species of knowledge, known to one man and not to another. It is plain that the knowledge of the one and the ignorance of the other does not change the relation of the thing in respect to God, but this must remain on the contrary, one thing in relation to God and God's providential government.

Plato refers to this principle in the Dialogue on *the nature of things* (*Cratylus*, under the Hermetic form of an inquiry into language), where he calls the disposition to explain *things* by the "machinery of the gods," used by "writers of tragedies," the "not very clever evasions on the part of him who is not willing (or not able) to give a reason" for the original nature of things.

In the third place, many things that are very mysterious to some men are, philosophically speaking, very plain to others, and may become so to themselves by experience, study, and contemplation ; and we may remember particularly that *marvels* in relation to uncommon men, reported by the ignorant and the credulous, are extremely apt to be without foundation.

There is one recourse in determining such difficulties, entirely open to a man of plain sense, which the Swedenborgians are in danger of closing up in their desire to exalt Swedenborg above humanity ; and that is, a belief that he was not only a fallible man himself, but that he lived among fallible men, from whom we have received such relations as appear out of the order of nature.  In addition to which we, ourselves, who may feel called upon to judge of these matters, are fallible also; and it does not become us to assign supernatural powers to any mortal man, as if we could infallibly determine the limits and powers of nature in man.

No one can, in any proper sense, be said to be exalted except *in his nature*, and according to it.  A man may become "more a man" and be honored accordingly; but he cannot become more *than* a man without severing his connection with the race and losing the sympathies of his brethren.

Swedenborg was a true man, greatly yet altogether a man; a wise man, indeed, but still a man; and it is certain that he must have desired that his doctrines should be studied and received upon their own ground, and not upon his authority.

The members of the "Society" of Angels of which Swedenborg speaks, *veiled* their doctrines expressly with a view, as one object undoubtedly, of not veiling nature; that is, they desired that no one should appeal to their writings as authority for eternal truth, which can only be taught by the eternal itself, but should be compelled to look through and beyond their writings to the same inexhaustible fountain (the "Fountain" of Trevisan, the alchemist) whence they themselves had drawn a doctrine of life and love.

There is deep significance in the words recorded in *John* 16. 7 : *It is expedient for you that I go away : for if I go not away, the Comforter will not come unto you ; but if I depart I will send him unto you.*

This Comforter is called in the 13th verse of the same chapter, the "Spirit of Truth :" [as also in ch. 14. v. 17.] By this Spirit of Truth we may now understand, that so long as the apostles had the bodily presence of Christ with them, and could look to him for a decision upon all questions concerning truth, they would have no grounds of teaching from any light, on questions not specifically settled by him.

To the end, then, that the apostles should have the infinite source of truth opened to them, it was necessary that its representative in the humanity of the Lord should be withdrawn.

It is not otherwise now. We, too, in this age, need some freedom from the letter, in order that the spirit may be liberated ; for so long as any one looks to a record as containing the whole body of truth, he draws a veil over his eyes, and the "fountain" of truth becomes invisible.

Lord Bacon thought it an injury to the progress of knowledge when any science became reduced into formularies supposed to embrace the whole body of the science. If this is so of a special science, what must be thought of the attempt to put limits upon the science of science, the queen of the sciences? This science emphatically refuses to be confined in old bottles and is forever bursting them.

What then is the true "fixation" of the *matter* of the Philosopher's Stone,—of which so much is said in Hermetic books? What is it but the "law of liberty," wherewith the Spirit of Christ doth make us free; by which we are free even to remember that Christ himself, the greatest teacher the world ever saw, left no writing behind him whatever.

In this spirit, as it appears to me, the Hermetic philosophers, one and all, virtually say to us: Read our writings, indeed; we have written them for you, but "test them by the possibility of nature" [Sandivogius]; and "do not attempt to practise upon our bare words" [Eyræneus Philaletha].

In one word, every man dies alone. We brought nothing into this world, and it is certain we can carry nothing out. This ought to warn us that nothing in this world can have any other than an instrumental value, and among the things of this world are the books of so-called philosophers. When we make them other than instruments and depend upon them as the substantial truth, we lean upon broken reeds or upon reeds that shall surely be broken.

But every one must determine for himself the difference between liberty and license,—between genuine freedom and positive slavery.

Here lurks the peculiar danger of semi-enlightened times, when men attain light enough to distinguish or to suspect error, but want the power of discovering truth. This condition is perfectly described in the 7th book of Plato's Republic, under the story of the supposititious child,—nurtured and protected by those who were not his parents, for whom his respect declined when he discovered the cheat ; while yet, unable to find his true parents, he fell a victim to "flatterers," and was ruined.

A very useful volume might perhaps be written on *interpretation*, but for the single difficulty, that such a volume might need to be interpreted. Indeed, our libraries are already filled with works of this kind,—critical works, and commentaries without number, with commentaries upon commentaries. The readers of Swedenborg's interpretations may fancy that those writings are exempt from the universal law, yet many books have already appeared on the exposition of Swedenborg's works.

It was the same with the *Mysterium Magnum* of Jacob Behmen, which is an interpretation of the Pentateuch and other parts of the sacred writings.

Jacob Behmen wrote as magisterially, claiming an inspired insight, as any one who ever attempted an explanation of any part of the Holy Scriptures. He claimed an illumination from at least as high a source as Swedenborg could possibly pretend to, and yet who has ever looked into his interpretations, without feeling at once the need of an interpreter of the interpreter? The Pentateuch is light itself compared to the darkness of Jacob Behmen's interpretations.

In what now do Swedenborg and Behmen agree? Certainly in nothing but a mutual denial of the *letter*. But in this respect they were both preceded by multitudes of interpreters, equally denying the letter with themselves, and yet who has given us a light to be depended upon?

With regard to the *letter*, who has been more

absolute in its denial than Origen, who tells us, addressing us from the middle of the third century, that "the source of many evils lies in adhering to the carnal or external part of Scripture! Those who do so (says he) shall not attain to the kingdom of God. Let us seek therefore after the spirit and substantial fruits of the Word, which are hidden and mysterious;" and he says also that "the Scriptures are of little use to those who understand them as they are written."

In this view Origen flooded his time with rolls of books to interpret the Scripture, not according to the letter, but according to the spirit;—but according to what spirit? Here lies the original question, which neither Origen nor any other man has ever settled or can settle, except for himself.

In truth, any book whatever, that is read at all, calls for and meets with some sort of interpretation, which in the last resort is the judgment of the individual reader. When individual opinions are multiplied in favor of any work, it becomes a standard work: if a work be generally condemned, it disappears, unless in cases where it has a depth of real meaning beyond the penetration of ordinary readers. In this case, an approval from half a dozen thinkers in each age may carry the work down to the latest posterity, and in its progress it may be said to accumulate testimonials in its favor, so as largely to outnumber any one generation. That any work should live for many ages is undoubtedly something in its favor; and yet Lord Bacon has compared time to a river, which carries down the scum, but allows the more weighty and valuable substances to sink to the bottom.

The oldest books in the world,—Hindoo, Persian, Egyptian, Jewish,—are all obscure, and admit of various interpretations, and this may be one reason for their preservation; for a dark, mystical book tasks the inventive faculties to discover its meaning, an agreeable exercise in itself, and as vagueness allows a latitude of interpretation, more individuals may thus *please themselves*, perhaps the chief secret of approbation, by assigning a meaning to it; and under such circumstances it is not strange that approving interpreters are multiplied.

All of the great poems in the world are more or less allegorical, and are addressed to both the reason and the imagination of man, where interpretations are multiplied according to the variety of tastes and states of cultivation brought to the task, or the pleasure, as may be, of interpretation.

No one at all acquainted with Homer imagines that the interest he commands in the world is at all due to the historical element found in him, the reality of which has, indeed, been plausibly denied without diminishing in the least the interest in his great poems, where his classical admirers find pictures of life including both worlds, the seen and the unseen. There has always been a class of his admirers who see in the Iliad and the Odyssey both religion and philosophy, and this class will continue in the world; and yet if those who see religion in Homer could be brought together, they would not at all agree among themselves, while each would not the less insist that his own opinions are fully shadowed out by the Grecian bard.

What vast numbers, in like manner, have been called, or have allowed themselves to be called, *Platonists*, or admirers of Plato; while yet if a party of such admirers could be brought together, scarce any two individuals would propound the same views of the great Grecian intellectual realist, who is, by some, considered the most mystical of idealists.

If we take the Sacred Scriptures, what a field is open for this sort of inquiry! The so called

Jewish Cabala was nothing but a sort of tradition-
ary secret interpretation of the ancient Hebrew
Scriptures,—itself capable of expansion and con-
traction according to the genius of the class
amidst whom it might fall.  Much of the Cabala,
it is supposed, was never written.  Much that was
written is supposed to have been lost, but we
have one remarkable work of Jewish interpretation in the writings of Philo.  He denies the letter as *emphatically* as Swedenborg, and interprets
it according to *his* spirit.  Does his interpretation
and that of Swedenborg agree?  Certainly, in but
very few particulars, unless we force them into
harmony by interpretations of our own.  It is
true that Philo regards the Israelitish history as
symbolical of the progress of the natural man to
the spiritual man—from Egypt as the Land of
Darkness, to the Holy Land as the Land of Light,
—and gives us many very acceptable interpretations of the books of Moses ;—a little too diffuse,
indeed (like Swedenborg in this respect), often
tedious, and frequently very far-fetched ; but in
many instances, as I have said, very acceptable
as making sense of what otherwise seems very
unimportant.  He, too, as well as Swedenborg,
uses the sun, by similitude, for the " *mind*," or
says that Moses so used it.  The wicked idolaters

and inhabitants of Canaan, who were to be exterminated, are the bad passions and affections of the natural man, which must be eradicated, says Philo, before the divine possession, the Holy Land, can be entered upon. But where the two writers differ from each other, who shall decide? We must not allow Swedenborg to claim precedence upon his own assertion that his internal sight was opened by the Lord. This is merely his own declaration, and possibly Philo had what was to him as complete authority, but was too modest to place it upon extraordinary grounds,—appealing only to reason.

How are *we* to judge between them? Philo was a learned Hebrew, acquainted with the writings of his fathers, and possibly in possession of time-honored traditions received from the reputed wise men of his nation. Shall his interpretations be thrown aside and those of a modern philosopher accepted on his mystical declaration that the Lord had opened his internal sight and privileged him to look into what he called the spiritual world?

It is plain that this is a case where every man is thrown upon his own spirit and must interpret the interpreters, and it is not possible in the nature of things to supersede this necessity either by volumes of interpretations themselves or by works on the *principles* of interpretation.  Those who cannot understand the original may be deluded by either Philo or by Swedenborg, or by commentators in turn upon either of these.

In short, we cannot think by the intellect of others any more than we can see by their eyes. We may do both under certain conditions and limitations; but in the last resort, every man must judge for himself.

As to interpretation—every discourse, every sermon upon a text of Scripture, is in some sense an interpretation of Scripture, and what are all organized sects in Christendom but expressions or exponents of interpretations of Scripture? Luther interpreted the Scripture; Calvin interpreted the Scripture; Arminius, John Knox, Wesley—what are all these, and hundreds of others, but interpreters of Scripture?   And amidst this vast crowd Swedenborg comes forward and interprets the Scripture, claiming for this purpose a special Light from the " Lord "— denying, however, that there was any thing miraculous in his age.

This diversity may show that if the Scriptures are taken literally they do not yield an open sense equally accessible to all who may be equally earnest in their efforts to read aright ; or, if taken metaphorically or symbolically, the spirit of interpretation is not universally recognized.

The Catholic Church has acted upon the opinion of Origen and others, Fathers in the Church, and at one time refused to allow the laity access to the letter of the Scripture. Many have attributed this to sinister motives, and have proclaimed it a mere artifice to gain power and accumulate wealth. But it had no such origin. The Fathers of the Church, observing the vast diversity of individual opinions, sought first a remedy through the judgment of a council, by which certain books were set apart as authentic and canonical, and all others had the mark of Cain put upon them, by which they fell into disrepute, and ceased to furnish materials for heresy. But this was found to be only a partial remedy ; for disputes arose upon the sense of the retained books, and these disputes it was thought expedient to have determined by the decisions of councils also, until finally the authority of the Church took precedence over both individual opinions and the literal reading of the canon. But this was not the product of either ambition or avarice. Those who think otherwise know but little of the spirit of such men as Origen and St. Augustine.  It was merely the result of that sort of moral necessity, under which many men labor, of looking to others, *supposed to know*, for a decision upon questions involving eternal interests, under a sense of inability to decide for themselves.  Nowhere in the world has a sense of this inability been more deeply felt than in the Church itself, as evidence of which the writings of St. Augustine alone are sufficient.

As the Church on earth is composed of men, it was impossible to exclude from it human elements and human infirmities, which in the course of time manifested themselves from a double cause—a decline of earnestness and wisdom in the Church itself, and an advance of intelligence and spirit among the laity.  It was unavoidable that this should in time bring into question the doctrine of the infallibility of the Church, and thence it followed with the same certainty and necessity that the old questions arose, questions that occupied the Grecian sages, and have equally been the subject of study upon the banks of the Nile and those of the Ganges.

The reformation was no doubt a necessary product of the ages, but its effects are not confined to the reformers.  It has worked back upon the Catholic Church, and reformed that also; for, in enlightened countries, the Catholic Church is not now what it was prior to the days of Luther.

Among the reformers we find a vast variety of sects, and the number seems constantly increasing, while, in our day, a feature formerly unknown has become very prominent. I refer to the Congregational organizations containing an element of independence, by which, while they acknowledge the authority of the sacred Scriptures, they separate almost altogether from hierarchical domination and creeds, giving freedom to the spirit—carefully preserving at the same time educational influences full of good fruits.

Amidst all this variety of sects, organizations, and individual opinions, the philosophers being also divided into sects, there being no system of philosophic doctrine generally received, a writer comes forward with a learned work in our age, with this opening passage :

" Wherever a religion, resting upon *written* records, prolongs and extends the sphere of its dominion, accompanying its votaries through the varied and progressive stages of mental cultivation, a discrepancy between the representations of those ancient records, referred to as sacred, and the notions of more advanced periods of mental development, will inevitably sooner or later arise. In the first instance, this disagreement is felt in reference only to the unessential,—the external form : the expressions and delineations are seen to be inappropriate ; but by degrees it manifests itself also in regard to that which is essential : the fundamental ideas and opinions in these early writings fail to be commensurate with a more advanced civilization.  As long as this discrepancy is either not in itself so considerable, or else is not so universally discerned and acknowledged, as to lead to a complete renunciation of these Scriptures as of sacred authority, so long will a system of reconciliation by means of interpretation be adopted and pursued, by those who have a more or less distinct consciousness of the existing incongruity."

This is an ominous commencement of a critical examination, and would prepare almost any reader for a work of destruction.  Many have hailed it with joy, and have been fully prepared to accept conclusions, whose first effect might seem to be unalloyed freedom :—but some few, very few perhaps, not satisfied with the *letter*, still less satisfied with what seem fanciful and fallible interpretations, are yet least of all satisfied

to see violently assailed a system upon which the
" human heart has nourished itself for ages."
These become silent and reserved.  They withdraw from all public demonstration of their opinions, become thoughtful, and enter into solemn
resolutions with themselves, to take no active
part for or against any externally marked system,
—to perform punctually all the duties of life
without ostentation,—to lead perfectly innocent
and blameless lives, and see whether time and
the blessing of God will not bring to them some
kind of solution of the great problems that have
always occupied the attention of man.

# CHAPTER IX.

Can it be thought strange, amidst the confusion of the world on the subject of religion, that a class of self-secluded men should come into existence, the individuals of which, through contemplation, reading, and observation,—the duties of life being all punctually performed,—should reach a satisfactory condition, accompanied with the conviction, that others will not attain to it so long as they remain partisan advocates of a more or less externally formalized creed?

From this class, some of whom may be found in all enlightened countries, has come a small body of Hermetic philosophers,—a very few of whom have written, though very obscurely, of certain principles attained in secret, and maintained in secrecy ; for, if published at all, it has always been under a veil.

Many men have sprung up from time to time with the idea that they had reached the secret of this doctrine, and have audaciously and presumptuously written books to publish it to the world, affecting obscurity in imitation of the genuine writers, as if obscurity was the badge of truth, and a virtue in itself. For the most part, these men have known nothing of the secret.

Most of the real adepts have written nothing at all, while those who have published any thing have limited themselves to very small tracts, published, not so much with the object of making known a doctrine, as to indicate to the initiated their claim to brotherhood, and these works have almost invariably been anonymous.

From the nature of the case, the members, to call them such, of this " society" (referred to so frequently by Swedenborg) are scattered, both as to time and space, there being a few in every age, but not many in any age ; and from the same necessity they do not and cannot form an organized body, for this would be to put limitations upon that which in its nature is absolutely free. Yet they truly exist, and know each other by signs more infallible than can be made effectual by any organized society whatever ; and why ? —because they live in the fear of the Lord, and have become the depositors of his secret (Ps. 25, 14).

The members of this *society* have in former times communicated with each other by a secret language, which has had many forms, and will have many more, but which can never utterly perish.

" It is not unknown to you (says the translator of *An Easy Introduction to the Philosopher's Gold*, addressing the reader) that there is a certain tongue, which is the tongue of mysteries, called by FICINUS *Lingua Magica*, and sometimes *Lingua Angelorum;* and, indeed, it is *Lingua Ipsius Ternarii Sancti;* for almost all the Hagiography is in it; all the Cabalism of the Hebrews, and, without the ambit of that, there is nothing that is admirable.  This tongue is not only absolutely necessary, and wisely fitted to veil nature's secrets from the unworthy and profane, but is also bravely proportioned to the Olympus or the intellectual imaginations of man ;—That MAN—who is descended from God, who has in himself a sense of Him, and turns his mind towards him—might, like a generous scholar, be taught by mystic words.—And yet it is not every artist who has attempted this tongue that has a right felicity in the use of it; nay, indeed, not very many out of the whole *Sacra Corona* can be shown who have offered so much as a Rose to the true Venus of the language, the sweet and secret Cytheria."

We have all heard of Roger Bacon as a Magician. He was indeed an Alchemist—a Hermetic Philosopher—and wrote many works himself in the mystic vein of that mysterious class of men, and in one of his works (*The Admirable Force of Art and Nature*) he has taken such especial pains to prepare his reader for his mystical writing, that it seems wonderful how the *subject* at least of his treatise should have escaped observation, as it appears to have done. He recites many species of secret writing, and explains, as openly as need be, why they were adopted, expressly telling us that *he himself will use some of them.* The first part of the Treatise is devoted to purely natural things, designed to show the power of *Art*, "using nature as an instrument." It is in this work that the monk gives us reason to believe that he was acquainted with the composition of (gun) powder, and seems to predict the use of steam power, both for propelling ships and railway carriages. He speaks of what we now call the hydraulic press, and of the diving bell; he describes the kaleidoscope as if he had one before him, and foretells the making of "instruments to fly withal, so that one sitting in the middle of the instrument, and turning about an engine by which the wings, being artificially composed, may beat the air after the manner of a flying bird." One object of this Tract appears to have been to defend himself from the accusation of magic, and to give reasons for his own use of secret writing, of which he gives us an example; for he says:

"Thus, having produced certain examples, declaring the power of Art and Nature, to the end that out of those few we might collect many, out of the parts gather the whole, out of particulars infer universals, we see how far forth it is altogether needless for us to gape after *Magic*, whereas Nature and Art are sufficient. Now I intend to prosecute every one of the aforesaid things in order, and deliver their causes, and the method of working them particularly. But, first of all, I consider that the secrets of nature contained in the skins of goats and sheep [he is speaking of *men*] are not spoken of, lest every man should understand them; as Socrates and Aristotle commandeth. For Aristotle, in his Book of *Secrets*, affirmeth, that he is a breaker

of the celestial seal that maketh the secrets of Art
and Nature common ; adding, moreover, that
many evils betide him that revealeth secrets.
And in the book entitled *Noctes Atticæ*, in the
comparing of wise men together, it is reputed a
great folly to give an Ass lettuce, when thistles
will serve his turn ; and it is written in the book
of *Stones*, that he impaireth the majesty of things
who divulgeth mysteries.   And they are no
longer to be termed secrets, when the multitude
is acquainted with them—having regard to the
usual division of the multitude, which evermore
gainsay the learned.   For that which seemeth
[appeareth] unto all, is true, as also that which is
so judged of by the wise, and men of best account.   But that which seemeth only to the
many, that is, to the common people, so far forth
as it seemeth such, must of necessity be false.

"I speak here of the common sort, in that
sense, as they are distinguished from the learned.

"For in the common conceits of the mind,
they agree with the learned, but in the proper
principles and conclusions of arts and sciences
they disagree, employing themselves about mere
*appearances*, and sophistications, and quirks, and
quiddities, and such like trash, of which wise men
make no account.

"In things proper, therefore, and in secrets, the common people do err, and in this respect they are opposite to the learned; but in common matters they are comprehended under the law of all, and therein do agree with the learned. And as for these common things, they are of small value, and not worthy to be sought after for themselves, but only in respect of their use for things particular and proper.

"Now, the cause of this concealment among all wise men, is, the contempt and neglect of the secrets of wisdom by the vulgar sort, who know not how to use those things that are most excellent. Or if they do conceive any worthy thing, it is altogether by chance and fortune, and they do exceedingly abuse that their knowledge, to the great damage and hurt of many men, yea, even of whole societies; so that he is worse than mad that publisheth any secret, unless [by mystical writing, is meant] he conceal it from the multitude, and in such wise deliver it that even the studious and learned shall hardly understand it.

"This hath been the course which wise men have observed from the beginning, who by many means have hidden the secrets of wisdom from the common people.

"Some have used characters and verses, and

divers other riddles and figurative speeches, as *Aristotle* witnessed in his book of *Secrets*, where he thus speaketh: 'O *Alexander*, I will show thee the greatest Secret in the world: God grant that thou mayest keep it close, and bring to pass the intention of the Art *of that Stone, which is no Stone, and is in every man, and in every place, and at all seasons, and is called the* END *of all philosophers.*'

" And an infinite number of things are found in many books and sciences obscured with such dark speeches, that no man can understand them without a teacher.

" Thirdly, some have hidden their Secrets by their modes of writing; as, namely, by using consonants only: so that no man can read them, unless he knows the signification of the words:— and this is usual among the Jews, Chaldeans, Syrians, and Arabians, yea, and the Grecians too: and, therefore, there is a great concealing with them, but especially with the Jews; for *Aristotle* sayeth in the above-named book, that God gave them all manner of wisdom, before there were any philosophers, and all nations borrowed the principles of philosophy from them. And thus much we are plainly taught by Albamasar in his book named the *Larger Introductory,* and by other philosophers, and by Josephus in his Eighth Book of Antiquities.

"Fourthly, things are obscured by the admixture of letters of divers kinds; and thus hath *Ethicus* the astronomer concealed his wisdom, writing the same with Hebrew, Greek, and Latin letters, all in a row.

"Fifthly, they hide their Secrets, writing them in other letters than are used in their own country, to wit, when they take letters that are in use in foreign nations, and feign them according to their own pleasures.  This is a very great impediment, used by Artephius [an alchemist] in his book of the Secrets of Nature.

"Sixthly, they make certain forms, not of letters, but such as used by diviners and enchanters, which according to the diversity of arrangement have the power of letters:  and these likewise hath Artephius used in his Science.

"Seventhly, there is a yet more cunning mode of concealment by the help of Art notary: an Art whereby a man may write or note anything, as briefly as he will, and as swiftly as he can desire.  And in this sort have the Latin authors hidden many Secrets.

"I deemed it necessary to touch these tricks of obscurity, because haply myself may be constrained, through the greatness of the secrets which I shall handle, to use some of them, so that, at the least, I might help thee to my power.  I give thee therefore to understand, that my purpose is orderly to proceed in the exposition of those things, whereof I made mention before; as, *to dissolve the philosopher's egg, and search out the parts of a philosophical man.* And this shall serve for a beginning to the rest."

One would think that here is a sufficient warning not to understand literally what follows :

" Take SALT (says he, and I will tell the reader that Bacon here, like other Hermetic philosophers, is writing of *man*, and intends to indicate a method of making him 'the salt of the earth '), —Take salt, and rub it diligently with water— [wash the matter, say all these philosophers] and purify it in other waters; afterwards by divers *contritions*, rub it with *salts*, and *burn* it with sundry *assations*, that it may be made a PURE EARTH, separated from the other elements—which I esteem worthy of thee for the stature of my length.  Understand me if thou art able : for it shall undoubtedly be composed of the elements, and therefore it shall be *a part of the stone, which is no stone, and is in every man ; which thou shalt find at all times of the year in his own place,"

&c., &c.    But here is enough.    The reader may think more than enough.

I might perhaps have satisfied myself with a simple reference to these writings, but I desired to show decisively the fact, that in former times there existed secret modes of writing, and something of the reasons for them, that the reader may credit me in the assertion of the fact, and be in a better position to understand something of those reasons.

*Sandivogius* addresses the *Courteous Reader* as follows :

"Seeing that I may not write more clearly than other philosophers have written, haply thou mayest not be satisfied with my writings ; especially since thou hast so many other books of philosophers already in thy hands: but believe me, —I have no need to write books, because I seek neither profit nor vain-glory by them.    To conclude, if you will not be wise and wary by these my writings and admonitions, yet excuse me, who desire to deserve well of thee : I have dealt as faithfully as it was lawful for me, and as becomes a man of a good conscience to do.    If you ask who I am,—I am one that can live anywhere. If you know me and desire to show yourselves good and honest men, you shall hold your tongue.

If you know me not, do not inquire after me.
* * * Now I do not wonder, as before I did,
why philosophers, when they have attained to
this medicine, have not cared to have their days
shortened; because every philosopher hath the
life to come set as clearly before his eyes as thine
may be seen in a glass. And if God shall grant
thee thy desired end, then thou wilt believe me,
and not reveal thyself to the world."

While I feel obliged to declare my opinion,
as I have in the foregoing pages, that Swedenborg was a Hermetic philosopher, I feel equally
bound not to place him in the foremost rank
among those men. I believe that he had studied
the writings of the Hermetic class, and had im-
bibed some principles from them; but I am sure
that he did not precisely "lay hold" of the very
secret itself. If he had fully possessed the art,
he would have written less, and especially he
would not have attempted to disclose the hidden
sense of the books of Moses, in which attempt he
has most assuredly departed from the Hermetic
practice, and has placed himself on the footing
of Philo and other allegorists.

The Hermetic writers do indeed assert that
the letter of the Mosaic books is a *veil;* but their

reference to the first verses of Genesis is rather to illustrate or *hint*, perhaps I ought to say, the nature of their own doctrine, than to set forth openly a secret sense of those verses. Swedenborg here mistook their design, and, departing from the genuine Hermetic rule, he undertook a vast work, which would have remained incomplete, had he lived and labored to this day. I am disposed to say, therefore, that, although Swedenborg had caught a glimpse of Hermetic doctrine, and wrote under its influence, he was not, as I must believe, in a condition to breathe the prayer, " Father, I thank thee that thou hast hidden these things from the wise, and revealed them to babes."

If Swedenborg has justly expounded the True Christian Religion, in his work with this title, it is certain that none but the deepest students can penetrate the doctrine, and the general mass of mankind can be but little benefited by the preaching which is to derive its life through or by means of a comprehension of the principles discussed in that work. Swedenborg's doctrine of substance, of discrete and continuous degrees, of time, of space, and even of love itself, will never be generally acknowledged and made popular; and therefore, as a fruit of study, can never become generally useful.

Is not this, it may be asked, still less likely to result from the Hermetic writings, which have already fallen into deserved oblivion? It may be so; but there is this to be said of those writings—No one can attain to any doctrine from Hermetic books as a result of direct teaching. The consequence is, that whatever be derived from those works can be said only to manifest the individual character of the student; hence no one can be said, in any proper sense, to be or to have been injured by that sort of reading. The Hermetic books may be said to have been written purposely as enigmatical as nature itself, and every one who comes to their study brings with him a certain *design* or *intent*. Now this, for the time being, expresses the very essence of his life, and will work itself out. If this *intent* be the truth, the student will not be misled by Hermetic books, for their aim is to throw the student upon the truth itself for a solution of its problems, and they do not aim to furnish a solution which may be carried, folded up, in one's pocket. The result of reading Hermetic writings is not to enable their readers to urge that they say *thus and so;* but that (something) *is,* thus and so.   But, for the most part, the readers of Swedenborg seem content to know that *he*, the Swedish seer, says thus and so.   In other words, a doctrine is received by the Swedenborgians, or at all events by many of them, because "the master has said it."   They look to him and not to the author of all truth, and some of them are in danger of forgetting that Christ, while in the body, would not allow even his followers to call him good.   "There is none good but one, *that is*, God."

Still, I desire to bear my testimony in favor of Swedenborg's writings as of immense *instrumental* value.   His influences are good, and his followers, so far as I have observed, are amiable, excellent citizens, people to be loved and admired.   But they should be on their guard against the error of imagining that Swedenborg understood the doctrine of life better than John, or that there is any positive need of twelve octavo volumes in exposition of only two books of the Pentateuch, Genesis and Exodus.

The doctrine of Christianity cannot need large and learned volumes to expound it.   The principle by which it may be understood lies much nearer home :—" Blessed are the pure in heart, for they shall see God."

" Keep thy heart with all diligence, for out of it are the issues of life."

# CHAPTER X.

THE multitude of interpretations that different portions of the Sacred Writings have met with might discourage us, if we could not draw from this very variety a reconciling consideration ; for what does it prove but the " many-sidedness " of those Scriptures, and their adaptation to the wants of every condition of life; while, at the same time, we may be sure that it is not essential for us to rest upon any one interpretation exclusively; but, if we will have explanations, or whatever they may be called, we are at full liberty to cull them from all quarters upon one single condition, that we domesticate nothing in our hearts except under the law of conscience.

Those who feel the want of an interpretation of Genesis, or of the Pentateuch as a whole, may undoubtedly seek for it wherever it may be found, and accept such portions of different interpretations as may seem just and rational.  Thus, many

very beautiful interpretations may be found in
Philo, though his criticisms are evidently a little
cramped by a *theory* in great part manifestly
drawn from Plato.  Swedenborg also drew from
Plato and others, and had a theory to which the
Mosaic writings were compelled to submit in
passing through his alembic.

It may be that every interpreter, at all advanced beyond the sensuous state, has some theory constantly present in reading mystic writings,
or writings having an indeterminate element in
them.  The merely didactic mind will perhaps
never see in the story of the Garden of Eden any
thing but a veritable history ;  but the same story,
under the examination of a genius a little exercised in poetry, appears as a mixture of history
and allegory, while many see nothing in the story
but the allegory, and consider it idle to imagine
that it ever had a historical basis of any sort.

It is the same with nearly every part of the
most ancient Scriptures ; with, for example, the
Tabernacle of Moses and the Temple of Solomon.
With perhaps the majority of readers the Temple
of Solomon, and also the Tabernacle, were mere
buildings ;  very magnificent indeed, but still
mere buildings for the worship of God.  But
some are struck with many portions of the ac-

count of their erection admitting a moral interpretation, and while the buildings are allowed to
stand (or to have stood, once), visible objects,
these interpreters are delighted to meet with indications that Moses and Solomon, in building
the temples, were wise in the knowledge of God
and of man; from which point it is not difficult
to pass on to the moral meaning altogether, and
affirm that the building, which was erected without "the noise of a hammer, or axe, or any tool
of iron" (I Kings 6. 7), was altogether a moral
building, a building of God, not made with
hands :—in short, many see in the story of Solomon's Temple a symbolical representation of
MAN, as the temple of God, with its HOLY OF
HOLIES deep seated in the centre of the human
heart.

This class of readers or interpreters dismiss
all idea of an external building, and study the
details of the Temple (or of the Tabernacle) as
significant of the nature of MAN, with its two
pillars, Jachin and Boaz, used, perhaps, by every
"image" of God in going to and fro in his daily
avocations; and the Hermetic writers might possibly see their sulphur and mercury, as the attributes of their sacred Trinity, symbolized in the
*Two Cherubims*, from "between" which GOD, as

the Spirit, gave his commands to Moses for the Children of Israel; or, finally, it may come to this, that the Temple is Moses himself, whose conscience speaks forth the commands of God, to our consciences, where they are verified and acknowledged. Thou shalt not kill, said the conscience of Moses, seated in the "midst" of the Temple of the Lord, from "between" the *Soul* and the *Body*, as the two cherubims;—and where is the human heart that does not say, speaking from the same point, Amen?

To understand the power and authority of this Amen, we need only ask ourselves what authority Moses would have in the absence of it;—or, let us imagine that his commands had violated that oracle of God in the human breast! It is evident that the authority of Moses does not in the least depend upon the history of the miraculous accompaniments at the enunciation of the commandments; but, contrarily, the reasonableness of the commandments has supported a belief in the miracles.

From this mode of looking at the subject we may understand why Swedenborg regarded Moses as a Hermetic philosopher;—writing, as he says, in "correspondences," or, in other words, in Hermetic Symbolism; for this is the meaning of

the Swedish philosopher, himself a Hermetic
writer. Swedenborg tells us again and again
that all the ancient wise men wrote in " *Correspondences*," undoubtedly including MOSES,—for
the interpretation of whose writings, or two books
of them only, he devoted twelve octavo volumes!
Now, this word, " correspondence," can itself
have no other meaning than that of Symbolism.
It is plain, therefore, that, in the estimation of
Swedenborg, Moses was a Hermetic philosopher;
and Swedenborg, having seized as he supposed
his point of view, comes forward in modern
times as his interpreter, yet without wholly lay-
ing off the veil himself. He has, in fact, rather
taken up the mantle of Moses, and assumes to
speak to us as if " the Lord had been seen of
him,"—to use his own language.

But does this lessen the authority of Moses?
Not in the least. On the contrary, it may show
us the true ground of that authority, when we
find it not only in Swedenborg, but in ourselves,
and upon this foundation we may be enabled to
predict the permanent authority of Moses, whose
commandments will live and be respected forever;—and why?—because they proceeded from
the human heart and speak to the human heart.

We believe in Moses, because we believe in ourselves.

To enable the reader to understand these allusions more distinctly, let him study the real import of the following citations from Scripture:

*Exodus* xxv. 17.—And thou shalt make a mercy seat of pure gold : * two cubits and a half shall be the length thereof, and a cubit and a half the breadth thereof.

18. And thou shalt make two cherubims of gold, of beaten work shalt thou make them, in the two ends of the mercy seat.

19. And make one cherub on the one end, and the other cherub on the other end : even of the mercy seat shall ye make the cherubims on the two ends thereof.

20. And the cherubims shall stretch forth their wings on high, covering the mercy seat with their wings, and their faces shall look one to another ; toward the mercy seat shall the faces of the cherubims be.

21. And thou shalt put the mercy seat above

---

* Let us, for a moment, consider this *mercy seat* to be a human heart, and the *gold* of which it is to be made is that of which we read in *Rev.* iii. 18,—" tried in the fire,"—said to make us " rich." With all reverence, be it spoken, this is Alchemic gold.

upon the ark; and in the ark thou shalt put the testimony that I shall give thee.

22. And there I will meet with thee, and I will commune with thee from above the mercy seat, from between the two cherubims which are upon the ark of the testimony, of all things which I will give thee in commandment unto the children of Israel.

*Numbers* vii. 89.—And when Moses was gone into the tabernacle of the congregation to speak with him, then he heard the voice of one speaking unto him from off the mercy seat that was upon the ark of testimony, from between the two cherubims: and he spake unto him.

viii. 1.—And the Lord spake unto Moses, saying, &c.

1 *Kings* vi. 23.—And within the oracle he made two cherubims of olive tree, each ten cubits high.

24. And five cubits was the one wing of the cherub, and five cubits the other wing of the cherub; from the uttermost part of the one wing unto the uttermost part of the other were ten cubits.

25. And the other cherub was ten cubits:

both the cherubims were of one measure and one size.

26. The height of the one cherub was ten cubits, and so was it of the other cherub.

27. And he set the cherubims within the inner house; and they stretched forth the wings of the cherubims, so that the wing of one touched the one wall, and the wing of the other cherub touched the other wall; and their wings touched one another in the midst of the house.

*2 Kings* xix. 15. And Hezekiah prayed before the Lord, and said, O Lord God of Israel, which dwellest *between* the cherubims, thou art the God, even thou alone, of all the kingdoms of the earth; thou hast made heaven and earth.

*Psalm* lxxx. 1. Give ear, O Shepherd of Israel, thou that leadest Joseph like a flock: thou that dwellest *between* the cherubims, shine forth.

*Psalm* xcix. 1. The Lord reigneth; let the people tremble: he sitteth *between* the cherubims; let the earth be moved.

*Isaiah* xxxvii. 16. O Lord of hosts, God of Israel, that dwellest *between* the cherubims, thou art the God, even thou alone, of all the kingdoms of the earth; thou hast made heaven and earth.

*Ezekiel* x. 1. Then I looked, and, behold, in the firmament that was above the head of the cherubims there appeared over them as it were a Sapphire stone, as the appearance of the likeness of a throne.

2. And he spake, &c.   *   *   *

15. And the cherubims were lifted up. This is the living creature that I saw by the river of Chebar.   *   *   *

19. And the cherubims lifted up their wings, and mounted up from the earth in my sight * *.

20. This is the living creature that I saw under the God of Israel, by the river Chebar; and I knew that they were the cherubims.

It cannot be thought strange that with such descriptions and allusions as these a symbolic representation should be supposed, to the comparative disregard of the historical elements, though without denying them, and that some men may even yet be living who believe that the Lord,—the eternal, the unchangeable,—still speaks from " between " the cherubims to those who enter the temple, and penetrate the seat of mercy, their own hearts, unveiled. But further, and still more to this point:—

*Exodus* xxxiv. 33. And till Moses had done speaking with them [the children of Israel], he put a veil on his face.

34. But when Moses went in before the Lord, to speak with him, he took the veil off, until he came out. And he came out, and spake unto the children of Israel that which he was commanded.

35. And the children of Israel saw the face of Moses, that the skin of Moses' face shone: And Moses put a veil upon his face again, until he went in to speak with him.

St. Paul's commentary upon this *veil* is remarkable, and might very well excuse us for supposing it a purely Hermetic veil, and that St. Paul himself thought no otherwise of it.

2 *Cor.* iii. 3. Forasmuch as ye are manifestly declared to be the Epistle of Christ ministered to by us, written not with ink, but with the Spirit of the living God; not in tables of stone, but in fleshy tables of the heart.

4. And such trust have we through Christ to God-ward.

5. Not that we are sufficient of ourselves to

think any thing, as of ourselves; but our sufficiency is of God.

6. Who also hath made us able ministers of the New Testament; not of the letter, but of the Spirit; for the letter killeth, but the Spirit giveth life.

*          *          *          *          *

12. Seeing then that we have such hope, we use great plainness of speech:

13. And not as Moses, *which* put a veil over his face, that the children of Israel could not steadfastly look to the end of that which is abolished.

14. But their minds were blinded; for unto this day remaineth the same veil untaken away in the reading of the Old Testament; which veil is done away in Christ.

15. But even unto this day, when Moses is read, the veil is upon their heart.

16. Nevertheless when it [the heart] shall turn to the Lord, the veil shall be taken away.

17. Now the Lord is that Spirit; and where the Spirit of the Lord is, there is liberty.

Philo's interpretation of the cherubims is inadmissible, or it needs a further interpretation; for he says that, " by one of the cherubim is understood the extreme outermost circumference of the entire heaven, in which the fixed stars celebrate their truly divine dance," &c. :—" the other (he says) is the inner sphere which is contained within that previously mentioned, which God originally divided into two parts: "—referring no doubt to the 6th verse of the 1st ch. of Genesis, or possibly to the 1st verse: "In the beginning God created the heaven and the earth." But Philo's description would seem to refer to an outer and inner sphere, as if one was contained in the other, in which case one would be larger than the other; whereas, we read that the cherubims were of "one measure and size."

Swedenborg's idea of mind and body would come nearer to the requisitions of the text; for, according to him, these may be regarded as the two extremes of the universe,—of matter on the one side, and spirit on the other;—yet, so answering to each other as to be exactly united, as he says, by *correspondence;* and he further says, that there is nothing in the one which is not in the other; in the midst or "between" which we may suppose to be the *place* referred to in the text, which every man carries with him.

The *Hermetic* PHILALETHE had two certain impressions upon his mind, which he refers to in the following language:

" When I consider the system or fabric of this world, I find it to be a certain series, a link or chain, which is extended *à non gradu ad non gradum :*—From that which is *beneath* all apprehension, to that which is *above* all apprehension. That which is beneath all degrees of sense is a certain horrible, inexpressible darkness ; the magicians call it *tenebræ activæ,* and the effect of it in nature is cold, &c.  For darkness is *vultus frigoris,* the complexion, body, and matrix of cold, as light is the *face, principle,* and *fountain* of heat.  That which is above all degree of intelligence, is a certain *infinite inaccessible fire or light.* Dionysius calls it *caligo divina,* because it is *invisible* and *incomprehensible.*  The Jew styles it EIN, that is *nihil* or *nothing,* but in a relative sense, or as the schoolmen express it, *quo ad nos.* [This nothing is simply no thing, or not a thing.] In plain terms it is *deitas nuda sine indumento.* The middle substances, or chain between these two, is that which we commonly call nature. This is the *scala* of the great *Chaldee,* which doth reach *à tartaro ad primum ignem,* from the *subternatural darkness to the supernatural fire.*"

This, to be sure, throws no light upon the subject, and I only recite it to show how men's minds have labored upon a certain two things,

which Moses has shadowed out by two cherubims, equal to each other, whose outer wings
touched the extreme outer walls, while their inner wings touched each other within the *house*,
from *between* which God communed with Moses,
and gave him his commands for the people of Israel, to wit, the " congregation," who, according
to some interpretations, are all of the passions and
affections, and indeed all the capabilities of our
nature, the whole of which are actually ruled by
the Spirit of God, whether we know it or not.
The wise are said to know it ; but the unwise are
ignorant of it, and think they possess and enjoy
an independent life.

The Masonic Society is said to make great use
of the story of the temple of Solomon, as symbolical and typical of a temple not made with hands ;
but I am not a Mason, and may be supposed not to
know any thing on the subject ; and yet Dr. Oliver's *Landmarks of Masonry*, an authorized Masonic work, very plainly shows how the subject is
understood by the truly initiated within a lodge.
Dr. Oliver gives a very minute account of a certain *rebuilding* of the temple, which any one may
see has no reference whatever to a building of
masonry and carpentry.

The second Temple, it appears, must be built

upon the foundations of the first; which, interpreted, means that the man of grace must be created from the natural man.

"The foundations of the Temple (says Dr. Oliver) were opened and cleared from the accumulation of rubbish, that a level site might be procured for the commencement of the building. While engaged in excavations for this purpose, THREE fortunate sojourners [?] are said to have discovered our ancient stone of foundation, which had been deposited in the secret crypt by Wisdom, Strength, and Beauty [Dr. O. has already told us that these represent the trinity], to prevent the communication of ineffable secrets to profane or unworthy persons. The discovery having been communicated to the prince, priest, and prophet of the Jews, the stone was adopted as the chief corner-stone of the re-edified building; and thus became, in a new and expressive sense, the type of a more excellent dispensation. An avenue was also accidentally discovered, supported by seven pair of pillars [?], perfect and entire, which, from their situation, had escaped the fury of the flames that had consumed the temple, and the desolation of war which had destroyed the city. The secret vault, which had been built by Solomon as a secure depository for

certain valuable secrets that would inevitably
have been lost without some such expedient for
their preservation, communicated by a subter-
ranean avenue with the King's Palace [?]; but,
at the destruction of Jerusalem [?], the entrance
having been closed by the rubbish of falling
buildings, it had been now discovered by the
appearance of a key-stone [?] amongst the foundations of the Sanctum Sanctorum," &c.

In reading this account of the rebuilding of
the Temple, it is difficult not to think of the *three*
sojourners in the "image" of the trinity;—of the
seven virtues, as prudence, temperance, courage,
fortitude, hope, faith, and charity, which in themselves are indestructible, however much they
may be disregarded by man;—of the passage
through these to the WISDOM crowning life; and,
finally, one may hope that the *key* is not so absolutely lost but that it may be found by the faithful, the simple, the true.

While one class of interpreters surrender the
historical character of the first verses of Genesis,
and another disregard the historical account of
the building and rebuilding of the Temple, another class of interpreters think it no impicty to
go so far as to deny that there ever was such a
people as the Israelites, and affirm their belief

that the whole history is symbolical and typical of the progress of man in the process of regeneration.

A peculiarly earnest and pious writer, Mr. THOMAS BROMLEY, evidently a man of great learning, published a very extraordinary volume in 1744, entitled—*The Way to the Sabbath of Rest, or the Soul's Progress in the Work of the New Birth: together with the Journeys of the Children of Israel,*" &c., in which the whole account of the Exodus is explained as symbolical and typical, the historical character being, not denied, indeed, but entirely disregarded:—and this account is given purely in the interest of piety. The wonders at Sinai, the waters of Horeb, the heavenly quails and manna, &c., &c., are all spiritualized, and may thus be said, in some sense, to be naturalized. The story itself is treated as a divine parable or allegory.

The *fire* in the *bush* is interpreted to be the Spirit of God in Moses—God, in Scripture, being often called a fire; the *waters* flow from the *stony* heart of man, softened by the Spirit of God; the *quails* and the *manna* become heavenly truth, the divine food of the spiritually-awakened man.

The Alchemists, or some of them, symbolize this *truth* by *dew* from heaven; hence the er-
10*

roneous opinion prevailing that the Alchemists thought that *dew* was the universal solvent! They thought that the Spirit of God was the universal solvent, and they tell us, in their jargon, to gather *dew* upon the *tops of mountains* by spreading *clean* linen cloths, &c., &c. Their writings fell into the hands of an unbelieving generation, and this age has inherited their misunderstandings.

The story of Robinson Crusoe has been believed true by those who could in nowise believe that *dew* is the universal solvent! Yet this class of readers have no difficulty in believing that quails and manna have been rained from heaven! But the actuality of the history of the transition from Egypt—as the Land of slavery and darkness—to the Holy Land flowing with milk and honey, the Land of Light and peace, is manifestly subordinate to the spiritual sense, and without a spiritual sense would be on a footing with other histories; whereas, the spiritual sense might remain in full beauty and power, without a historical basis, and thus free the story from seeming grounds for captious criticism.

This mode of interpretation has one important advantage, which many have seen, and which, in an inquiring age like this, ought by no means to be overlooked; and on this point the Swedenborgians have just reason to commend their system. It strikes a fatal blow at one of the strongholds of the literal reading infidel. This system of interpretation may be applied to many parts of Scripture—to the sacrifice of Isaac, for example.

The *literal* reading infidel cries out against this story as a dishonor to God,—as imputing to him a violation of one of the purest instincts of life, implanted by God himself in the breast of a loving father. The infidel dwells with exultation upon the horror of imagining, that the infinite Father of all could command a loving parent to butcher his own son, and then burn his remains upon a funeral pyre, as an offering to himself.

To tell him that the event was in the control of God, and was not permitted to be consummated,—that a substitute was provided,—does not satisfy him. He insists that this explanation only changes a dishonorable tragedy into an equally disreputable farce, absolutely beneath and derogatory to the divine majesty.

If now this story be classed with other symbolic or allegoric illustrations of principle and eternal truth, what is the truth it poetically teaches? It is plainly this:—that there is but one object of supreme love for man, and no man is right-minded towards God, whose entire affections are centred upon any subordinate being. What now is stronger than the love of a father for a son,—for an only son,—for an only son in his old age? These conditions are all seized upon in this story, and the sacrifice of the son is poetically put for that of the *love* which, it was the object of the allegory to show, should be subordinate to the love of God. The literal reading may cheerfully be surrendered to the infidel, but the eternal truth it teaches will preserve the story as a divine allegory in the admiration of all wise men.

Philo interprets at great length the story of the flood, of the *ark*, and of the preservation of the "just," as a piece of poetic symbolism. According to Philo, *man* is the *ark*, his sins are the overwhelming flood, from which is saved the principle of truth and good ;—as true to-day as when the story was written.

It is plain that he did not consider the story as historical, or, if he did, it is certain that he attached no value to it as history.

All such stories are beautiful as allegories, but when their historic truth is not only insisted upon, but, as often happens, is made the chief interest, it is calculated to drive away from their study the more mature intellects, who often thus lose the benefit of ancient wisdom altogether.

As in the parables of the New Testament, so in the allegories of the Old, the truths taught have no need of historical reality for their support.

That which distinguishes the sacred writings from all other books, profane books so called, is not their historical verity, but it is the spiritual truth enclosed in the divine representations contained in the sacred volume. The historical character of the entire record, from Genesis to Revelation, may be surrendered without the loss of one "jot or tittle" of the eternal WORD, by which it was produced. When Jesus declared that "*Heaven and earth shall pass away, but my words shall not pass away,*" he did not speak of written words; for, as respects what he said, his words were not then written; nor did he in a narrow literal sense refer even to his spoken words, but he referred to that eternal truth in God, by whose authority and teaching he represented himself as speaking; for he said expressly, "My doctrine is not mine, but his that sent me;" and in a great many forms he is represented as repeating this declaration, as if it was an important part of his mission to guard against being misunderstood on this point.  .

Those who are accustomed to dwell upon the literal reading of Scripture, are apt to fear that the truth itself is in danger when the literal sense is brought into question; but this is to mistake the effect for the cause, and imagine that the Bible is the cause of religion, instead of a product of it.   Some, still further removed from the truth, if possible, are of opinion that the preservation of religion depends upon the building and endowment of churches, not seeing that the ancient temples and modern churches and mosques have all been produced by what is called the religious sentiment in man, which can never be destroyed but with the destruction of his nature.   The external forms and ceremonies of religion may be perpetuated by synagogues, churches and mosques, but the sentiment or the idea of religion, or whatever may be the name of the spiritual essence of religion, can never be lost, nor are churches essential to its preservation.   Our Lord himself compared the Old Testament, or its forms and ceremonies, to old bottles, by which we are taught to consider that all external appliances for the preservation of eternal truth are forever growing old, and are but the shell, the husks, the outside of religion.   To respect these things is the duty of all good men in every country; but to insist

upon them as the essentials of religion, is to rouse
opposition in a certain class of middle intelli-
gences, many of whom fancy it an evidence of
high enlightenment to denounce religion as a
dream, when they only mean to repudiate the
show of religion; for even infidelity itself cannot
destroy the core of religion in the human heart.
To be certain of this, it is only necessary to know
what it is.

But religion is not the only field for allegory
and symbolism. Truly, all the great poems and
romances in the world would be worthless if not
interpreted by the spirit of life. Dante, Tasso,
Ariosto, Milton,—are all allegoric writers. Goethe is the great modern master in this art. His
Travels of *Meister* are nothing but sketches of
the deepest soul experiences that man can know.

To perceive this, let the reader of Meister divine the meaning of the chapters in which the
story of Mary and Joseph passes before him, and
of the chapter on the Lily-stalk;—and then follow Meister into the prison with impassable walls,
and study the design of the author through those
mysterious chapters where the hero is so impressed by a sense of stillness and silence; and
gather the meaning of the songs introduced, and
of the "strange" noise, which "sounded as from

a distance, and yet seemed to be in the house itself:"—And then, there is the New Melusina
episode, beautifully illustrating a not uncommon course of experience known to men of
genius.

The New Melusina (16th chapter in Carlyle's
translation) is a symbolic representation of the
rise and career of an artistic genius;—its start
from ordinary life (the "cook and landlady");
its joyous elevating power (careering in a car-
riage with seemingly inexhaustible "pouches of
gold and silver," imagination and fancy); its decline under the lowering influences of its employ-
ment on inferior subjects; the doubts raised
about the wisdom of obeying its impulses, and
the reassurances under a decision to employ it
under the guidance of reason (improved "by a
certain balsam"); the incompatibility of its as-
sociation with "moroseness and caprice;"—and
then is shadowed out the successive developments of "dwarfs" (imagination); "dragons,"
(animal passions); "giants," (intellectual passions, ambition, &c.);—and finally the "knights"
(reason), the last acquisition in the perfecting line
of life.   And then we see how the author has
contrived to "marry" a *knight* and a *dwarf* from
time to time in the world, as in Shakspeare, in

whom reason and imagination seem to have been in equilibrium. The whole thing is filled with characteristic touches;—the improvidence of the poetic temperament, commencing a journey with "extra post, and fronting the end on foot;"—its aversion to industry ("ants"); the loss of its, the imagination's, "twin brother" (truth); its opposition to mere mechanical views of life and of nature ("music-makers"); and its "never doing any thing in the right-handed way." Finally, the imagination sets its subject down where it was taken up, in common life, "with the cook and landlady."

Goethe's Meister, notwithstanding Jeffrey's criticism, is a more profound study than Faust itself, though either of these works hold materials for many a month's study to any one who looks beyond the surface, and who reads for something besides pastime and amusement;—to any one who has learned that life is full of vast realities, which we must face and examine if we would not be crushed by them.

But the reader of such works, and of all symbolic works, should be constantly on his guard against fictitious interpretations, and no less against attaching an undue value even to the

true unriddling of mysterious writings, for they
are not all of equal value, and some are of no
value at all.  Here, in this walk, I know of no
art that can supply the want of genuine good
sense.

# CHAPTER XI.

It will not be out of place to refer here to Bouterwek's History of Spanish Literature,—(translation by Ross, Bohn's Edition).

I find in this work a multitude of allusions to Hermetic philosophy, in the extracts from Spanish writings, apparently not recognized by the author, showing that the principal writers of the middle ages in Spain, as elsewhere, were more or less imbued with a secret science or art, no doubt greatly modified by the particular genius receiving it, and thus appearing in a great variety of forms. I do not pretend that all are of equal value. Many may be worthless,—mere caricatures and absurdities, not deserving so much as to be named by the side of the Romaunt of the Rose, one of the most perfect examples of Hermetic writing.

I will adduce but one example from Bouterwek, and will show how the piece is to be interpreted.

The historian of Spanish Literature thinks it would be unjust to the history of Spanish dramatic poetry during the first half of the sixteenth century, not to notice two tragedies by Geronimo Bermudez, a Dominican monk of Galicia, who published them under the assumed name of Antonio de Silva.  Bouterwek supposes that these two tragedies were founded upon what he calls " the well-known story of the unfortunate Inez de Castro."

The " titles " of the two tragedies he says, " are whimsical and affected : "—though they will not appear so when properly understood. " The one is denominated Nise Lastimosa (the Lamentable Nise, the anagram of Inez); and the second, Nise Laureada (the glorified Nise); and under these titles (says Bouterwek) they are reprinted in the Parnaso Espagñol, vol. vi."

The very titles of these dramas might induce us to look a little beyond the surface for their signification.  Bouterwek, however, seems to see nothing in them except some excellence in a merely literary point of view.  He treats them as belonging to the current dramatic literature of the time, and as if they had been actually represented on the stage, though, in my opinion, the author never intended them for actual scenic representation, but addressed them to a class of readers more common in the Middle Ages than is generally supposed, who would distinguish their spiritual significance without asking for or desiring a visible exhibition.

To assist the reader in seeing what I shall urge as the true meaning of these dramas, I will copy entire all that Bouterwek says of them.

" The first of these tragedies (says he) sufficiently proves what may be effected by a dramatist of even moderate talent, when thoroughly penetrated with a poetic subject, and at the same time possessing the power of eloquent expression. The *Nise Lastimosa*, it is true, is far from approaching the ideal of tragic perfection; but some of the scenes fulfil all that the theory of the dramatic art can require; and energy and dignity of expression are not wanting even in those passages where the action is tedious and the incidents ill-connected. The plot is simple, and towards the conclusion its interest declines. But Bermudez has introduced, by turns aptly and inaptly, a chorus composed of Coimbran women, which is sometimes interwoven with the action of the drama, and sometimes quite independent of it. The unities of time and place the author has totally disregarded. The first act opens with a soliloquy by the Infante Don Pedro, in which the prince deplores his separation from his beloved wife. This soliloquy is succeeded by a long conversation between the Infante and his secretary, in which the latter, with all due courtesy, hints that the attachment of the prince for a lady, not of royal birth, is incompatible with the welfare of the State. The scene then changes, and the chorus of Coimbran women is very absurdly introduced to moralize on love. Thus closes the first act. In the second, the scene changes to the court, and exhibits the king amidst his assembled council; the advice of the ministers prevails over the good disposition of the monarch, and he consents to the death of Inez de Castro. A soliloquy by the king follows, in which he offers up his prayers. The scene again changes, and the fair Coimbrans once more appear to moralize on happiness. In the third act, however, a new spirit is infused into the piece, and the chorus partakes in the action. Inez de Castro appears. The women of the chorus form her attendants, and offer her consolation and advice. Inez is informed of the reports that are circulated respecting her fate; but throughout this act, the progress of the story is nearly suspended. The fourth act may however, be regarded as almost a masterpiece.  Inez, attended by her children, and the chorus, appears before the king to receive her sentence.  Nothing can be more expressive than the dignity with which she demands justice, or more affecting than the tenderness for her children, which continually breaks forth in her discourse.  At length she pictures to herself in vivid colors the sorrow that awaits her husband, till, exhausted by her feelings, she begins for the first time to think of her own situation, and anticipating the horrors of death, she swoons, exclaiming, *Jesus Maria!*  This scene exhibits a picture so replete with real pathos, that it may be truly said, modern tragic art has seldom attained so hight a point of perfection.  The fifth act is merely a tedious supplement.  The prince is made acquainted with the death of his wife, and he vents his sorrow in long lamentations.

" The tragedy of *Nise Laureada* is far inferior to that just described.  The story is below criticism ; and towards the end becomes revolting to feelings not blunted by inquisitorial horrors, or sunk to the level of brutality.  The Infante Don Pedro, who has now ascended the throne, orders the remains of his judicially murdered wife to be taken from the tomb ; he then, with great solemnity, invests the corpse with the dignity of queen, and the ceremony of the coronation is followed by a marriage. Two of the counsellors, whose perverted and inhuman patriotism had urged them to sacrifice the unhappy Ines, receive sentence of death, and are executed. This is the whole plot, if so it may be called; and among the acting and speaking characters, the executioners play a prominent part. The first act contains many beautiful passages; but when the last judicial ceremonies commence, horror and disgust fill the mind of the reader. The hearts of both culprits are extracted from their bodies, the one through the breast, and the other through the back. The most brutal exclamations accompany the execution of the royal sentence, and the chorus utters shouts of joy, while the executioner discharges his barbarous task. That these horrors might be regarded as pathetic incidents by the Spaniards of that age, accustomed as they were from early childhood to stifle every sentiment of humanity, and to allow fanatical exultation to overcome the natural emotions of the heart, whenever a brutal sentence was pronounced by ecclesiastical or royal authority, is, unfortunately, but too probable. Had it not been for this perversion of feeling, a people, otherwise so noble-minded, could not have attended the cruel festivals of their church, and witnessed the burning of Jews and heretics with as much pleasure as the exhibition of a bull fight."

What now do these tragedies signify? They never could have been intended for representation upon a stage. They shadow out the author's opinion of the fall of man, and of his restoration:—his fall is represented under a symbolic figure, by turning away from the love of truth, the true wife, to the false;—to a *lady* not of *royal* descent; that is, to an *object* not approved by truth and reason, which is always "incompatible with the welfare of the *state;*" that is, for this is the meaning, with the MAN, who is the *state* in this tragedy. In ordinary language, the fall of man is involved in the love of the world, as opposed to the love of God. The truth itself, in the Tragedy, is personified in the queen, and is represented as being put to death at the instigation of certain evil counsellors. This is the substance of the first tragedy.

In the second tragedy, which Bouterwek evidently considers a mere drama of outward life, placing it below criticism, the author represents the Prince as ascending the throne; which means that the fallen man, the subject of the drama, has returned to the possession of Reason, the *Sol*

11

of the Hermetic writers; and the first thing that declares or evinces it, is the scene by which the murdered queen, the Truth (the conscience, for this is what is signified), is recovered from her tomb, and fully reinstated as the true wife, the true object of love. She is fully reinvested with the dignity of queen, and is crowned; and, after the coronation, reason and truth are married;— and this is the true "conjugial" marriage so largely discussed and eulogized by Swedenborg under the names of truth and good; meaning that, in the perfect man, the understanding and the will must act as one:—a mere truism, I admit, and yet we see but few examples of it in life.

The false counsellors are then represented as undergoing the punishment of death, for deluding the prince and seducing him from his true love —the hearts of both being extracted from their bodies, one through the breast and the other through the back:—and what can this be supposed to signify?—why were there just two sufferers, and no more; and why was the heart of one extracted through the breast and the other through the back? What can we suppose the meaning of all this to be but that the spirit, in assuming its proper supremacy over the enticing

blandishments of the soul and the body, is represented as executing these latter attributes of the
one man, distinguishing one of the two by the
*honor* of having its heart extracted through the
breast, while the heart of the personified body is
drawn forth through the back, as the most igno
ble of the two.

This is the interpretation of these two tragedies, whether it be worth any thing or not. It
supposes a theory with regard to man which
makes him a triple person of Body, Soul, and
Spirit (Salt, Sulphur, and Mercury;—Swedenborg's Ens, Cause, and Effect, or " proceeding");
and while either of the two first have the ascendency, the true queen of life is deposed and
dishonored; and, in order to a restoration, she
must be reinstated with all her dignities. This
was the *Hermetic* opinion of Bermudez, the
Dominican Monk, and this was what he intended
to teach in these anonymously published tragedies.

If the reader asks why the poet resorted to a
fictitious representation in teaching so simple a
truth, several reasons might be given. Some of
the most important truths in the world are necessarily truisms, and ought to be so, as being not
denied to the most humble in life; but they are

not the less neglected on this account, and need
to be presented in a great variety of forms to
arrest attention and thus secure an important element in their success.   In the case of Bermudez,
also, we may easily see that he was endeavoring
to teach perhaps the most important of all truths,
the necessity of a union in the perfect man, of
reason and truth, the understanding and will,
without appealing to the Church, which, in his
age and country, assumed the exclusive control
of the consciences of all men, and professed to
hold the only authentic chart by which its followers were to be guided to bliss.   But there
were many, even in the Church, who did not indeed teach a different doctrine from that of the
Church, but taught it differently, and thought it
no prejudice to the truth to put it upon grounds
which the Church, in its external and formal
character, endeavored to suppress whenever such
exhibitions were recognized.   The literature of
the Middle Ages will never be understood by
any one who fails to see that, whenever the truth
in those ages attempted to walk abroad, she was
compelled to go *veiled*, or encounter the most
horrid persecution.   All genuine literature,
dramas, novels, romances, essays, &c., have a
higher purpose than amusement; and to read

books for mere pastime and amusement may be a little, but a very little, better than other dissipations. The *Preacher* no doubt understood how to read even books of amusement, when, in the midst of all of his trials and experiments upon life, he kept his "wisdom" by him, and we should do the same in our reading.

It may be thought that I am extending the field of Hermetic philosophy beyond its proper limits, and using it as a *one-idea* hobby.

I should be sorry to incur just censure upon this ground, but as I am persuaded that the learned men of the Middle Ages were extensively imbued with that philosophy, and wrote chiefly under its *veil*, I cannot but so express myself. I by no means say that the philosophy was equally well understood by all who used the *veil*. Very far from it; and still less would I urge that the mere shadowing out one's opinions in a fiction—a novel, a romance, or a poem, though all of these forms were used by Hermetic writers—would bring an author under this class of writers.

To distinguish the members of this class readily, some study of Hermetic philosophy may be supposed necessary,—and in the books by Hermetic writers themselves; because it is very difficult to give any intelligible *external* account of it.   It may be emphatically said, that there is no " royal road " to this sort of learning.   A mere verbal statement of a theory expressing something of it, would be very unsatisfactory, particularly if the writers on the subject are correct when they tell us, that it must first be seen out of books, and then it may be discovered in them. A plain, direct, right-minded man, feeling sure that the truth has nothing to fear, and can have no foe but falsehood, may ask, why make a mystery of this thing; why not speak out plainly? The only answer I can imagine to this is the one given by the Hermetic writers themselves, that the secret is the mystery of God, and is reserved in the power of God, to be given to whomsoever he will; and yet they tell us that this will is not arbitrarily exercised, and that the science is a true science; by which they mean that the will of God is exerted under fixed laws, themselves expressing the very nature of God.

I will take this opportunity to enforce the opinion I have already intimated, that Plato was a Hermetic philosopher, and that he appears in this character in his Republic.

A difference of opinion exists among critics,

as to whether Plato's writings have any other than a *surface* meaning.   Those who perceive no underlying sense must of course be expected to deny its existence ; yet Plato, in his seventh Letter, universally admitted to be genuine, has expressly withdrawn *one* subject from the field of *open* writing, and gives some reasons for it, saying that " a matter of that kind cannot be expressed by words, like other things to be learnt ; " —and further, " But if it had appeared to me that such matters could be written or spoken of sufficiently before the masses [meaning the masses of his day], what could have been done by us more beautiful in life than to impart so great a benefit to mankind, and *to bring nature to light before all ?* "

Here he tells us *openly* the subject upon which he has not *openly* written.   He goes on to say that the attempt to promulgate such matters would benefit only a few, who " are able (he says), with a little showing to make discoveries themselves."

By this passage we may understand that Plato's writings are to be regarded as attempts to show us a " little " of *something*, which we are to study out for ourselves ; and this is entirely in accordance with his opinion of the defect of writing, as a channel or instrument of teaching, given towards the end of *Phædrus*, where he tells us that " writing has this inconvenience, and truly resembles painting ; for paintings stand out as if they were alive ; but, if you ask them any question, they observe a solemn silence :—and so it is with discourses ; you would think that they spoke as though they possessed some wisdom ; but if you ask them about any thing they say, from a desire to understand it, they give only one and the self-same answer.   And when it is once written, every discourse is tossed about everywhere, equally among those who understand it, and among those whom it in no wise concerns, and it knows not to whom it ought to speak, and to whom not.   And when it is ill-treated and unjustly reviled, it always needs its father to help it ; for, of itself, it can neither defend nor help itself."

He then contrasts that teaching of God, written, as St. Paul said after him, not upon tables of stone, but upon the fleshy tables of the heart :— thus showing us plainly where he sought knowledge.

There is a remarkable passage in the Protagoras, referring to the use of " veils " by the ancient wise men, which, though attributed to Protagoras himself, we may presume was introduced by Plato, expressly as a caution to his own readers to look beyond the letter, the more especially as we know why the master of Plato was put to death.

The passage in Protagoras is sufficiently striking to justify its citation in proof of the point I aim to establish.   Socrates is represented as seeking *Protagoras* for instruction, and, on meeting him, he asks first whether their conversation shall be conducted publicly or in private, to which Protagoras answers :

" You very properly take precautions on my behalf.   For a stranger who visits powerful cities, and persuades the most distinguished of the youth to quit the society of others, both kindred and not kindred, both old and young, and associate with him, in the expectation of being improved by his society, ought in doing this to be very cautious, for things of this kind are attended with no slight jealousies and enmities, and even plots.   For my part, I say that the art of a Sophist is ancient, but the men who professed it in ancient times, fearing the odium attached to it, sought to conceal it, and veiled it over, some under the garb of poetry, as Homer, Hesiod, and Simonides; and others under that of

11*

the Mysteries and Prophecies, such as Orpheus
and Musæus, and their followers ; and some I
perceive have veiled it under the gymnastic art,
as Iccus of Tarentum, and one of the present day
who is a Sophist, inferior to none, Herodicus of
Selymbria, who was originally of Megara. But
your own Agathocles, who was a great Sophist,
concealed it under the garb of music, as did
Pythoclides of Ceos, and many others. All
these, as I say, through fear of jealousies employed these arts as *veils*."

The readers of Plato, therefore, may be ex-
cused for supposing that there is something
underneath the surface of his writings, to be discovered by study under a suitable preparation,
possibly justifying *Apuleius* in referring to what
he calls "those sublime and divine Platonic doctrines, understood by very few of the pious, and
absolutely unknown to every one of the profane."

*Olympiodorus* also says that "Plato, above
all men, is difficult to be understood; for, like
Homer, he may be taken which way you will,
either Physically, Ethically, or Theologically."
*Diogenes Laertius* also tells us that "Plato made
use of various *names* to preserve his writings from
being thumbed by rude and illiterate readers."

These testimonies, it is true, are not required

by those who see the Hermetic character of Plato's writings. On the other hand, they should not be urged as a pretence or excuse for seeking in the mere imagination for a sense to Plato's Dialogues never dreamed of by himself. Let his reader, I would say, keep strictly to the *real*, but with the consideration that things unseen may be quite as real as those that are visible, and when truly known may come to be understood as the only truly real, all visible things being manifestly shadows; but they are shadows of something unseen, and the unseen is the principal subject of Plato's writings. Even the Timæus is not an exception, and should be read as the conclusion to the Republic, and ought not to be separated from it.

Very severe criticisms have been made upon Plato on account of many things in the supposed *model* of a government called the Republic, particularly in regard to the seeming recommendation of a community of women, so highly commended in that work. Excuses or apologies have been made by Plato's admirers for admitting into his idea of a Republic a tenet so destructive to civilized life; but no adequate explanation of a notion so extraordinary is current among reading men, so far as I know.  Plato's age has been condemned for both ignorance and corruption of manners by way of apology for this blot upon his writings, but I find nowhere any attempt at an explanation, which nevertheless seems at hand, and may at least change the ground of censure, if nothing more.

This repulsive feature in one of Plato's greatest works calls loudly upon us to remember the caution of St. Augustine, of Origen, of Philo, and others, not to understand literally what appears an abomination in ancient writings.  I will venture a suggestion with regard to the object of Plato in the Republic, for the consideration of the more learned and curious on the subject, drawn from Hermetic philosophy, which all the writers say is older than Plato.

The Hermetic philosophers claim to see (metaphorically, I mean), first, ONE (thing, which is not a *thing*); then Two, then ONE again; then three and one, or one and three: and in these, as principles, they affect to see the infinite diversities of nature in the particular subject of their philosophy, without going beyond their principles.

The reader may wonder what this has to do with the Republic of Plato; but I will endeavor to show something of its application, as hints to be pursued at leisure; for the subject is not studied out in a day.

Call the ONE *esse, being, substance,* or by any other name; but be in no haste to imagine what this ONE is. Conceive yourself in the centre of it; imagine no origin to it, and be sure it has no end :—assign no limits to it, and suppose it hermetically sealed so that nothing can pass into it but what belongs to it, and nothing pass out of it unless known to be " superfluous." Then suppose two attributes coexistent with and in the ONE, and call these, under the same reservation as to knowledge, active and passive, to which, however, other names may be given; yet " they are not two, but one," as the Hermetic writers say : and thus, or by some other more efficacious means, endeavor to comply with the requisition of Plato in the Sophist, and be able to " perceive one *idea* every way extended through many things, the individuals of which are placed apart from each other; and many ideas, different from each other, externally comprehended under one; and one idea through many wholes conjoined in one; and, lastly, many ideas, every way divided apart from each other."

To be able to do this perfectly, Plato considers the science of a free man. In fewer words, it is to be able to see the one in all, and all in one; and this is the claim of Swedenborg, when he says that in turning entirely around and looking in every direction he saw the *Lord*, the ONE thing, or one in all; or, whether he calls it the Lord, or God, or Grand-man, or Substance, he says it is all the same.

Now, apart from this mere statement for the present, consider man as, physically and to the natural eye, a double organism in one, having a right side and a left side, each of the same "measure and size," and observe that this double nature extends to every part of his system; his tongue, as all physiologists know, being double, yet united into one,—as a hint, say some, that we ought to speak the truth.

A fanciful theorist might possibly see in these two "like" things, the cherubims we read of in Exodus, from the midst of which God spake to Moses.

Swedenborg tells us that, to the angels, the Lord is seen through the *right* eye as a *sun*, and through the *left* eye as a *moon*. But he only means to suggest the double attributes of the ONE, whom he calls the LORD.

Let this notion be now carried within man,

and let us see there two things, metaphorically called the *head* and the *heart;* that is, thought and will, or the intellect and the affections ; or, what Swedenborg calls truth and good. And now let us see in these two things the *Sol* and *Luna* (the " fixed and unfixed ") of the Hermetic writers,—which they also call masculine and feminine, brother and sister, &c., and think it no sin to marry them together. Call the intellect *masculine*, I say, and the affections *feminine*, neither of them alone securing the perfection of man ;—for a man may be intellectually able, and yet be an accomplished villain ; and the poet tells us that " mere good nature is a fool." Conceive, then, the two to be united and to act as one, that is, in unison ; and call this one both a MAN and a STATE. This STATE is under a legitimate monarchy when " reason rules ;" but it is subject to an oligarchy, and to other forms of government, and finally, in the descending scale, to an anarchy, when inferior principles usurp the ascendency.

If we suppose a perfect development of all the powers and faculties of man, under the influence of *true* thoughts and *right* feelings, working in *unison*, we shall have, I think, Plato's perfect republic, in which the *feminine* principle and its brood or family of affections in man are equally free with the so-called *masculine* principle, and they all share equally in the government and in the burdens of the state,—as represented in the Republic,—there being an entire comity and " COMMUNITY " of all things in the perfect man. But this community is only good in the perfect man;—in the imperfect man it is evil.

Plato's Republic is not a theory or ideal of a government among men, but the ideal of man in the abstract, whose condition is determined internally by the action and reaction of internal elements under a certain freedom which no external law can reach. In this STATE all the thoughts and feelings exist in common, or as a " community," under no restraints or compulsions not derived from their internal nature. Under these circumstances, the *family* of thoughts and feelings *generated*, will represent the character of the STATE, whether noble or base, elevated or depraved. If *true* thoughts and *good* affections are united, that is, are married, in the jargon of these writers, and act as one, the man lives on the ascending side of life and tends towards heaven, that is, towards a knowledge of and a union with the principle of life itself, which is in God only.

A mere common-place reading of the Republic will show many passages, no doubt, seemingly incompatible with this view, but a more careful study will bring this explanation within probability. Such books should be read with an allowance for a considerable external latitude, but under an internal law of truth that cannot be too strictly applied. The form of all Hermetic writings is always full of variety, and is purposely made so by the writers themselves, but, for reasons which have less weight in this age than formerly.

The *inhabitants* of Plato's Republic are the thoughts and feelings, that is, the internal or spiritual principles of man *personified*, the external form being a Hermetic veil. When *wealthy* citizens are spoken of in comparison with the *poor*, no more is intended than to indicate some *disproportion* of natural power among the elements within man. Wisdom is often called *wealth* in Plato; as in Cratylus, where HERMOGENES is represented as being covetous of *wealth*, but without acquiring it. In this dialogue HERMOGENES personates the *natural* man, incapable of appreciating the knowledge of CRATYLUS and of SOCRATES on the nature of things,—which is the subject of that dialogue, under the Hermetic

form of an inquiry into the origin of language.
All of the critics appear to regard this beautiful
dialogue as devoted by Plato to an inquiry into
the origin of the Greek language, and no one
seems to perceive that this is a mere veil, the external form of an inquiry of a totally different
character; and they are all puzzled with the dialogue, and express astonishment at what they
regard as Plato's puerilities and absurdities in
regard to the .language, whose origin is the professed object of inquiry.   One of the recent
translators of Plato, BURGES, has even ventured in
some places to deny Plato's knowledge of his own
language, instead of feeling himself invited, by
the absurdities he saw, to look beyond the letter.

Thomas Taylor had good reason for declaring
that philology is not philosophy.

But to return to the Republic.

Before taking leave of this subject, I desire to
suggest, as a study for those who interest themselves in such questions, that Plato's *idea* of the
perfect man, as indicated in the Republic, is substantially the same as Swedenborg's *idea* of the
*grand-man*, whom he places in Heaven, where
the Greek philosopher also places his perfect man,
—as may be seen towards the close of the 9th

book of his Treatise; or, to be minutely exact, the "pattern," described by Plato as in Heaven, is the *pattern* of Swedenborg's grand-man; and the perfect man formed after that pattern is Swedenborg's angel, or what he calls "heaven in its least form."

Hermetic writers recommend the reading of many, but *good* books, upon their subject; because, as they say, "one book openeth another;" in view of which sound advice, I have no hesitation in saying that both Plato and Spinoza will very greatly assist in *opening* Swedenborg; for they are something like fountains to his stream, the *color* of which will show, however, the Hermetic soil through which it has passed, to those who make themselves acquainted with that soil. This may startle those who are not accustomed to consider *ideas* under *words*, and are unable to find what some of the writers call the centre of this subject. If truth is one, as everybody says, it is theoretically certain that the best philosophers must approach each other in their main principles, and must ultimately occupy the same ground. Hence, students of this subject have placed the great masters, Plato, Zeno, and even Epicurus, nearer to each other than their respective followers, who appeal to their authority, and lose sight of that essential truth which the best philosophers all know is most real, and yet most purely ideal; for these, in the last analysis, are two phases of one thing. Plato points at this ONE in the 6th book of the Republic, as something beyond the visible sun (Swedenborg's sun of the natural world, and the Lord, as seen through the "left eye"); and beyond the intellectual sun (Swedenborg's sun of the spiritual world, and the Lord, as seen through the "right eye"). Plato calls it the GOOD, and says "it is not essence, but beyond essence, and is superior to both (suns) in dignity and power;" and this is the *One*, called by Swedenborg the Lord, who is seen "everywhere" in power, but nowhere in essence.

If now any one cries out against this view, and declares that nothing of these similitudes can be found in Plato, either to Swedenborg, or to those who wrote of salt, sulphur, and mercury, in the middle ages, I feel much disposed to say that such a critic would be in danger of seeing no men in a foreign country, because dressed perhaps in a different fashion from what he is familiar with.

That all men have something in common, is only saying that all men are men; but that which ought to be common among philosophers, and should mark them as a class, is necessarily their *idea* of man, and this must necessarily tend to unity : but, in proportion as it does so, it must more and more be. removed from external manifestations, and must finally be found in Heaven, with Plato's *pattern* and Swedenborg's grandman; where also is to be found the "City of God" of St. Augustine, and no less the "City" of Antoninus, who saw. it only in his meditations ; for on earth it is not seen, except by "art," as they say : and yet it is said to be the most real of all things, and may become visible even on earth to the clarified eye.

All good men strive to see this city, and it is the struggle of life to be worthy of it; for to live in that city is to live in Heaven, and this, independently of all considerations of time,—if what they tell us of it is true.

For a description of life in this city of the blessed, I would refer to the little poem placed in the preface to my Remarks on Alchemy,— which "may be held a fable;" but the poet tells us that,

> "Who first
> Made and recited it, hath in that fable
> Shadow'd a Truth."

Those who doubt the possibility of such a

*state* or *condition*, and feel disposed to ridicule
the idea of it as fantastical and unsuited to a
world of practical labor and trial, might do well
to consider whether such a doubt does not exhibit one who lives in the calamitous condition
of being ignorant of the true worth and possibili-
ties of his own nature. Here is a theme for
earnest eloquence, but I am not a practised
writer, and strive only to express myself with
clearness. I therefore waive a topic that might
possibly suffer from my inexperienced and didactic pen.

I will merely remark, in concluding this
chapter, that Plato's opinions upon government
must not be sought in the Republic, but in the
longest, though perhaps not the most studied of
all his works, the Laws.

# CHAPTER XII.

Having thus pointed out the Hermetic character of Swedenborg's writings, I feel that my notice of their remarkable author will be incomplete unless I indicate also his connection with or dependence upon the writings and principles of a man who flourished about one hundred years before him; one of the most extraordinary men of modern times, whose name the whole world at one period seemed anxious to load with obloquy, but whose reputation for purity of life is now universally acknowledged, while his philosophy is beginning to be recognized as worthy the careful study of all those who desire to know the power of the human intellect as manifested in works of thought upon abstruse and difficult subjects.

It is most remarkable that, although Swedenborg, especially in his philosophical writings, shows the most intimate acquaintance with all the learning of his day, quoting largely from a great number of works upon the anatomy, physiology, and philosophy of man, never so much as once, so far as I now remember, makes the least allusion to the name of BENEDICT SPINOZA, the born but anathematized Jew, who nevertheless furnished him with some of the most profound principles announced and developed in his religious works.

The similitude, or rather the identity of the doctrines or principles of these two men, is a most interesting and curious fact, which can be established by citations from their respective works with so much clearness that the most hasty reader cannot fail to recognize it.

Some years ago, in 1846, I printed for circulation among my friends a series of parallel extracts from the writings of Spinoza and Swedenborg, the object of which was to show, as a speculative curiosity, the remarkable identity of the doctrines of the two men, regarded from a scientific point of view. I called attention to the fact, that while one of the two men had been reviled as the veriest Atheist the world has produced, the other has been held forth, by a con-

siderable body of followers, as expressly illuminated for the purpose of teaching the True Christian Religion.   It struck me that reflecting men
might see in the parallel I presented, matter
worth their serious consideration, and I still think
the subject worthy the attention of all considerate
men.

The parallel to which I refer ought to teach
us moderation and charity, and must suggest the
probability, at least, that if Spinoza's enemies
were right in their abuse of his writings and
character, the friends of Swedenborg can hardly
fail to be in error in their admiration of the
Swedish Philosopher; while, on the other hand,
if the followers of Swedenborg are justified in
their approval of his doctrines, the revilers of
Spinoza must have been in error.

But the reader may say that I am in too much
haste in making inferences and comments, and
ought first to point out the likeness between the
two men, if indeed it exists.

I shall show presently its prominent features;
but I desire to say that, in the pamphlet to which
I refer, it was not my purpose, neither is it now
my purpose, to approve or condemn the doctrines
in question.   I remarked in the pamphlet, and I
repeat now, that, in the estimation of some, the

dissimilarities between the two men in their writings may be even greater than their points of likeness, but that it is not easy to see how men, whose groundwork is the same, can very widely separate from each other without subjecting one of the parties, at least, to the charge of inconsistency or inconsequentiality.  But the most inveterate enemies of Spinoza, I believe, do not accuse him of inconsistency in the doctrines he develops from his principles.  On the contrary, it is generally asserted by those who have examined his writings, that if his definitions and axioms are granted, his entire system follows without the possibility of being overthrown. Accordingly, a recent writer has undertaken to destroy the whole system of Spinoza's Ethics by objecting to his first definition.

For my own part, I will confess that I have never been able to follow Spinoza's demonstrations through, connectedly, from first to last.  As a demonstrable system, therefore, the *Ethics* of Spinoza has never taken hold of me.  I am not therefore a Spinozist.  Yet,—and this may seem singular,—the two last parts of the Ethics, seem very beautiful and fascinating, without any reference to the formal basis laid in the preceding parts; and I must say, especially, that the very last proposition of the entire work seems more clear to me than the first, and would sooner be assumed by me, as the basis of a system, than almost any thing in the whole work,—if I desired to make a system myself.

Spinoza, after defining *Substance* to be *that* which exists of itself, and is conceived by itself; and *modes*, to be the *affections* of substance, announces, as his *first* proposition, that, Substance is prior in nature to its affections: and he refers, for proof, to his definitions.

I say now, that this proposition is not demonstrated; because, we may conceive the coexistence of the two, substance and its affections, without conceiving the priority of substance. It is true that the affections of substance cannot be conceived without the idea of substance, but this does not necessarily suppose priority. This first proposition is not so clear to me, therefore, as the very last in the work, which is in these words; Prop. 42, Part 5: " *Happiness* (Beatitudo; Bliss) *is not the reward of virtue, but it is virtue itself; and we do not enjoy* (or possess) *it, because we restrain our bad or evil desires* (libido, evil propensities), *but, on the contrary, 'tis because we possess or enjoy it that we are enabled to restrain our lusts.*"

This proposition is almost self-evident, and scarcely needs any thing for its proof but a little experience and observation of life. In the external world of nature and time, rewards and punishments, both being temporal, *follow* the conduct of man, and are of a nature altogether different from the conduct itself, and are often wholly unforeseen ; but these are incidents in life, and do not constitute its real happiness or misery. The true bliss lies in the very substance of life itself, and not in its affections ; and this substance of life is what Spinoza in this proposition calls virtue, elsewhere calling it power ; by which he means, in fact, the power of God, in which alone man is secure against the evil affections, because all affections are subordinate to this one power. Hence, a sense of its possession is the glory of man, though its attainment may require the *transmutation* so much talked of by the Hermetic writers :—a change from a state of nature to a state of grace.

I admire the Fourth and Fifth Parts of Spinoza's Ethics so much that I can almost accept the First Part upon my faith in the last ; but I cannot reverse this order and receive the latter portions of the Ethics upon any convictions derived from the demonstrations in the First. I therefore prefer to read the Ethics *backwards*, and stop somewhere in the Fourth Part. If any one can read the beautiful developments in the last Two Parts of the Ethics of Spinoza without imbibing a great respect for their author and a deep sense of gratitude for so much light and instruction as may there be found, he is much to be pitied. But to return to my subject.*

If I make good the point I suggest, of a likeness between the doctrines of Spinoza and those of Swedenborg, it will appear remarkable that many of them should be found, where they will be found, in one of the latest and most religious of Swedenborg's works,—that entitled *The True Christian Religion.* If the principles to which I refer were discoverable only in his philosophical works, written before what he called the opening of his internal sight, it might be imagined that under the correction of a higher light they had been abandoned; but, in truth, they may all be found in his religious works,—introduced there indeed with studied precision.

It is generally said that every system of thought, where thought takes the form of a sys-

* I hope Mr. Lewes will fulfil the promise made in his Life of Goethe, and soon give us an English version of Spinoza's entire works.

tem, depends very much if not altogether upon the idea of God. It is true indeed, that the contrary statement is also made,—that, every man's idea of the Deity expresses his individual character and mode of thought; that, instead of saying that God made man after his own image, it may be said more truly that man *imagines* God after his image.

However this may be, it was Spinoza's opinion that some idea of God must be presupposed in every attempt to form any system of doctrines whatever; for he says in Chapter 4th of his Tract on Theology and Politics, that,—" since all our knowledge, and certainty which removes all doubt, depends only upon the knowledge of God, —because nothing can be, or be known without God, and because we may doubt of all things while we have no clear and distinct idea of God, —it follows, that our perfection and chiefest happiness depends only upon the knowledge of God."

In this passage God is conceived as the immutable; because, as any one may see—unless something fixed and unchangeable be supposed, there can be no science or knowledge of any thing. Unless something *permanent* be assumed, we could not depend upon the continuance of our knowledge of any thing whatever for one single moment.   The world is only not a chaos, because there is something unchangeably holding it in order, even amidst all its apparent changes. Hence, with Spinoza, the existence of God was a first principle—the most immediate and absolute of all intuitions—above all demonstration, since every demonstration assumes it.   Still, he carries his readers through a series of propositions demonstrative of the existence of God, though such demonstrations have never convinced any human being who needed a demonstration at all.   So far, however, were these demonstrations from convincing Spinoza himself, that, evidently, on the contrary, they were the mere product of his own convictions antecedent to them—as all demonstrations indeed must be antecedently in the mind of the demonstrator.   To Spinoza there was nothing so evident as the existence of God; but his demonstrations close with the declaration that He cannot be made known or described by any "mark" whatever; his Being, being altogether "UNIQUE"—not falling within the possibility of being *imaged* by any thing whatever. This is truly the Mosaic doctrine—"Thou shalt not make to thyself any graven image," &c.— only Spinoza extends the prohibition virtually to *writings*, and would have us understand that

God not only cannot be imaged by the graver, but cannot be described by human language.

But Swedenborg held the same doctrine, as may be seen by the following passage from the True Christian Religion, to wit:

"The esse of God, or the Divine Esse, cannot be described, because it is above every idea of human thought, into which [human thought] nothing else falls than what is created and finite, but not what is uncreate and infinite: thus not the Divine esse."

Why, then, it may be asked, did they write about God?

The genuine Hermetic writers saw this point with perfect clearness, and hence, among other reasons, they wrote about *Salt*, *Sulphur*, and *Mercury*, and left the reader to discover for himself, under the blessing of God, that which is not of a transferable nature among men.

"Our practice," says a Hermetic writer, "is in effect a track in the sands, where one ought to conduct one's self rather by the North Star than by any footsteps which are seen imprinted there. The confusion of the *tracks*, which an almost infinite number of people have left there, is so great, and one finds so many different paths, almost all of them leading into most frightful deserts, that it is almost impossible not to stray from the true Road, which only *Sages* favored by Heaven have happily known how to find out and discover." "It is a Path (says another of the same class of writers, quoting Job) which no Fowl knoweth, and which the Vulture's eye hath not seen."

One would think that Spinoza had taken sufficient and praiseworthy care to remove the notion that by God he meant external and visible nature, expressly denying it, among other evidences, in a published letter to Oldenburg; yet he has by some been charged with making nature God. Others, driven from this point, have gone to the other extreme; and, seeing how carefully Spinoza has endeavored to guard against the notion of an *imaged* God, which with him was an *imaginary* God, have denied that his idea of God was any thing at all:—so difficult is it for man to reach an *idea* independently of an *image*. Some say it is impossible to have such an idea— an idea without an image. If this is really so, then, indeed, I do not see to what purpose any one can write or read, or even think of God; for it is certain that no image or imagined thing can represent the eternal, invisible, immutable Being we call God. Our idea of God may be imperfect, and may contain sensuous imagery which may need to be eliminated, but to deny altogether the possibility of freeing it from the cloud in which it may first be recognized, is equivalent, it seems to me, to a denial of the possibility of both a true religion and a true philosophy; for it is undeniable that these must not only rest upon some idea of God, but will be true only so far as that idea is true. Let the searcher, therefore, examine his idea of God, and continue his examination until he feels satisfied that he has one upon which he can repose, and yet it must be that such an idea cannot be found in books alone, unless by some very remote analogy.

Mathematicians have what they call the idea of a triangle, as also the idea of a circle, of an ellipse, of a parabola, &c., all coexisting in one mind without jostling each other; and from the idea of a triangle, for example, they demonstrate innumerable properties without affirming the existence or reality of any triangle in nature, while yet from the force of the idea alone they affirm, conditionally, that if any triangle exists in nature it must exist necessarily under the law of the idea.

Spinoza seems to have carried this notion of an IDEA, to the IDEA of GOD as [a] self-existence,

of such a nature as to include all possible exist-
ences of a specific or finite nature, so that nothing
can exist specifically except in conformity with
the nature, that is, with the law of the *uncreate,*
—the self-existence;—and this in theological language is expressed by saying that all things exist
by the will of God (except God himself, the uncreate—the self-existence); because, in Spinoza's
sense, the will of God, and the nature of God,
and the law of God, are one and the same.

In saying that something immutable must be
conceived before there can be any science or
knowledge whatever, nothing more is expressed
than a demand of the intellect.   It is involved in
the mere expression, that if *something* be not
fixed, then *nothing* is fixed, and of course no science.   The postulate in itself is simple enough,
and is acceptable to every one.   The difficulty
lies in determining what that is which is immutable, and here it is that Spinoza, following his own
ancestor of the Pentateuch, declares that it cannot be known by any " mark " whatever.   This,
say the Hermetic writers, is to be " seen by the
eye of the mind," and though the fixed is not the
movable, yet when the fixed is known it is understood in what sense the movable is fixed also,
because its motions all take place according to

the law of the fixed.　In Hermetic language, call the fixed, *sulphur;* the movable, *mercury;* and find their *unity*, which may then be called *salt*, and the problem of the Hermetic Trinity will be solved.　But this problem is never solved on paper until after it has been solved in another fashion.　Thus, say several of the writers,—virtually all Hermetic writers,—it may be found by a profound contemplation upon experience in life, and "not otherwise;" and then it may be recognized in books.　To make this discovery man must, like Moses, enter the tabernacle unveiled.

I thought proper to premise thus much because Spinoza made the existence of God a prerequisite in his system, and devotes the first part of his *Ethics* to the proof of it, while yet the principle is beyond and above all proof, and never fails to confound the intellect that would hold it otherwise than by submission to it.

That Swedenborg attached the same importance to this first principle may be inferred from his efforts to establish the doctrine of the one substance, the *Esse* of God, at the commencement of his most systematic works; as, for example, in his work on Divine Love and Divine Wisdom; his work on the True Christian Religion; and also his volume on Heaven and Hell. But those who read these works ought not to imagine that they understand this thing until they can reconcile Swedenborg's declaration that "the *Divine Esse* is above every idea of human thought," with his no less positive affirmation, that God is the Lord, that the Lord is Life and is seen everywhere.

Swedenborg's works are extremely valuable, but their author never intended that they should supersede the gospel of John in enabling us to understand the WORD that was with God and was God in the beginning, and was "made flesh."

But it is time now to show the parallel to which I have referred.

I. OF GOD, according to Swedenborg.

" Every one who thinks from clear reason, sees that all things were created out of a Substance, which is substance in itself, for this is the real Esse [Being] from which all things that are can exist : and as God alone is Substance in itself, and thence the real Esse, it is evident that the existence of things is from no other source." *Angelic Wisdom concerning Divine Love*, par. 283.

Again, "It is acknowledged by many, that there is *an only Substance*, which is also the first, from which all things are." *Ang. Wis. conc. Divine Providence*, par. 6.

Again : " Where there is Esse [Being] there is also existere [existence]; one is not possible without the other, for Esse is by Existere, and not without it." *Angelic Wisdom concerning Divine Love*, par. 14.

Again: "He who in any degree of thought can conceive and comprehend an *Esse and Existere* in itself, will perfectly conceive and comprehend that such *Esse and Existere* is the self-subsisting and sole-subsisting Being." *Ibid.* par. 45.

Again: "As things all and each are forms, it must be that He who created all things is form itself, and that from form itself are all things which were created in forms: This is therefore what was demonstrated in the treatise comcerning the Divine Love and Divine Wisdom, as, *That the Divine Love and Divine Wisdom is Substance, and that it is Form.*" *Angelic Wisdom concerning Divine Providence*, par. 40—43.

Again: "Who does not from reason perceive and acknowledge, that there is an only Essence, from which is all essence, or an only Being, from which is all being? What can exist without being? And what being is there from which is all being, unless there is Being in itself? And what is being itself is also the only Being and Being *in itself.* Since it is so, and every one perceives and acknowledges this from reason, and if not, can perceive and acknowledge it, what else then follows, than that this Being, which is the Divine itself, which is Jehovah, is the all of all things which are and exist? *It is the like, if it is said that there is an only Substance, from which all things are;* and because a Substance without form is not any thing, it follows also that there is an only form, from which all things are." *Ibid.* par. 157.

Of God, according to Spinoza.

"*By God*, I understand a Being absolutely infinite ; that is, a *Substance* consisting of infinite attributes, each one of which expresses infinite and eternal essence." *Ethics*, part 1, def. 6.

"*By Substance*, I understand that which is in itself, and which is conceived by itself : or, that, the conception of which does not need the conception of another thing, from which it must be formed." *Ibid*, def. 3.

"Existence belongs or pertains to the nature of Substance." *Ibid.* prop. 7.

"No Substance can be conceived except God." *Ibid.* prop. 14.

"Whatever is, is in God, and nothing can be, or be conceived without (out of) God." *Ibid.* prop. 15.

"The Existence of God, and the Essence of God are one and the same." *Ibid.* prop. 20.

"By a *Self-Cause*, I understand that, the essence of which implies or involves existence ; or, that, the nature of which cannot be conceived except as existing." *Ibid.* def. 1.


Let us now see the similarity of the two thinkers on the subject of *things*, i. e. *modes*.

II. Modes, according to Swedenborg.

"With respect to the existence of things, sound philosophy teaches us, that things which are much compounded take their origin from things less compounded ; the less compounded from things still less so ; these from their individual substances or parts, which are least of all limited ; and these again from things simple, in which no limits can be supposed, except one; from which circumstance also they are called simples. But whence is this simple, in which only one limit is to be conceived? And whence that limit? It cannot exist by itself; for there must be something by which it may exist, if it have a limit, if it be simple, or if it be capable of giving origin to two or more limits. Extending the inquiry therefore, by the same philosophy we rationally proceed to the conclusion, that such a simple derives its existence from the Infinite; but that the Infinite exists of itself. Again, if we contemplate the successive progression of causes, it will be found highly reasonable to conclude, that nothing finite can exist without a cause; that things which are much compounded, or which consist of many individual parts, neither could be compounded, nor can subsist, without a cause, by which they were compounded, and by which they may consist: for a cause always precedes and afterwards accompanies that which exists from it. The individual parts of such a composite must in like manner be compounded of and subsist from their individual parts still smaller; and these again, by the order of their succession, from things simple. But still things simple can neither exist nor subsist from themselves. Wherefore there must be an Infinite Something; there must be something infinitely intelligent, which may be considered both as a cause in itself, and at the same time as an operator of effects out of itself; or as an inherent force, and at the same time as a positive agent; or as a power capable of producing, and at the same time as actually producing the existence of other things. It follows, therefore, *that things composite derive their origin from things simple; things simple from the Infinite; and the Infinite from itself, as being the sole cause of itself and of all things.* It was before observed, that all finite things came into existence successively; for nothing can be at once such as it is capable of becoming, except the Infinite. Every thing finite acknowledges, or is indebted to, *a certain mode,* by which it is what it is, and nothing else; *a mode,* by which it is of such a figure, and no other; *a mode,* by which it occupies such a space, and no other. *In a word, all things are modified;* and therefore they acknowledge a mode prior to their modification, and according to which it takes its place: they acknowledge also a time, in which they were so modified. Hence nothing is at once what it is capable of becoming, except the Infinite. All finite things must necessarily undergo different states successively; but not so the Infinite. And thus we perceive that *all things out of the Infinite have their modifications, but that in the Infinite there is no such thing as a mode:* He being the original cause of all modifications." *Principia,* vol. 1, p. 47.

Modes, according to Spinoza.

" By a *Mode,* I understand the affections of a Substance, or that, which is in another thing through or by means of which other thing it is conceived. *Ethics,* part 1, def. 5.

Observe, that Swedenborg has said of Simples, out of which Compounds are made, that they cannot exist by themselves; i. e. as Spinoza expresses it, they must be conceived as existing in something else, which something else *is in itself,* &c.

Again (Spinoza says), " I understand by Body, a mode

by which the essence of God, in so far as he is considered as Extension (res extensa, an extended thing), is expressed in a certain and determined manner or mode." *Ibid.* part 2, def. 1.

Again. " Particular things are nothing but affections of the attributes of God, or modes in which the attributes of God are expressed in a certain and determinate manner." *Ibid.* part 1, *corol.* to prop. 25.

Again. " The Essence of things produced by God does not involve existence." *Ibid.* part 1, prop. 24.

Again. " There must be a certain cause of the existence of each thing which exists.   *   *   *   It must be concluded absolutely (universally) that, every thing according to whose nature many individuals may exist, must necessarily have an external cause of such existence." *Schol.* prop. 8, part 1.

Hence, in the Ethics of Spinoza, man and all things in nature are considered as not having in themselves necessary existence; but they are regarded as modes, things existing in another thing, i. e. affections of the attributes of God, existing only in God.

Let us now notice what each of these extraordinary thinkers has to say of our *knowledge*, and it will be seen that each of them point out three different sources or kinds of knowledge, and that the two authors harmonize in a most remarkable manner.

III. Of Kinds of Knowledge, according to Swedenborg.

" Moreover, it should be known that there are three degrees of Love and Wisdom, and thence three degrees of Life, and that the human mind, according to these degrees, is formed as it were into regions, and that life in the highest region is in the highest degree, and in the second region in a lower degree, and in the last region in the lowest degree. These regions are successively opened in man; the last region, where life is in the lowest degree, is opened from infancy to childhood, and this is done by the senses. The second region, where life is in a higher degree, from childhood to youth, and this is done by knowledges from the sciences; and the highest region, where life is in the highest degree, from youth to manhood and onwards, and this is done by the perception of truths, both moral and spiritual. It should be further known, that the perfection of life consists not in thought, but in the perception of truth from the light of truth; the differences of the life with men may be thence ascertained; for there are some who, as soon as they hear the truth, perceive that it is truth. [This is Spinoza's third kind of knowledge.] There are others who do not perceive truth, but conclude it from confirmations by appearances. [To conclude or infer a truth, means to reason out a truth, and this is Spinoza's second kind of knowledge.] There are others who believe a thing to be true, because it was asserted by a man of authority." [And this last answers to Spinoza's first kind of knowledge, which he afterwards shows to be the source of error and falsehood, because things are seen in their *apparent* order in nature, in which their true causes do not appear; these being only seen by the third kind of knowledge, in the intellect. And in this too, the two thinkers agree, Swedenborg attributing error to seeing or judging of things from *appearances* as effects, and not seeing them in their causes—as we shall see presently.] *True Christian Religion*, page 37.

OF KINDS OF KNOWLEDGE, according to Spinoza.

" We perceive many things and form universal notions from single things represented to us through the senses, mutilated, confused, and without relation to the intellect : and also from signs; for example, reading or hearing certain words, we call things to mind, and form certain ideas of them like those, by which we imagine things. These I will in future call knowledge of the first kind. [Swedenborg's lowest degree.] Secondly, we form them from our having universal notions and adequate ideas of the properties of things, and this I call reason and knowledge of the second kind. [This is Swedenborg's second degree.] Besides these two kinds of knowledges, there is a third, as I will show in the sequel, which we will call intuitive knowledge. And this kind of knowing proceeds (or descends) from the adequate idea of the formal essence of certain attributes of God to an adequate knowledge of the essence of things." [This is Swedenborg's highest degree.]

Both writers make very great use of the distinctions above set forth, of which, one or two examples may suffice. The above extract is from the Ethics, part 2, scholium 2, prop. 40.

IV. OF THE DIFFERENCE OF SEEING THINGS IN THEIR EFFECTS AND IN THEIR CAUSES, according to Swedenborg.

Explaining his reasons for treating certain matters as he has, Swedenborg says, " To treat of them otherwise than from their original source, would be to treat from effects and not from causes ; and yet effects teach nothing but effects, and when they are considered alone, they do not explain a single cause ; *but causes explain effects;* and to know effects from causes is to be wise ; but to inquire into causes from effects is not to be wise : because then fallacies present themselves, which the examiner calls causes, and this is confounding wisdom." *Angelic Wisdom concerning Divine Love,* par. 119.

On this point, Spinoza, in the 4th axiom to the first Part of the Ethics, states his doctrine, that, " the knowledge of an effect depends upon (or is involved in) a knowledge of its cause."


V. OF THE INTUITIVE KNOWLEDGE, (or highest degree,) according to Swedenborg.

" There are two things proper to nature, *space and time.* From these in the natural world man forms the ideas of his thought, and thence his understanding. If he remains in these ideas, and does not elevate his mind above them, he never can perceive any thing spiritual or divine ; for he involves it in ideas which he derives from space and time, and in proportion as he does this, the light of his understanding is merely natural. Thinking from this merely natural light, in reasoning of things spiritual and divine, is like thinking from the darkness of night of those things which only appear in the light of day; hence comes naturalism. But he that knows how to elevate his mind above the ideas of thought which partake of space and time, passes from darkness to light, and becomes wise in spiritual and divine things. *Ibid.* par. 69.

Of Intuitive Knowledge, according to the Ethics.

Spinoza, in the Ethics, after stating the *three* kinds of cognition (knowing), i. e., 1st, from the senses : 2d, from reasoning : 3d, from intuition, states the proposition, that the third kind of knowing (corresponding to Swedenborg's spiritual knowledge) cannot possibly arise from the first kind of knowledge; and in various places throughout the Ethics sets forth the same doctrine; while in his Tract on Theology, treating of the Divine Law, chap. 4, he has the following passage, referring to the impossibility of the natural man's knowing the things of the spirit.

" These things cannot but be unintelligible to a carnal man, and must seem vain and unsubstantial to him in consequence of his meagre (jejune) conceptions of God; and because in this highest good, consisting solely in contemplation and pure mind, he can find nothing to touch or eat, or which in any way affects the bodily senses, wherein he takes his chief delight. But they must be the most substantial of all things to those who know that there is nothing more excellent than reason and a sound mind." [By reason, is not meant here the faculty of reasoning (argument), but that element or principle in man, by which he is man, and without which he would not *be* at all—in short the *divine* in man; which, as both Swedenborg and Spinoza agree, is from God.]

The admirers of Coleridge will readily see, above, the grounds of the doctrine so zealously set forth by him, i. e. the distinction between the understanding and the reason; all knowledge depending upon the first being uncertain and unstable, while through the reason, according to this doctrine, knowledge is absolute, and admits of no appeal.

We have now seen how nearly similar these two thinkers are in their doctrines *of God, of things,* of the different *kinds of knowledge,* and of the *impossibility of the natural man's knowing the things of the spirit.* We will next pass to a vital point, to which particular attention is invited, namely, their doctrine of *Salvation.*

It is important to observe, that the language of Swedenborg, soon to follow, has a very distinct signification, where he distinguishes the wish of one to make another happy " from " himself; the idea being, to make another happy with a total disregard of one's own happiness;

this being the test of a true love, independent of consequences.

### VI. OF SALVATION, according to Swedenborg.

" The third essential of the love of God, *which is to make them happy from itself*, is acknowledged from eternal life, which is blessedness, happiness, and felicity without end, which God gives to those *who receive his love in themselves ;* for God, as he is Love itself, is also blessedness itself; for every Love breathes forth from itself a delight, and the Divine Love breathes forth blessedness itself, happiness and felicity to eternity. Thus God makes angels happy from himself, and also men after death, which is effected by conjunction with them." *True Chrn. Relig.* p. 38.

And again, at page 262, same work, is the following :

" If therefore man becomes rational-spiritual, and at the same time moral-spiritual, he is *conjoined to God*, and by conjunction has salvation and eternal life."

### OF SALVATION, according to Spinoza.

" Our intellectual love of God is the same love with which God loves himself; not, as he is infinite, but in so far as he can be explained (or represented) by the essence of the human mind, regarded under the form of eternity; or in other words, the intellectual love of the mind for God, is a part of the infinite love with which God loves himself. Hence it follows that, in so far as God loves himself, he loves men or mankind, and consequently, that the love of God for men, and the intellectual love of the mind for God, are one and the same thing."   [ This is the Conjunction of Swedenborg.]   " We see clearly now wherein consists our salvation or happiness (bliss or blessedness), or in other words, our liberty (or freedom), to wit, in a constant and eternal love for God, or, in the love of God for men, (God's love of us;) and the sacred scriptures have not without reason given to this love the name of glory."   *Ethics*, part 5, prop. 36.

The brevity of these last extracts must present the doctrine of salvation in some degree obscurely, there being, especially in the Ethics, very many propositions necessary to its full exposition; but a similitude will hardly fail to be seen in the above extracts.

Here are certainly shown very remarkable points of contact between these men, on the most essential doctrines, of God, of Knowledge, and of Salvation, sufficient to excite curiosity at least, if not astonishment, considering the fate, thus far, of the two men : and as these are all important doctrines, necessarily having an influence over those who hold them, it might be expected that a likeness should also appear in other portions of the works of these men.   I am now to show that this is the case in some remarkable particulars; in doing which there will be some further confirmations of what has already been adduced.

VII. *Swedenborg.* "The Esse of God, or the Divine Esse, cannot be described, because it is above every idea of human thought, into which [human thought] nothing else falls than what is created and finite, but not what is uncreate and infinite; thus not the Divine Esse." *True Chn. Relig.* page 16.

*Spinoza*, treating of God, says, "If any one should ask me to give an example for the full explication of what is here intended, I must reply, that no instance can adequately explain what is in itself *unique.*" *Ethics*, part 2, prop. 8, schol.

VIII. *Swedenborg.* "The Divine Esse is esse in itself, and at the same time existere (existence) in itself." *True C. R.* page 16.

*Spinoza.* "Existence belongs or pertains to the nature of a substance." *Ethics*, part 1, prop 7.

IX. *Swedenborg.* "The Divine Esse and Existere in itself cannot produce another divine, that is esse and existere in itself: consequently another God of the same essence is not possible." *T. C. R.* p. 16.

*Spinoza.* "One substance cannot produce another substance." *Ethics*, part 1, prop. 6.—And the conclusion of the demonstration is, that "there cannot be many substances, but only one." And prop. 14 is, that "No substance can be conceived except God."

The above I note as remarkable.


X. *Swedenborg.* "In relation to subsistence, all finite things, produced in the way here described, [i. e. from the Infinite,] do actually subsist from the same cause and mode, which brought them into existence." *Principia*, page 54.

*Spinoza.* " God is not only the cause of the beginning of the existence of things, but of their continuance in existence."   *Ethics*, part 1, prop. 24, corol.

XI. *Swedenborg.* " Jehovah God is esse in itself * * * beginning and end, &c, from eternity to eternity." *T. C. R.* p. 17.

*Spinoza.* " Substance is that which is in itself, and is conceived by itself." *Ethics*, part 1, def. 3.   And " whatever *is* is in God."   Prop. 15.   And " God is eternal." Prop. 19.

XII. *Swedenborg.* " The unity of God is most intimately inscribed on the mind of every man." *T. C. R.* page 20.

*Spinoza.* " The human mind has an adequate knowledge of the eternal and infinite nature of God." *Ethics*, part 2. prop. 47.

XIII. *Swedenborg.* " That the infinite divine is in man, as in its images, is evident from the word where this is read," &c.   *T. C. R.* p. 29.

*Spinoza.* " Hence it follows that the mind of man is a part of the infinite intellect of God."   *Ethics*, part 2, prop. 11, coroll.

XIV. *Swedenborg.* " In him (man) the soul is not life, but a recipient of life.   *   *   Life in himself is God.   *   *   *   The Divine Esse, because it is One, the same, the Itself, and thence indivisible, cannot be in several." *T. C. R.* page 22.

*Spinoza.* " The Being (Esse) of Substance (God) does not belong to the essence of man, or, does not constitute the form of man."   *Ethics*, part 2, prop. 10. And " the absolutely infinite Substance is indivisible." Part 1, prop. 13.   And " Every thing according to whose nature many individuals may exist, must necessarily have an external cause," [i. e. man has not life in himself.]   Part 1, prop. 8, schol.

XV. *Swedenborg.* " Wherefore *infinite* is an adjective, belonging to the essentials and attributes of God, all of which are called infinite."  *T. C. R.* page 33.

*Spinoza.*   The Ethics speaks of the attributes of God as infinite, but only in their own kind; thus, *thought* is infinite thought, but is not infinite extension; and again, extension is infinite extension, but is not infinite thought.   While God is the *absolutely* infinite Being.

XVI. *Swedenborg.* " Every one should prepare the way for God, that is, should prepare himself for reception; and this should be done by means of knowledges."   *T. C. R.* page 20.

*Spinoza.* " The highest effort (aim or striving) of the mind, and its supreme or greatest virtue, is to know God by the third kind of knowledge."  *Ethics*, part 5, prop. 25.   See No. III.

XVII. *Swedenborg.* " Every quality has its quality from that which is *the itself* from which it is [derived], and to which it refers itself [as to its cause] that it may be such."   *T. C. R.* page 21.

*Spinoza.* " The power of an effect is defined by the power of its cause, in so far as the essence of the effect is explained by the essence [*the itself*] of the cause." *Ethics*, part 5, ax. 2.

XVIII. *Swedenborg.* " Wherefore the Lord says, that He is in the midst of them: also, that He is in them and they in Him."   *T. C. R.* page 21.

*Spinoza.* " Our mind in so far as it knows itself

and the body under the form of eternity, possesses necessarily the knowledge of God, and knows that it is in God, and is conceived by (or through) God." *Ethics*, part 5, prop. 30.

XIX. *Swedenborg.* "*   *   and yet the substantial and material things in the universe, considered individually, are infinite in number." *T. C. R.* page 26.

*Spinoza.* " There must be infinite things in infinite modes in nature." *Ethics*, part 1, prop. 16.

XX. *Swedenborg.* "*   *   the life to eternity, which every man has after death, is not communicable but from an eternal God." *T. C. R.* page 27.

*Spinoza.* " The human mind cannot be entirely destroyed with the body, but something remains of it, which is eternal." *Ethics*, part 5, prop. 23.   And the demonstration connects this portion with God as the cause.

XXI. *Swedenborg.* " Let every one therefore be cautious how he persuades himself that he lives from himself; and also that he is wise, believes, loves, perceives truth, and *wills* and does good from himself." *T. C. R.* page 36.

*Spinoza.* " There is no absolute or free will in the mind ; and it may be demonstrated that the mind has no absolute faculty of understanding, desiring, loving." &c. *Ethics.* part 2, prop. 48, schol.

It is proper to remark here, that although both writers deny the freedom of the will of man, as *of himself*, yet the two writers do not hold to the doctrine in the same manner. Spinoza adhered strictly to this doctrine, and gave a reason for the general prevalence of the opinion that man is free, saying that *man thinks himself free because he is conscious of his desires, but not conscious of the causes that impel him to desire.* Yet Spinoza contends for a certain freedom in man, when he acts from what he calls adequate ideas, which he says are in God and in man at the same time; and it comes to this, that the freedom of man arises from his knowledge of God, which Spinoza calls the power of reason, to the elucidation of which he devotes Part *Fourth* of his Ethics. Man is free in obeying God *knowingly*, and no otherwise.

Swedenborg theoretically denies the freedom of the will as completely as Spinoza, as must be seen above; yet he cannot do without it in his system. He adopts, however, extraordinary language for a philosopher in reference to it, saying that, although man is not free as of himself, yet he must act "as if" he was free, while he must "know" that "all freedom is from the Lord."

It must be confessed that Swedenborg gives us no light on this question. If he saw the truth himself, he has not been able to explain it, and on this long disputed question he leaves his reader where he finds him,—unless the student of Swedenborg may "fancy" he knows what he does not know at all ;—I mean, as a result of Swedenborg's teachings.

Without assuming to solve this controverted question myself, I will remark that the chief difficulty seems to arise, not from a " pre-established harmony " in the ideas we have of God and man, but from preconceived ideas irreconcilable with each other; which ought to satisfy us that one set of them, at least, cannot be true.  To maintain the idea of God's omnipotence in the usual sense, and of the eternity and immutability of his decrees, as extending to all things, and, at the same time, the notion of man's free agency, as if he possessed an actual power of his own, is impossible.  Whoever holds these two opinions must necessarily carry about a conflict within himself.  One or both sets of ideas should be *purified*, in order to introduce harmony.  If the Philosopher's Stone could solve this one question, it might be worth seeking, if for nothing else. Let the power of God—I say it reverently—be called *sulphur*, and the power of man *mercury :* then find a *salt* that shall be their unity.  This is the problem.

The student of this problem need not go out of himself, to find the root of the controversy between necessity and freedom, and may be able to understand the principal question between Augustine and Pelagius, between Calvin and Arminius, and between the "Old School" and the "New School" of more recent times. He may find that the controversy lies between two of the elements or principles of man, and must last until the third principle becomes recognized, which, though last discovered, is first in order, and stands above, as it were, the other two, and, though it decides, it takes no part in the controversy. This third principle, when awakened in man, constitutes Swedenborg's Celestial State ; that is, in this state man is an angel, and no longer " opines " about things, but " knows." This I understand to be Swedenborg's view, and it does not differ essentially from that of Spinoza,—that which is said by one of *reason*, being said by the other of the *spiritual* in man.

But to return to the parallels :

XXII. *Swedenborg.* "It is to be held that all things in the universe were created in their orders, so that they may subsist each one by itself, and that from the beginning they were so created, that they may conjoin themselves with the universal order, to the intent that each particular order may subsist in the universal, and thus make one." *T. C. R.* page 47.

*Spinoza.* "*  *  *  and if we thus go on *ad infinitum*, we may easily conceive that all nature is one

Individual, whose parts (that is to say, all bodies) vary in infinite modes, without any change in the total Individual:" [i. e. all bodies make one.] *Ethics*, part 2, lemma 7 after prop. 13.

The doctrine at page 57 of the True Christian Religion, of God being "order itself," and that the "laws of order are myriads," and that "God cannot act contrary to them," is precisely Spinoza's doctrine, as may be seen in many places. The doctrine is argued at length in the *Ethics*, part 1, prop. 17, schol.: the proposition being, that "God acts by the mere laws of his own nature, and is not necessitated."

As a further illustration of this point, I add the following from Swedenborg. "Those who do not understand the Divine Omnipotence, may imagine either that there is no order, or that God can do contrary to order, as well as according to it, when yet, without order, there could be no creation.  *  *  *  Yea, God himself cannot do contrary to his own divine order, since this would be to do contrary to himself." p. 347.

The corresponding passage to this in the Ethics, is in the 2d schol. to prop. 33, part 1, where Spinoza says, "It clearly follows from the preceding propositions, that things have been produced in the greatest perfection by God; seeing, indeed, that they have followed necessarily from His·most perfect nature.  Nor does this opinion argue any imperfection in God; for it is his very perfection which has compelled us to affirm it.  Nay, it follows from the contrary opinion, that God is not wholly perfect;

13*

for if things could have been produced in any other mode, we must attribute to God another nature, different from that which we have been compelled to attribute to Him, from the consideration of the most perfect Being (*Ens.*)"

And further, in the same scholi. Spinoza remarks, that the supposition that God could create things otherwise than according to order, would imply that God could change his own decrees, while all agree that God's decrees are unchangeable.

XXIII. *Swedenborg.* "It is at this day a prevailing opinion that the omnipotence of God is like the absolute power of a king in the world, who can at his pleasure do what he wills," &c. [and this opinion Swedenborg very severely condemns.] *T. C. R.* page 48.

*Spinoza.* " The vulgar understand by the omnipotence of God, the free will of God, and his right or authority over all things which exist, and which are therefore generally regarded as contingent. Moreover, they often compare the powerof God with the power of kings. But we have refuted this in Corollaries, 1st and 2d, prop. 32, part 1."

Here it will be seen that the same illustration is taken by each writer, and the popular opinion equally condemned.

XXIV. Swedenborg's doctrine of space and time is the same with that of Spinoza. Each author denies that these terms apply to God.  " The sun itself," says Swedenborg, " would be near the eye unless intermediate objects discovered that it is so distant; " and Spinoza, in the schol. to prop. 35, part 2, had already taken the same example, the sun, to illustrate the same principle.

XXV. *Swedenborg.* " * * * They acknowledged that there is a God, and that nature was created to be subservient to the Life which was from God ; and that nature in itself was dead, and that thus, it does nothing from itself, but is actuated by Life," [i. e. by God.] *True C. R.* page 65.

*Spinoza.* " A thing which has been determined (moved) to *act* has necessarily been so determined by God, and what is not determined to act by God cannot determine itself." *Ethics*, prop. 26, part 1.

Spinoza makes a distinction between nature active and nature passive. The first is nature regarded as *absolute*, and is always active ; the second regards nature as relative, in which sense one thing is acted upon by another. Every single thing partakes of each ; it has a certain power of action, but from the active power of other things it may be acted upon. But God is regarded as the really acting cause in both cases, or as the only *activity*.

XXVI. *Swedenborg.* " Now, because the Word is such, *appearances* of truth, which are truths clothed, may be taken for naked truths, which, when they are confirmed, [by reasonings founded on the mere appearances of things as presented to the senses,] become fallacies, which in themselves are falses. From this, that *appearances* of truth may be taken for naked truths and confirmed, have sprung all the heresies which have been, and still are, in the Christian world. *Heresies themselves do not condemn men;* but confirmations of the falsities, which are in a heresy, from the Word, and by reasonings from the natural man and an evil life, do condemn." *T. C. R.* p. 192.

*Spinoza.* "But the reason why men have not an equally clear knowledge of God and of common notions is, they cannot imagine God as they do bodies, and they have connected the name of God with images of things which they are in the habit of seeing; [which last, according to both Swedenborg and Spinoza, are only *appearances* of truth,] and this is the origin of most controversies, that men either do not correctly express their own meaning, or do not correctly interpret the meaning of others. * * * I wish you to remark, that *the imaginations of the mind, regarded in themselves, contain no error;* or, the mind does not therefore err *because* it imagines; but only inasmuch as it is without an idea which precludes the existence of those things which it imagines to be present. For if the mind, when it is imagining non-existing things as present to itself, knows at the same time that the things do not exist, it will certianly attribute this power of imagining, not to any defect, but to the action (power) of its own nature." *Eth.* part. 4, props. 17, 47, & schol.

XXVII. *Swedenborg.* "But bare knowledge only enters the understanding, and this has not any authority over the will, and so is not in man otherwise than as one who stands in the entry, or at the door, and not as yet in the house." *T. C. R.* page 193, also p. 397.

*Spinoza.* "The true knowledge of good and evil

cannot, as truth, [i. e. as "bare knowledge "] restrain any affection, but only in so far as as it is itself considered as an affection." *Ethics*, part 4, prop. 14.

XXVIII. *Swedenborg.* " There is not any thing in the mind, to which something in the body does not correspond; and this which corresponds may be called the embodying of that." *T. C. R.* page 267.

This is a very important proposition in Swedenborg's works, and it has a remarkable parallel in Spinoza; but to see it, the notion of Spinoza must be stated, that the *mind* is *the idea of a body existing.* This idea is not single, but compounded of many ideas. Then follows the 12th prop. part 2, Ethics, namely, " Whatever takes place in the object of the idea constituting the human mind, [i. e. the human body,] must be perceived by the human mind, or, the human mind will necessarily have an idea of it."

Spinoza elsewhere states that *man* is constituted by modifications of two attributes of God, to wit, thought and extension, i. e. mind and body; but, because these are, in the *absolute* nature of God, a unity, they must be developed under the same uniform law, and hence their operations or manifestations are simultaneous, or, in a certain sense, the *same*, only regarded in two ways, one as thought, the other as body. And by this would be explained the curious problem touching the correspondence between the most abstruse mathematical results, arrived at in the closet, and the motions of the physical heavens, or heavenly bodies; for they are the same essence manifested in two ways, and make but one, as all things make one, in God.

It is not my object to exhibit any thing more than the *likeness* between the two writers; but at this point, I cannot help suggesting that possibly, in the curious proposition above stated, may be found the true ground of Swedenborg's visions into what he calls the spiritual world; for it may not be impossible that some men may so habitually contemplate the physical things of the world in their essence, i. e. in God, as measurably to cease to regard them in their inferior character as *modes* or modifications; and as all things in God are eternal, these modifications may be regarded as eternal, when thus recognized by the intellect, instead of being regarded simply by the senses as mere appearances. In this way, whatever is the object of knowledge, even through the senses, becomes, when seen in the intellect, spiritual and eternal; and hence man, if he can conceive himself thus to see things in their essence, may speak of this vision as a vision of the spiritual world. The spirits of departed men, as of Plato, Cicero, Luther, Calvin, &c., may be considered as seen in their works, which have come down to us, through which we become acquainted with them, as we do with living men. The spirits of departed men are then seen in their essence, i. e. our knowledge of them is thus seen and regarded as eternal. This may be considered as a tolerably legitimate result of Spinoza's doctrine; for by prop. 22, 23, 24 of part 1, Ethics, he undertakes to demonstrate the *eternity* of *modes* or *things*, not regarded *as things*, but as seen in the intellect, and referred to God. It should be recollected that Swedenborg saw, in the spiritual world, whatever is seen on earth, and no small power of ridicule has been expended upon him for alleging, that in the spiritual world there are a sun and earths, with inhabitants in cities, having dwellings, with every species of furniture, &c.; in short, our own natural system seen in the spirit, i. e. referred to God as the sole cause of both the essence and existence of all things, and thus conceived under the form of eternity, as God is eternal.

"In the spiritual world," says Swedenborg, " or, in the world where spirits and angels are, similar things appear as in the natural world, or where men are; *so similar, that as to external aspect there is no difference.*" *Heaven and Hell*, par. 582.

And again : " It is not yet known that the Divine Providence, in all progression with man, looks at his eternal state; for it can look at nothing else, because the Divine is infinite and eternal; and the infinite and eternal, or the Divine, *is not in time*, and hence all future things [and so also all past things] are *present* to it. And because the Divine is such, it follows, that in *each and every thing* which it does is the eternal. *Yet they who think from time and space, perceive this with difficulty*, not only because they love temporal things, but also because they think from the *present in the world*, and not from the *present in heaven;* this is as absent from them as the end of the earth. But they, who are in the Divine, do also think *from the eternal when from the present*, because from the Lord, saying with themselves, What is that which is not eternal?" &c. *Angelic Wisdom concerning D. Prov.* par. 59.

It would be easy to multiply passages like these from the writings of Swedenborg. They are profusely scattered throughout his works, and if they signify any thing, it must be on the supposition that the universe is identified in some way with God, "*not as he is infinite*," [Spinoza] but as he is manifested by the universe, which is to be seen truly only when seen in God; in which case, " each and every thing " becomes invested with a divine aspect, and has the signification of eternity. In the last of the above passages, Swedenborg has warned us that those *who think from time and space* can with difficulty perceive this. He may as well have said, at once, that they cannot perceive it at all, and then have added, that, neither can those who think from time and space, judge of the doctrine of either himself or of Spinoza.

XXX. *Swedenborg.* " That which a man loves above all things is continually present in his thought, because in his will, and makes his veriest life. As for example, *he who loves riches*, whether money or possessions, above all things, continually revolves in his mind how he may procure them for himself; he inwardly rejoices when he gains ; he inwardly grieves when he loses; his heart is in them. * * * All the delight, pleasure, and happiness of every one, are from his ruling love, and according to it ; for that which a man loves, he calls delightful, because he feels it ; but that which he thinks, but does not love, he may also call delightful, but it is not the delight of his life. *The delight of the love is what is good to a man, and the opposite is what is evil to him.* * * * * A man is altogether such as the ruling principle of his life is; *by this he is distinguished from others ;* according to this his heaven is made, if he is good, and his hell, if he is evil; it is his very will, his proprium [that which belongs peculiarly to him], and his nature; for it cannot be changed, because it is the man himself." *T. C. R.*

*Spinoza.* " For we have proved above that we do not desire a thing because we judge it to be good, but on the contrary, we call it good because we desire it, and consequently we call what we are averse to, evil; so that every one judges or estimates what is good, what bad; what better, what worse; what best, what worst; according to his passions. *The miser thinks a plenty of money the best thing and the want of it the worst. The ambitious,*" &c. &c. *Ethics*, part 3, prop. 39, schol.—and the schol. to prop. 51, p. 3, remarks— ' Hence *when we compare men together, we distinguish them by the difference of their affections alone.*' "

Here are in fact *three* points of contact instead of one ; to wit, that our love or desire is the foundation of our judgment of what is good : 2d, the love of *wealth* and *the miser*, taken as an illustration : and lastly, the notion of each writer, that men are to be distinguished from each other by their passions, loves, affections, and not by reason, which is uniform in all men.

XXXI. *Swedenborg.* " For those who put reward in the first place, and salvation in the second, thus, this for the sake of that, invert order, and immerse the interior desires of their mind in their proprium, and in the body defile them with the delights of their flesh." *True C. R.* page 310.

*Spinoza,* after proving that virtue and religion are their own reward, remarks, that " most persons seem to think themselves free only when they are allowed to consult their own pleasure, and feel as if they were surrendering something of their rights when they yield obedience to the divine law; as if the service of God were not perfect freedom and perfect happiness. Piety then and religion, and in short whatever belongs to fortitude or strength of soul, are looked upon as burdens, which they hope to lay aside after death, and receive the reward of their services, to wit, of their piety and religion." *Ethics*, part 5, prop. 41, schol.

XXXII. *Swedenborg.* " It is quite otherwise with those who regard reward in works as the end itself. These are like those who enter into friendship for gain, &c. * * * The case is similar with those who claim recompense for their merit in the things of salvation." *True C. R.* page 310.

*Spinoza.* This is but a repetition, with the particular allusion to *interested friendship;* in regard to which Spinoza says, in prop. 71, part 4, that " the mutual kindness or favor of men, who are governed by blind desire, is a trade or traffic," &c.

XXXIII. *Swedenborg.* " God alone *acts,* and man suffers himself to be acted upon, and co-operates in all appearance as from himself, although inwardly from God." *True C. R.* page 397.

*Spinoza.* " God alone *acts* by the sole necessity of his own nature, and therefore God alone is a free cause." *Ethics*, part 1, prop. 17, corol. 2.

Yet it should be remarked, that Spinoza contends for a freedom in man in so far as he acts from adequate ideas referred to God as their cause; but he considers that in so far as man is *acted upon* by external causes, blindly, unconscious of the existence of these causes in God, he is not free, but a slave. But even here there is an opening for freedom in the man who can

recognize God *in* all these external causes, and
when *by love to God* he yields joyfully to them,
converting them as it were into his own acts, by
regarding them as God's acts, with which his
love of God places him in harmony, in relation
or in conjunction.   See No. VI.

As a further illustration of the above, I take
the following passage from

*Swedenborg.*   " Concerning the elevation of the interior of a man's mind, this also is to be observed;
there is from God in every created thing a re-action:
Life alone has action, and re-action is excited by the
action of life: this re-action *appears* as if it belonged
to the created thing, because it exists when the being
is acted upon; thus in man it appears as if it were his
own, because he does not perceive any otherwise than
that life is his own, when nevertheless man is only a
recipient of life.   From this cause it is that man, from
his own hereditary evil, re-acts against God; but [and
here is the doctrine assimilated to that of Spinoza] so
far as he believes that all his life is from God, and
every good of life from the action of God, and every
evil of life from the re-action of man, re-action becomes
correspondent with action, and man acts with God, as
from himself.   The equilibrium of all things is from
action and joint re-action, and every thing must be in
equilibrium." *Angelic Wisdom conc. Div. Love*, p. 23.

XXXIV. *Swedenborg.* " It is to be known that the
faculty of elevating the understanding, even to the intelligence in which the angels of heaven are, is from

creation inherent in every man, in the bad as well as the good." *True C. R.* page 397.

*Spinoza.* " The intellectual love of God (the perfection of the mind) is eternal," and " the mind has eternally those perfections we have supposed it to acquire." *Ethics*, part 5, prop. 33, schol.

XXXV. *Swedenborg.* " But yet no one can be said to be reformed by the mere knowledges of truths; for man, from the faculty of elevating the understanding above the love of the will, can apprehend them (truths) and also speak, teach, and preach them. But he is reformed who is in the affection of truth for the sake of truth." *True Chr. Relig.*

*Spinoza.* This is but a repetition of the doctrine in No. XXVII., though its similitude to Spinoza's prop. 14, part 4, is more clear and striking.

XXXVI. *Swedenborg.* " It is commonly believed, that life is in man his, so that he is not only a receptacle of life, but also life. That it is commonly so believed is from *appearance*, because he lives, i. e. feels, thinks, speaks, and acts, altogether as from himself." *True C. R.* page 335.

*Spinoza.* This is a repetition of XIV. The essence of man, according to Spinoza, does not involve necessary existence, and men believe themselves free, of themselves (and not from God), because " they are conscious of their desires, but not conscious of the cause of them."

XXXVII. *Swedenborg.* " Most [men] at this day are natural, and few spiritual; and the natural man judges from appearances, and thence fallacies, and these are diametrically opposite to this truth, that man is only a receptacle of truth." *True C. R.* page 335.

*Spinoza.* This also is a repetition.

XXXVIII. *Swedenborg.* " God, because he is infinite, is life in itself. This he cannot create, and thus transcribe into man, for this would be to make him God." *True C. R.* page 335.

*Spinoza.* See No. IX.

XXXIX. *Swedenborg.* Speaking of the conjunction of man with God, and its possibility, Swedenborg says, " that man does not know this from any light of reason, is because fallacies from the believed appearances of the external senses of the body overshadow that light." *True C. R.* page 336.

*Spinoza.* This is Spinoza's doctrine, referring to what he calls knowledge of the first kind (see No. III.), which is sensuous, and founded on the *images* of things from without; which, so far from giving us a knowledge of God and divine things, " obstructs that knowledge, and never leads to it." *Ethics*, part 2, prop. 41, 42.

XL. *Swedenborg.* " For the principal cause and the instrumental cause act together as one cause, according to a maxim known to the learned world." *True C. R.* p. 336.

*Spinoza* must be considered as included in what Swedenborg calls the learned world, for this is his doctrine. Many philosophers speak of two causes, the efficient, and the occasional or transient cause, but Spinoza, with Swedenborg, knows of but one cause, and that is God.

XLI. *Swedenborg.* " Who denies, or can deny, that all the good of love, and all the truth of wisdom, are solely from God; and that, as far as man receives them from God, so far he lives from God, and is said

to be born of God, that is, regenerated.  And, on the
other hand, as far as any does not receive love and wisdom, or, what is similar, charity and faith, so far he
does not receive life, which *in itself* is life, from God,
but from hell, which is no other life than inverted life,
which is called spiritual death."  *T. C. R.* 335, 6.

*Spinoza's* language wholly differs from this, but
nevertheless the idea conveyed above corresponds to
the doctrine of the Ethics, as far as I can make out
what was intended, and it may be stated something
after this manner:   God is the sole *absolutely* Infinite
Being, with attributes, as before stated (No. XV.); not
absolutely infinite, but infinite in their own kind.  Of
these attributes man is acquainted with but two,
thought and extension;  and this for the reason, that he
is composed of these.  Thought and extension are both
infinite, but man is not thought and extension itself, or
in himself;  but he is a modification of these attributes,
and may conceive himself in two ways, as *nature active*
and *nature passive*.  In the first case, man conceives
himself as existing in God, " in whom are all things,"
and in so far as he does this, and acts from this idea
(reason), he is *nature active;* he is something *positive*
and *free*.  But man does not stand alone in the world;
he is surrounded by infinite other things, every one of
which has, as well as himself, a *nature active;* and
now, in so far as man loses sight of the idea of God, as
He " in whom are all things," and is acted upon by
outward things, he represents *nature passive;* i. e. he
does not *act*, but *receives an action*, and in so far as he
does this, he is a slave and not a free man.  When man
is thus overcome by outward things, and is swept along

the tide of time without carrying with him the idea of God, the man is blind, and a slave, and it may answer, as a figure, to say, as Swedenborg does, that he then acts from hell, and the idea of God being lost, he may be said to be spiritually dead.  He can only be brought out of this state by recovering the idea of God, &c. See XXXIII.

XLII. *Swedenborg.*  " All that a man loves, and from love wills, is free; for whatever proceeds from the love of the internal will, is the delight of his life; and because the same is the *esse* of his life, it is also his proprium, (that which is *himself*,) which is the cause that *that* which is received in a free state of this will remains, for it adds itself to the proprium.  The contrary is the case, if any thing is introduced not in a state of freedom."  *T. C. R.* page 347.

Again: " All freedom, which is from the Lord, is real freedom, but that which is from hell, and thence with man, is servitude."  *Ibid.*

Spinoza's definition of action and passion is in the 3d part of the Ethics, as follows: " I say that we act, (are in a state of action) when any thing takes place either within us or without us, of which we are the adequate causes; that is, when any thing follows from our nature, either within us or without us, which can be clearly and distinctly understood from our nature alone.  On the contrary, we are passive, (we suffer, receive an action) when any thing takes place in us, or when any thing follows from our nature, of which we are only the partial cause."  His doctrine upon this is, that all we do in virtue of our own essence, referred to God as the cause, is free and necessarily good, but that many things *done unto us*, where we are acted upon by outward nature, are limitations upon us, and are called evils, and are felt to be such so long as they are not themselves referred to God.

I presume it will hardly be questioned by any one that a very clear and manifest similarity has been shown, by the foregoing extracts, between the doctrines of Swedenborg and Spinoza, so far as they appeal to our natural faculties. The dissimilarities between the two men may be still greater in the estimation of some, though it is not easy to see how men, whose groundwork, in a scientific point of view, is so nearly the same, can very widely separate from each other without subjecting one of the parties at least to the charge of inconsistency. Spinoza certainly made no claim to any peculiar insight into the spiritual world; no claim beyond the power of man's natural faculties; and it may he doubted whether the admirers of Swedenborg do not claim for him more than he ever claimed for himself; by no means an unusual case. I believe that many passages from his own writings may be adduced, giving a decidedly natural aspect to all his pretensions. Thus, he speaks of the *knowledge* of his day having attained an elevation suitably preparing the world for the truths he was commissioned to teach. He speaks of Calvin's conduct on earth after he became an angel, showing that regenerated men are considered as angels before death, &c., &c., but I do not design to discuss this point.

There are three opinions with respect to Swedenborg's claims to intercourse with the spiritual world, entitled to consideration.

1st. The followers or admirers of Swedenborg, or some of them, believe that he was actually inspired by God, in an especial manner, for a divine purpose; and the most intelligent among them defend this opinion, not by an appeal to miracles or outward signs, but by an appeal to the truths disclosed by him, which they think of such a character, that man in a state of nature could not have discovered them, though they affirm that men may, by their natural faculties, perceive and recognize their truth. It is therefore strictly by what is called an internal argument, that Swedenborg's pretensions are defended. This might be answered by an appeal to Spinoza's Ethics, where most assuredly the scientific grounds of Swedenborg were anticipated by nearly one hundred years, as must be evident from the foregoing extracts.

2d. Another opinion has been presented in a

systematic form by Herder, who supposes that Swedenborg's fancy had been so long and so intensely indulged in a particular direction, that its subjective operations became to him unconsciously objective; that, without the smallest intention to deceive others, he gave out that he had intercourse with the spiritual world, and talked with spiritual beings, while in fact he only held conversations with his own spirit, the operations of which became objective to him. Hence he made Cicero and other ancient philosophers, as Herder intimates, talk Swedenborgianism.

3d. There is still one other opinion, which has not yet had time to make its way in the world, that of Rossetti, a learned and ingenious professor of Italian literature in King's College, England. Rossetti supposes that a secret society has existed in Italy, embracing members in every part of Europe, since as far back at least as A. D. 1000: that this society was composed of the most learned and scientific men, whose intelligence was in advance of the world, enabling them to see the errors of the Roman church, which however by its power controlled and restrained these men from the free expression of their opinions: that, in consequence of this, the literary men of those ages avoided persecution, imprisonment and death, by the use of a conventional language, the exoteric or outward import of which appeared friendly to the party in power, while its esoteric or secret meaning was in direct hostility to the church, and clearly understood to be so by the initiated. Rossetti has employed great ingenuity in explaining the writings of Dante, Petrarch, Boccacio, and others, in conformity with his theory; and he intimates a rather decided opinion, that Swedenborg was a member of that society, which he thinks *is still in existence.* Rossetti asks, with a good deal of point, in reference to Swedenborg, " Has the thought never occurred to any one, that the man who displays so much vigor in a variety of works on poetry, philosophy, mathematics, and natural history, and who speaks continually of the language of correspondence, which gives a secret meaning to the smallest trifle, on the system of the ancient schools of the East, which he lauds to the skies; that a man, in short, who, even in his most extravagant fits, displays an immense store of sacred and profane learning, and an uncommon share of penetration, designedly concealed a profound meaning under his delusive language? Whoever reads his works, and attentively weighs his words, will see the real meaning of the language, which did him so

much discredit, as well as of his journeys to
heaven and hell, and his conversations with the
angels and demons; and will finally perceive
that the ravings of the madman explain the fictions of the sage."   [Disquisitions on the Antipa-
pal Spirit which produced the Reformation, &c.,
by Gabrielli Rossetti, translated by Miss Ward,
vol. 2, p. 177.]

It is worthy of note, that in several of his works
Swedenborg has drawn a line of separation between his
scientific views and what are called " relations," not exactly *revelations*.   That this separation was deliberately
made, with some special design, we may be sure, by a
letter from Swedenborg to the Danish ambassador, to
be found at page 173 of Swedenborg's Life, Boston ed.
1845, in which, referring to the Apoc. Rev., he says,
" In the same work are inserted various memorable relations of my intercourse with the spiritual world : they
are separated from the text of the work by asterisks,
and are to be found at the end of the explication of each
chapter."   The same arrangement was made of the relations in his work, entitled, " True Christian Religion."
Why did Swedenborg make the separation so plainly
between the scientific view and the relations ?   Did he
consider the one natural, the other supernatural ?   Some
of his followers seem to think he made such a distinction, but we have his own declaration to the contrary.
To M. Venator he writes, " I send to-day my reply to
the letter which his highness, your prince, has recently
sent to me ; and by his orders I speak to him of the

conversations which I have had with two personages in the spiritual world. But these conversations, as well as that between the queen of Sweden and her brother, when he was living, which was made known to me by him in the spiritual world, *ought by no means to be regarded as miracles." Life*, p. 178.

To the Landgrave of Hesse-Darmstadt he writes: " That which is reported of the daughter of the Prince Margrave in Sweden, is a fiction, invented by some foolish novelist, and I never even heard of it before. As to that which is related of the brother of the queen of Sweden, it is entirely true; but *it should not be regarded as a miracle*," &c. *Life*, p. 176.

To Dr. Oetinger, in 1766, he writes: " To your interrogation, *whether there is occasion for any sign that I am sent by the Lord to do what I do ?* I answer, that at this day no signs or *miracles* will be given, because they compel only an external belief, but do not convince the internal. What did the miracles avail in Egypt, or among the Jewish nation, who nevertheless crucified the Lord ?" *Life*, p. 43.

In the same letter he says, " Why from a *philosopher have I been chosen to this office ?* Unto which I give for answer, to the end that the spiritual knowledge, which is revealed at this day, might be rationally learned, and naturally understood; because spiritual truths answer unto natural ones, inasmuch as these originate and flow from them." *Life*, p. 44.

He says to M. Venator, referring to his work, *The True Christian Religion*, " You may see in the work above-mentioned, that *there are no more miracles* at this time; and the reason why it is, that they who do not believe because they see no miracles, might easily by them be led into fanaticism." *Life*, p. 178.

From the above passages, one point seems quite clear, that Swedenborg made no pretension to miraculous knowledge. We are bound therefore to give a rational interpretation to what he writes, or deny that it has any "significance for us."

As a further proof that Swedenborg did not regard his revelations of the spiritual world, and of "Representations and Correspondences," as miraculous, but merely natural, I would refer to the *Animal Kingdom*, vol. 1, p. 451, where, in a note to a purely philosophical allusion in the text to the "symbolical representation of spiritual life in corporeal life," and to a "perpetual typical representation of the soul in the body," he says: "In our doctrine of representations and correspondences, we shall treat of both these symbolical and typical representations, and of the astonishing things which occur, I will not say in the living body only, but throughout nature, and which correspond so entirely to *supreme and spiritual things*, that one would swear that the physical world was purely *symbolical of the spiritual world*. Insomuch that, if we choose to express any natural truth in physical and vocal terms, and to convert these terms only into the corresponding spiritual terms, we shall by this means elicit *a spiritual truth or theological dogma,* in place of *the physical truth or precept:* although no mortal would have predicted that any thing of the kind could possibly arise by bare literal transposition; inasmuch as the one precept, considered separately from the other, appears to have absolutely no relation to it.  I intend hereafter to communicate a number of examples of such correspondences, together with a vocabulary, containing the terms of spiritual things, as well as of the physical things, for which they are to be substituted."

In this note, from one of his merely philosophical works, we have a distinct expression of Swedenborg's intention with respect to what he subsequently accomplished in pointing out what he considered the spiritual truth corresponding to the *letter of the Scripture;* and when his philosophical system is penetrated it will be seen that his theological views necessarily result from it.  I do not say that the system is true or false; for I am not satisfied with my qualifications for an opinion on this point; but I am quite sure that the whole system, i. e. the whole life and pretensions of Swedenborg are to be regarded only from the natural point of view.

Those of his friends and followers, therefore, who persist in imputing to him supernatural endowments, are not faithful to his memory. To these people, I would use the advice of Miss Fuller, and urge them to *study the works of Swedenborg;* and I would add, study them until they learn from Swedenborg himself how to understand him; and they may suspect their own intellectual vision, until they can see him in a natural point of view, when they may rest assured his knowledge and genius will justify as much admiration as any one mere man should pay to another.

Some of Swedenborg's followers are now proposing the establishment of a *Hierarchy* in the name of their leader, while, in fact, there is no sign in any part of his writings that he ever expected or desired the institution of a separate sect of Christians, as a consequence of his revelations. The new Church, the new Jerusalem, is in Heaven, according to Swedenborg, and comes down to men in all of the churches when they are prepared to receive it. But its coming will not be hastened by the establishment of a new sect of Christians under his own or any other name; and much less can its coming be secured by a Hierarchy. Those who desire such an organization might do well to study the history of Romanism, and see how the Pontificate grew out of Catholicism, by the effort to confine the truth of God within the narrow limits of human organizations. I would advise all lovers of Swedenborg to remain in their respective churches, except where they discover something in conflict with their consciences, and then, by obeying the teachings of Swedenborg, there may be some hope of extending the good by their examples of "holiness and pureness of living." If Swedenborg's teachings are good, and those who profit by them withdraw from their accustomed associations, conscientiously formed, they deprive their friends of one of the greatest advantages for improvement, that of living examples.

A mathematical axiom occurs to me here, which I must notice; that, when two things are equal to a third thing, they are equal to each other.

I by no means say, in a strict sense, that Spinoza and the Hermetic writers are like Swedenborg, affording an inference that the Hermetic writers and Spinoza are to be classed together.

My position is that there is something in Swedenborg like Spinoza, to wit, chiefly, his scientific
principles; and something apparently drawn
from the Hermetic writers, as for example, their
doctrine of the one and three, but more especially
their mode, the Hermetic mode, of writing;—
writing of man in different senses, as a natural,
spiritual and celestial being;—affirming of one
phase of man's nature that which is denied of
another,—as, when he says, that angels can see
man but men cannot see angels, meaning merely
that man in his higher development may understand man in the lower states, but not contrarily,
&c.

Swedenborg seems to have attempted to com-
bine into one system the peculiarities of both
without sufficiently considering that something
like a contradiction would be observed in the result;—and yet such a contradiction is very visible. If we look at any of Swedenborg's systematic works on religion,—the Divine Love and
Divine Wisdom, or the True Christian Religion,
—we shall see a studied effort to lay down at first
some principles to be regarded as irrefragable,
after the manner of writing on science; as if he
intended that his work should be regarded from
a rational point of view only.    He endeavored

to set forth certain principles of *Being, Esse, Substance* and *Mode*, which we are bound to suppose he intended should be understood as a scientific basis for the superstructure to follow. We commence the study, therefore, as if our rational faculty was appealed to, and we naturally expect a continuance of the relation thus established between the author and his reader. But we soon come to something about *the opening of his internal spirit by the Lord*, by which the author separates himself from us and assumes, if we take him literally, to address us from another world with which we are not supposed to have any intercourse; and as a necessary consequence, his readers are no longer in a condition to decide upon what he communicates from the principles of reason so carefully laid down at first. The natural, in a certain degree, seems to run into the supernatural, the connecting link with which, if known at all, is known only to the author and not to the reader. The latter, then, is no longer in a condition to apply the principles at first inculcated with so much care; but, if not very watchful, he continues to read with the security of possessing a *test of reason* for what he reads, when, in fact, he is carried into the field of imagination,—unless it may happen, that the reader's internal sight shall be open also.

Now, Spinoza's Ethics is demonstrative, in form, throughout, though he exhibits many beautiful truths in no manner dependent upon his demonstrations. These truths, I might almost say, shine in his writings like the fire in the bush, though it may require the spirit of a Moses to apprehend them fully. But, although such truths do appear, Spinoza wrote from the scientific point of view, and asks nothing from his reader but the exercise of his rational faculties. He has much to say of substance and mode, like Swedenborg after him, but unlike Swedenborg he says nothing of the opening of his internal sight, and makes no demand upon our faith in his personal teaching.

The Hermetic writers have, on the other hand, nothing, or but very little to say of substance and mode;—and though they, least of all teachers of whom I know any thing, claim authority as teachers, they employ their utmost ingenuity to carry the mind of the student above, I do not say *reason* itself, but above *reasoning*. They would apparently have us believe that the most important principle that can be known is something subsisting independently of reasoning, and antecedent to all demonstration—upon which all true demonstrations themselves depend. I suppose, indeed, that Spinoza saw this principle (*vide* Letters 21 and 23 to Oldenburg, posthumous works, ed. 1802), and endeavored to represent it in a demonstrative form, contrary, as many think, to the nature of the thing. Those who think that the subject treated of can be brought within the field of science, will find nowhere, as I suppose, a more methodical and exact treatment of it than in Spinoza's Ethics. This form is very attractive to those who realize in themselves a strong intellectual power and delight in its exercise. A somewhat similar attraction is found in the writings of Swedenborg, for they present the same scientific basis that Spinoza wrote from, though the author does not use his principles in a demonstrative manner.

The older Hermetic writers aim at nothing of this sort. Neither do they elaborate systems from an assumption of the opening of an internal sight, though the possibility of the latter is strongly implied, and indeed in almost so many words asserted, not as actual with themselves simply, but as possible for their readers. They virtually say to us—we cannot teach you the " one thing," but God can; and " if he finds you sincere, he will not only show you a way, but help you to find it" [*Eyrenæus Cosmopolita*]. They tell us to purify ourselves and devote our affections to God; and that then we may learn something of God's mysteries, as if in that direction we might find the very "spirit of truth" itself, the "Comforter."

If this teaching should be thought similar to that of Jesus, enforcing the necessity of "doing" the will of his Father, it cannot on that account be thought less entitled to attention; while those who are in possession of the teachings of the Lord ought to rejoice that the deepest experiences of nature are testimonies of his truth. Even he had a mystic vein in his teachings, speaking "only" in parables to the people, but explaining all things openly to his disciples;— and this, says Roger Bacon, has been the way with "wise men from the beginning."

If the mystic writers had spoken out they might perhaps have instructed us in the language of Anebo to Jamblicus, or of Jamblicus to himself, to wit:

"In the first place, therefore, you say—'it must be granted that there are gods.' But thus to speak, ON THIS SUBJECT, is not right. For an innate knowledge of the gods is coexistent with

our very essence ; and this knowledge is superior
to all judgment and deliberate choice, and subsists prior to reason and demonstration.  It is
also co-united from the beginning with its proper
cause, and is consubsistent with the essential
tendency of the soul to the *good*.  If, indeed, it
be necessary to speak the truth, *the contact with
divinity* is not knowledge.  For knowledge is, in
a certain respect, separated or distinguished from
its object by a sense of *otherness*.  But prior to
the knowledge, which as one thing knows another, there is the uniform connection with divinity, which is suspended from (or caused by)
the gods, and is spontaneous and inseparable
from them.  Hence, it is not proper to grant
this, as if it might not be granted, nor to admit
it as ambiguous or doubtful (for it is always uni-
cally established in energy); nor are we worthy
thus to explore it, as if we had sufficient authority
to approve or reject it.  For we are comprehended in it, or, rather, we are filled by it, and
we POSSESS that very thing which we ARE in
knowing the gods.*  I shall likewise say the
same thing to you, concerning the more excellent genera that follow the gods, I mean *dæmons*,

* The readers of Faust may here be reminded of the answer
of Faust to Margaret.

heroes, and undefiled souls. For it is necessary to understand respecting these, that there is always in them one definite reason of essence, and to remove from them the indefiniteness and instability of the human condition. It is likewise requisite to separate from them that inclination to one side of an argument rather than another, arising from a reasoning process. For a thing of this kind is foreign from the principles of reason and [natural] life, which rather tend to secondary natures, and to such things as pertain to the power and contrariety of generated things. But it is necessary that the more excellent genera should be apprehended uniformly."

"The connascent perception, therefore, of the perpetual attendance of the gods, will be assimilated to them. Hence, as they have an existence which is always invariably the same, thus also the human soul is conjoined to them by knowledge, according to a sameness of subsistence; by no means pursuing, through conjecture, or opinion, or a reasoning process,—all of which originate in time,—an essence which is above all these, but through the pure and blameless intellections which the soul received from eternity from the gods, becoming united to them. You, however, seem to think that there is the same knowledge of divine natures as of any thing else, and that one thing, rather than another, may be granted from opposites, in the same manner as it is usual to do in dialectic discussions. There is, however, no similitude whatever between the two kinds of knowledge. For the knowledge of divine natures is different from that of other things, and is separated from all opposition. It likewise neither subsists in being now granted, or in becoming to be, but was from eternity uniformly consubsistent with the soul. And thus much I say to you concerning the first principle in us, from which it is necessary those should begin, who speak or hear any thing about the natures that are superior to us."

But I must hasten to show, by a brief extract from Iamblicus, that in thus speaking of the gods in the plural, he by no means denied the unity. " Since (says he) the order of all the gods is profoundly united, and the first and the second genera of them, and all the multitude which is spontaneously produced about them, are consubsistent in unity, and also every thing which is in them is one—therefore the beginning, middles, and ends in them are consubsistent according to the ONE itself; so that in these it is not proper to inquire whence the ONE accedes to all of them. For the very existence in them, whatever it is, is THIS ONE of their nature."

Those who judge by words, and not by ideas, may imagine that this ONE of Iamblicus differs from the ESSE of substance, defined by Swedenborg as above all *human thought*, but if they can, through the blessing of God, come into contact with that divinity, they may find reason to believe that *Iamblicus* was a true brother of man, a true member of the human family,—and rejoice at the discovery of a principle of union so extensive as to embrace the whole race of man.

# CONCLUSION.

As these pages are passing through the press, I have fallen in with an interesting *Biography and Exposition of Swedenborg*, by Edwin Paxton Hood,—interesting from the earnestness and eloquence of the writer. I have not time to read the whole work, for the compositors are pressing upon me. I observe in chapter second a somewhat elaborate defence of Swedenborg's claim to visions in the spiritual world, especially in reference to the MEMORABLE RELATIONS to be found in two or three of his works; and at page 104 the author recites one of the Relations, the object of which with Swedenborg was simply to give his opinion of a class of men, in regard to their *moral, intellectual*, and *religious* condition, of " a lethargic understanding, an indolent indisposition to think on spiritual subjects, or a laziness of the will in the execution of any useful purposes."

Mr. Hood admits that "there are some indications which might lead us to look upon the relations as simply allegorical, as figurative and representative portraits of spiritual things, a Pilgrim's Progress through the spiritual world; or as a gallery of paintings representing things on the earth, and in the course of happening among men." But this suggestion is immediately negatived by the course of argument by which the author labors to prove that Swedenborg actually saw into the spiritual world in a supernatural sense.

The point I have endeavored to set forward is, that Swedenborg regarded the inner or internal man as in the spiritual world, and he wrote the *Relations* simply from that point of view. Hence, in the example given by Mr. Hood, Swedenborg merely gives his *opinion* of the state of mind and religion of men of "lethargic understandings," &c., and of a preacher appropriate (or supported) by a congregation of such people. He describes the place as *cold*, &c., and the preacher "commences every sentence of his sermon with an ejaculation of praise of the grand mystery, and ended with an injunction to keep the understanding in obedience to the faith, affirming that man is only a man with respect to natural things; but that, upon religious things, he has no power to think, to will, to understand; let us keep our understandings in obedience to our faith, for our theology is like a bottomless abyss, into which if we suffer our understanding to look down, we shall become giddy, be drowned, and perish as in a shipwreck," &c.

As the preacher descends from the pulpit the people press around him saying, "We are ever bound to thank thee for thy most excellent discourse, so replete with the grandest wisdom." An imaginary traveller asks them,—"Did ye understand at all what the preacher was preaching about?" and they replied, "We took all in with open ears. But why dost thou ask whether we understand it? Is not the understanding quite stupid with respect to such subjects," &c., &c.

How is it possible for any one to stumble at the drift of Swedenborg in this sarcastic "relation?" It is nothing and can be nothing but a mode of expressing his opinion of certain dull, stupid people on the subject of religion.

Why, is it asked, did he throw the scene into the spiritual world? He tells us himself—first, because he regarded his thoughts, feelings, and opinions as spiritual; and then, in a letter to the Swedish Ambassador, without date, page 166 *Documents*, he says he introduced the Relations because "he thought that such remarkable particulars might probably excite the reader to their first perusal." What further explanation can be desired? But is not such a course at variance with truth? Not if we take Swedenborg with his explanations, instead of reading him fragmentarily. He gives us the key if we will only consent to use it, not only by his theory of man as body, soul, and spirit, but by his perpetually insisting upon the fact that all ancient wisdom has come down to us in correspondences and symbolism, not to be taken literally, but to be studied out in the spirit. It was thus he received the Bible itself, or the greater part of it, especially the beginning and the end, the Pentateuch and the Revelation, and now to be read literally himself he might well consider a hardship.

No one can be much accustomed to read works on speculative subjects, or reflect much upon what are called spiritual ideas, without being strongly impressed with the danger of misunderstanding what is written or spoken of such in-

visible matters.   Every thing in the " spirit-land "
may be named by many words, and, again, a single word may be employed to express many
things, and this to so great an extent, without a
design to make confusion, that many students
despair of attaining to clearness in that direction,
when, strange to say, in this very despair a light
is often generated, explaining the true cause of
the difficulty, which then ceases to be an obstacle
to farther progress.   I cannot conceal from myself that many may find such a difficulty in com-
prehending the meaning of the word conscience,
as the *spirit* which writes the "law of the Lord"
on the " fleshy tables of the heart."   But this difficulty seems unnecessary, if we would look at
things, and not attach too much importance to
words.   Whether we speak of *ambition* or of the
*spirit* of ambition, we surely speak of the same
thing; so, if we speak of duty, or the sense of
duty, of the right or the spirit of right, of justice
or the spirit of justice, we speak of the conscience, and of the conscience only, with this only
difference, that, in one case we may think of some
particular duty, and in another we may refer to
the law as a principle, or as the substance of duty,
and of right, and of justice.   This principle, law,
or substance of duty, is that which Kant called

the apodictic command, or the categorical impera-
tive, and in popular language is called the conscience, but in religious phraseology it may be
called the Holy Spirit; for it is certain there is
nothing in man more holy or more sacred, and
there is nothing of which men have labored to
speak more impressively, by way of instruction
and caution. "A palsy may as well shake an oak
(Dr. South is quoted as saying), or a fever dry up
a fountain, as either of them shake or impair the
delight of the conscience. For it lies within, it
centres in the heart, it grows into the very substance of the soul, so that it accompanies a man
to his grave; he never outlives it, and that for
this cause only, because he cannot outlive HIM-
SELF." On the other side, when it condemns,
Horace is quoted as saying that "not even for
an hour can you bear to be alone, nor can you
advantageously apply your leisure time, but you
endeavor, a fugitive and a wanderer, to escape
from YOURSELF, now vainly seeking to banish re-
morse by wine, and now by sleep; but the
gloomy companion presses on you, and pursues
you as you fly."

*Fuller* is quoted as saying: "If thou wouldst
be informed what God has written concerning
thee in *Heaven*, look into thine own *Bosom*, and

15

see what graces he has wrought in thee."—And *Shakespeare* makes one exclaim :

> " What stronger breast-plate than a heart untainted ?
>   Thrice is he armed, that hath his quarrel just ;
>   And he but naked, though locked up in steel,
>   Whose *Conscience* with injustice is corrupted."

*Crabbe* is quoted as saying :

> Oh, Conscience ! Conscience ! man's most faithful friend,
> Him canst thou comfort, ease, relieve, defend :
> But if he will thy friendly checks forego,
> Thou art, Oh ! wo for me, his deadliest foe ! "

Our own *Washington* calls the conscience a celestial fire, the very symbol of the Hermetic writers. " Labor," says he, " to keep alive in your breast that little spark of celestial fire, called Conscience."

*Cudworth* is quoted as saying that—" A good Conscience within will be always better to a Christian than health to his navel, and marrow to his bones; it will be an everlasting *cordial* to his heart; it will be softer to him than a bed of down. A good Conscience is the best looking-glass of Heaven."

This is said of a good conscience, as if there might be a bad conscience; but this is by a mere transference of terms. No man has a bad conscience, but a bad man may be very much troubled by a good conscience; for, so far as a man has a conscience at all, it must be good.

Many suppose that the conscience approves of some things known to be evil; but this is a mistake; for, in all such supposed cases the mischief proceeds from the immature state of the man, in whom the conscience does not act freely. It is on this account that the Alchemists have so much to say of what they call *separation*, or *dissolution*—or, in other words, the *analysis* of the soul in its operations, by which it attains to a knowledge of its true principles of action, when the conscience, eliminated from all selfishness proper to the natural man, shows itself always one and the same principle.

To guard their students on this point, Hermetic writers are careful to urge the necessity, in the student, of ascertaining the precise *intention* with which he sets about the study, one only intention being suitable to it, to wit, a love of the truth for the sake of the truth. They tell the student to consider the last intention as the first principle in his philosophy—as if they would warn us that every man's philosophy must take its color from the motive or intention leading the student to it.

As the Hermetic philosophers are constantly speaking of two things, as well as of one and three, so Swedenborg speaks of two consciences, an inward and an outward conscience; and if a distinction of this sort be considered as valid, I then would ask that the inward conscience be considered as here referred to—the inward, as the essential law of right within man.

To any one, however, who finds himself impeded in his studies and contemplations on this subject, I would suggest the effort to find some other *Spirit* whose office it is to write the Law on the heart, according to St. Paul's understanding of it, and so far as I have indicated any theory for the explanation of Hermetic Books, I have no objection to such a change of names, calling this for that which I have called the conscience, as may most clearly express the thing.

I have not merely spoken of the conscience, but of the conscience purified in the sight of God, or under a sense of God's presence; yet when I speak of purifying the conscience I mean always the MAN—not admitting that the conscience, considered in itself, is capable of defilement. As I have said in my *Remarks on Alchemy*, it can neither be bribed nor hoodwinked, and, when once aroused, it can never be silenced but by submission to it.  When it condemns, it is called, in Hermetic jargon, *wormwood*, the *juice of sour grapes*, and the like; but when it attains an acknowledged supremacy, it is called *oil*, and, finally, *elixir*, the elixir of Life.

It may interest the curious reader to assume for a moment—for experiment sake—that this is truly the Holy Spirit, and then observe how much of sacred writ, regarded as symbolical and figurative, may be referred to it, and how large a portion may be explained by it.

I pass by the first query that arises with many—Can any good thing come out of such a Nazareth as a common man (*John* i. 46), and the declaration also that it cannot do any mighty works, such as removing "mountains" of sin, because of "unbelief" (*Matt.* xiii. 58).  Not to think exaltedly of the Conscience—to have little or no faith in its efficacy—is to render it measurably of no avail; but let faith arise in it, though compared to a mustard seed in magnitude, and possibly it may grow to become the largest of trees, regulating, and taming, and giving "shelter" to all the thoughts and passions of man— themselves compared to *birds* and *beasts*.

But, as intimated above, let it be supposed

for a moment that the Conscience, even in the so-called natural man, is the Holy Spirit, and let us observe how aptly it may explain many things in the sacred writings.

This, then, is the *Spirit* which, in reference to the immature or imperfect man—the true chaos—is said to have been in the world, and yet the world, that is, the natural or carnal man, knew it not.

This is the *Light* which shineth in darkness, and the darkness, that is, the unregenerate man, comprehendeth it not.

This is the ubiquitous Spirit which is with us in Heaven, and no less in Hell, the "Maker" of both,—in the one case blessing us, and in the other condemning us, while yet it is but one and the same Spirit.

This is the Spirit which knocketh at the door of every man's heart, asking admission, and which we are warned not to grieve away.

This is the Spirit which *was* before Abraham, and whose coming has been the prediction of all time, at whose coming the world, that is, the man in whom it comes, is judged.

This is the Comforter which, when it comes to any man, reproves the man of sin because he has not believed in it.

This is the Spirit which appeals to the sinner in the affecting language, Come unto me, all ye that labor and are heavy laden, and I will give you rest:—for the *rest* here spoken of is moral rest and has no reference to mere physical evils, except that moral rest is the way to a power of endurance beyond the ordinary or natural power of man, having its root in a genuine humility:—for the genuine strength of man lies in the power of God.

Again: This is the Spirit at whose name every knee shall bow; and when all things shall be subdued unto it, then shall this Spirit be subject unto Him that put all things under *him*, that God may be all in all.

This is the Spirit, again, to whom, personified, we are commanded to go with a full confession of our sins, through whose vicarious suffering we are pardoned. This is a deep point in philosophy which however was well understood by Plato, who shows that a sinner can never be reinstated without a certain punishment as a purification. The sinner, according to Plato, is an unhappy man, miserable in the midst of his joys, until he is *punished;* yet the punishment referred to is not external but internal; meaning that the sinner must internally suffer the pangs of a wounded conscience, as the phrase is, before he can be recovered to a state of virtue. Now, in such a case the conscience is said to suffer; but this I have called a metonymy, or the substitution of one word for another; for, as I have said, it is not the conscience that suffers, but the man, that is, the sinner. The wicked man suffers under the judgment of a *sinless* conscience, which in itself does not and cannot suffer. The conscience, I repeat, is in itself both without sin and without suffering, and by its condemnation of the sinner the sinner is prepared for pardon; which is finally pronounced by the conscience itself, when the repentant state is perfectly completed, and not before. But the conscience, being substituted for man, is said to suffer, the innocent for the guilty; and this is expiatory suffering, which is not only necessary, but there is no other principle given under Heaven whereby man can feel himself redeemed.

Here, too, we see the importance of faith, for without faith in the Holy Spirit, no man will submit himself to it and make its commands the Law of his Life.

This is the Spirit of God which is in the world (man) reconciling the world to God—whose bid ding we are commanded to " do," if we would " know " that it is of God.

I may be told that the conscience is morbid in some men, and a most dangerous counsellor—that at the bidding of conscience the most terrible crimes have been committed; but I answer, no: men have abused the conscience, hoping to make it the means of attaining untold rewards, both in this and in another life. Men have desired to get to heaven—they have *intended* heaven, making conscience the instrument, but the conscience disowns such a use of itself, and " jealous " of its honor, will be served for itself alone. The *intention* must not look beyond the duty whose consequences must be valued less than the duty, and they must be received on trust—trnst in God.

I may be told that the Conscience fails in power, and leaves the man to suffer; but, can any other spirit save such a man? You will say, perhaps, that religion can save him: yes, truly, but it saves him through a purified Conscience, for an unpurified conscience and religion, that is, impiety and piety, can never coalesce. The Conscience, I have said, is the *Way;*—I have nowhere said it is the *End.*

This view may offer a theoretic explanation
15*

of the story of the destruction of children by
*Herod*.  Thus :—Among the infinity of principles or passions born in man, there is only one
absolutely innocent and immortal.  This one is
not, strictly speaking, born in man, but man is
spiritually "born in it."  This one opposes the
natural man while in what St. Paul calls the
natural state, and the natural man, the *Herod* in
this case, seeks to destroy it, which, however, he
cannot do.  In the attempt, on the contrary,
good is brought out of evil, and the other "children" of man, which, in respect to themselves,
are innocent also (but, as wild beasts are innocent), are cut off, and thus the divine in man is
preserved.  This mode of explanation might save
us the trouble of considering how it was possible
that any Roman governor could dare to destroy
all the children of a great city, under two years
of age, and not be called to account for it; and
it would relieve us also from the difficulty of
explaining how such an enormity could have
taken place without being so much as hinted at
by any Roman historian.  This mode of interpretation may also save us the trouble of explaining
why neither Josephus nor Philo say any thing
of Jesus Christ—the confessedly spurious passage
in the former being set aside—while both of them

give an extended account of the Essenes among the Jews, with doctrines corresponding to those of the gospels.

If we call this spirit the Son, we may easily conceive how his eternal generation is to be understood; how he is one with the Father, of his very substance, and how born of the eternal virgin mother of all things, and yet but one only Son, who, becoming flesh in "the man Christ Jesus," spake forth the commands of the Father, our "conscience bearing witness" that he spake the very truth. In this direction we may understand what the Hermetic writers mean when they speak of water mingling with water (spirit with spirit); for as Christ is one with God, so is he one with man, and to as many as receive this doctrine in spirit and in truth, God gives "the power of becoming sons of God,"—*John* 1. 12; or, as St. Paul expresses it—"As many as are led by the Spirit of God, they are the sons of God."

This view might be still further followed out by interpreting the scene of the Passion as designed to teach that, of the three principles of *Body*, *Spirit*, and *Soul*, one is essentially eternal. Personified, He is in the middle between the other two, who are called thieves because, while in the body, these assume and exercise an unlawful authority over the true Life, while yet one of the two may, by uniting with the Spirit, be ("to-day") in Paradise.  The soul, by uniting itself to the spirit, becomes immortal; but by yielding to the body it perishes with the body.  This soul, according to Swedenborg, is the spiritual body of man, the real individual man, which yet has no life in itself, but only in the spirit, the life of which is appropriated by Love.

No one need hastily suppose that in this view the historical is denied.  This is called the letter, and is no further denied than may be implied in the doctrine that the spirit (of the letter) is of more importance than the letter, and is essential to its interpretation, carrying its interpretations, —after the manner of Origen,—even to the miracles, all of which have a moral or spiritual significance.

Swedenborg did not deny the letter.  He called it the *ultimate*, and the *continent* of the spirit.  He also called it the *effect*, and to affirm the effect was also to affirm the spirit; but to understand the effect, it is necessary according to Swedenborg to understand or to know the spirit, which nevertheless is contained in the letter.  To hold to the letter and not seek the spirit, is like the endeavor to hold to the natural life; which, whoso seeks to save shall lose it, as we read; but to lose the letter in devotion to the spirit is to find the very truth from which the letter proceeded; while to lose the letter, except in devotion to the spirit, ["for my sake," as expressed in the gospel,] is to lose both the letter and the spirit; and this is to lose one's self, and to wander perpetually in the "dark wood" of Dante.

To find the spirit, and to walk in it, is to find the "law of the Lord" and "walk therein," and this is to "walk with God." When the law of the Lord is said to be "perfect," as we read in Scripture, the spirit is spoken of,—the eternal Law, the "Word,"—which St. Paul labored to make known for the purpose of showing its supremacy over the written law, which he speaks of as a veil, figuratively placing it over the hearts of the Jews; and this veil he tells us is "done away in Christ," that is, in the spirit, the unwritten law in the heart, which neither is nor can be any thing but the law of conscience, and we abuse ourselves when we seek for it elsewhere.

Hence the language, "When the wicked *man* turneth away from his wickedness that he hath committed, and doeth that which is *lawful* and *right*, he shall save his soul *alive*." What is it

to do that which is lawful and right?  Read all
the philosophy that has ever been written on the
subject, and in the end the rule is found in the
conscience, or it is not found at all;—but it must
be the conscience itself, and neither fear, nor
hope, nor any other passion mistaken for the
spirit itself, the spirit of truth, which, like the
law of the Lord, is also said to be "perfect."
There are many synonyms for the principle at
the root of this discussion, including justice—and
this in connection with perfection,—as, "The
path of the *just* man shineth to *perfect* day;"
and "mark the *perfect* man; and behold the *up-
right:* for the end of that man is peace."

This doctrine does not impugn the eternal
truth, that every good and perfect gift is from
above; in keeping with which, all of the mystic
writers, including Swedenborg, agree that their
secret is the gift of God; but the conscience is
the "way," the Nazareth, out of which it comes,
or in which, when the man is properly prepared,
the Spirit is manifested; which preparation,
nevertheless, however difficult it may be to understand it, is made by the Spirit; and this is so
true, that the Hermetic writers say that if any
man shall glory in its possession, and shall not
give the glory to God, he shall lose it—so little

does this doctrine minister to the presumption and idle vanity of man.

It is certainly remarkable that there seems to be three modes by which the Christian Religion is received in the world, not perhaps absolutely distinct from each other,—in this respect like the body, soul, and spirit of man,—yet sufficiently marked to be distinguished from each other. In one view it is received historically, and its truth is supposed to rest upon historical evidences so strong that no man in his senses can reject the testimony. From this point of view the miracles are especially appealed to; but I am not ignorant that in the class that appeals to testimony there is often with individuals a much higher evidence, that of the spirit, not always clearly discerned.

We next come to a class in which the intellect is cultivated, introducing the student into more or less incomplete philosophical principles; and here we find the chief controversies touching the externals of religion; and religion itself is treated as if so dependent upon these that it is supposed to share their fate. Here we find ingenious assaults upon the letter, and acrimonious defences of both the letter and the spirit.

A third class, more reserved and contemplative, say but little or nothing of the letter or external form, and seem to reach an idea of the truth, with more or less of fulness, as it is, or, speaking historically, as it was in Jesus,—the spirit of truth, the eternal Word, manifesting itself indeed in time, but existing eternally beyond and above all controversy.

In this latter class I place the genuine Hermetic Philosophers, including many misunderstood people in different ages of the world, under various names, as alchemists, astrologists, magicians, &c., and in this class I recognize the Swedish Philosopher, EMANUEL SWEDENBORG.

THE END.

## Agriculture & Rural Affairs.

| | |
|---|---|
| Boussingault's Rural Economy, | 1 25 |
| The Poultry Book, illustrated, | 5 00 |
| Waring's Elements of Agriculture, | 75 |

## Arts Manufactures, and Architecture.

| | |
|---|---|
| Appleton's Dictionary of Mechanics 2 vols. | 12 00 |
| Appleton's Mechanics' Magazine. 3 vols. each, | 5 50 |
| Allen's Philosophy of Mechanics, | 3 50 |
| Arnot's Gothic Architecture, | 4 00 |
| Bassnett's Theory of Storms, | 1 00 |
| Bourne on the Steam Engine, | 0 75 |
| Byrne on Logarithms, | 1 00 |
| Chapman on the American Rifle, | 1 25 |
| Coming's Preservation of Health, | 75 |
| Cullum on Military Bridges, | 2 00 |
| Downing's Country Houses, | 4 00 |
| Field's City Architecture, | 2 00 |
| Griffith's Marine Architecture, | 10 00 |
| Gillespie's Treatise on Surveying, | |
| Haupt's Theory of Bridge Construction, | 5 00 |
| Henck's Field-Book for R. R. Engineers, | 1 75 |
| Hoblyn's Dictionary of Scientific Terms, | 1 60 |
| Huff's Manual of Electro-Physiology, | 1 25 |
| Jeffers' Practice of Naval Gunnery, | 2 50 |
| Knepen's Mechanics' Assistant, | 1 00 |
| Lafever's Modern Architecture, | 4 00 |
| Lyell's Manual of Geology, | 1 75 |
| " Principles of Geology, | 2 25 |
| Reynold's Treatise on Handrailing, | 2 00 |
| Templeton's Mechanic's Companion, | 1 00 |
| Ure's Dict'ry of Arts, Manufactures, &c. 2 vols. | 5 00 |
| Youmans' Class-Book of Chemistry, | 75 |
| " Atlas of Chemistry. cloth. | 2 00 |
| " Alcohol, | 50 |

## Biography.

| | |
|---|---|
| Arnold's Life and Correspondence | 2 00 |
| Capt. Canot, or Twenty Years of a Slaver | 1 25 |
| Conan's De Longueville, | 1 00 |
| Croswell's Memoirs, | 2 00 |
| Evelyn's Life of Godolphin, | 50 |
| Garland's Life of Randolph, | 1 50 |
| Gilfillan's Gallery of Portraits. 2d Series, | 1 00 |
| Hernan Cortez's Life, | 38 |
| Hull's Civil and Military Life, | 2 00 |
| Life and Adventures of Daniel Boone, | 38 |
| Life of Henry Hudson, | 38 |
| Life of Capt. John Smith, | 38 |
| Moore's Life of George Castriot, | 1 00 |
| Napoleon's Memoirs. By Duchess D'Abrantes, | 4 00 |
| Napoleon. By Laurent L'Ardèche, | 3 00 |
| Pinkney (W.) Life. By his Nephew, | 2 00 |
| Party Leaders: Lives of Jefferson, &c., | 1 00 |
| Southey's Life of Oliver Cromwell, | 38 |
| Wynne's Lives of Eminent Men, | 1 00 |
| Webster's Life and Memorials. 2 vols. | 1 00 |

## Books of General Utility.

| | |
|---|---|
| Appletons' Southern and Western Guide, | 1 00 |
| " Northern and Eastern Guide, | 1 50 |
| Appletons' Complete U. S. Guide, | 2 00 |
| " Map of N. Y. City, | 25 |
| American Practical Cook Book, | |
| A Treatise on Artificial Fish-Breeding, | 75 |
| Chemistry of Common Life. 2 vols. 12mo. | |
| Cooley's Book of Useful Knowledge, | 1 |
| Cust's Invalid's Own Book, | 50 |
| Delisser's Interest Tables, | 4 00 |
| The English Cyclopaedia, per vol. | 3 50 |
| Miles on the Horse's Foot, | 50 |
| The Nursery Basket. A Book for Young Mothers, | |
| Pell's Guide for the Young, | 38 |
| Reid's New English Dictionary, | 1 00 |
| Stewart's Stable Economy, | 1 00 |
| Spalding's Hist. of English Literature, | 1 00 |
| Soyer's Modern Cookery, | 1 00 |
| The Successful Merchant, | 1 00 |
| Thomson on Food of Animals, | 50 |

## Commerce and Mercantile Affairs.

Anderson's Mercantile Correspondence, . . . 1 00
Delisser's Interest Tables, . . 4 00
Merchants' Reference Book, . . 4 00
Oates' (Geo.) Interest Tables at 4 Per Cent. per Annum. 8vo. . 2 00
"    "    Do. do. Abridged edition, . . 1 25
"    "    7 Per Cent. Interest. Tables. . . 2 00
"    "    Abridged, . . 1 25
Smith's Mercantile Law, . . 4 00

## Geography and Atlases.

Appleton's Modern Atlas. 34 Maps, 8 50
"    Complete Atlas. 61 Maps, . 9 00
Atlas of the Middle Ages. By Koeppen, . . 4 50
Black's General Atlas. 71 Maps, . 12 00
Cornell's Primary Geography, . 50
"    Intermediate Geography,
"    High School Geography,

## History.

Arnold's History of Rome, . . 3 00
"    Later Commonwealth, . 2 50
"    Lectures on Modern History, . . 1 25
Dew's Ancient and Modern History, . . 2 00
Koeppen's History of the Middle Ages. 2 vols. . . 2 50
"    The same, folio, with Maps, . 4 50
Kohlrausch's History of Germany, 1 50
Mahon's (Lord) History of England, 2 vols. . 4 00
Michelet's History of France, 2 vols. . 3 50
"    History of the Roman Republic, . . 1 00
Rowan's History of the French Revolution, . . 63
Sprague's History of the Florida War, . 2 50
Taylor's Manual of Ancient History, . 1 25
"    Manual of Modern History, 1 50
"    Manual of History. 1 vol. complete, . . 2 50
Thiers' French Revolution. 4 vols. Illus. . . 5 00

## Illustrated Works for Presents.

Bryant's Poems. 16 Illus. 8vo. cl'th, 3 50
"    "    cloth, gilt, 4 50
"    "    mor. ant. 5 00
Gems of British Art. 30 Engravings. 1 vol. 4to. morocco, . 18 00
Gray's Elegy. Illustrated. 8vo. 1 50

Goldsmith's Deserted Village, . 1 50
The Homes of American Authors. With Illustrations, cloth, . . 4 00
"    "    cloth, gilt, 5 00
"    "    mor. ant. 7 00
The Holy Gospels. With 40 Designs by Overbeck. 1 vol. folio. Antique mor. . . 20 00
The Land of Bondage. By J. M. Wainwright, D. D. Morocco, . 5 00
The Queens of England. By Agnes Strickland. With 29 Portraits. Antique mor. . 10 00
The Ornaments of Memory. With 18 Illustrations. 4to. cloth, gilt, 5 00
"    "    Mor. 10 00
Royal Gems from the Galleries of Europe. 40 Engravings, . 25 00
The Republican Court; or, American Society in the Days of Washington. 21 Portraits. Anti. mor. 12 00
The Vernon Gallery. 57 Engr's. 4to. Antique, . 25 00
The Women of the Bible. With 18 Engravings. Mor. antique, 10 00
Wilkie Gallery. Containing 60 Splendid Engravings. 4to. Antique mor. . . 25 00
A Winter Wreath of Summer Flowers. By S. G. Goodrich. Illustrated. Cloth, gilt, . 3 00

## Juvenile Books.

A Poetry Book for Children, . . 75
Aunt Fanny's Christmas Stories, . 50
American Historical Tales, . 75

UNCLE AMEREL'S STORY BOOKS.

The Little Gift Book. 18mo. cloth, 25
The Child's Story Book. Illus. 18mo. cloth, . . . . 25
Summer Holidays. 18mo. cloth, . 25
Winter Holidays. Illus. 18mo. clo. 25
George's Adventures in the Country. Illustrated. 18mo. cloth, . 25
Christmas Stories. Illus. 18mo. clo. 25

Book of Trades, . . . 50
Boys at Home. By the Author of Edgar Clifton, . . . 75
Child's Cheerful Companion, . . 50
Child's Picture and Verse Book. 100 Engs. . . . . 50

COUSIN ALICE'S WORKS.

All's Not Gold that Glitters, . . 75
Contentment Better than Wealth, . 63
Nothing Venture, Nothing Have, . 44
No such Word as Fail, . . . 65
Patient Waiting No Loss, . . 63
Dashwood Priory. By the Author of Edgar Clifton, . . . 75
Edgar Clifton; or Right and Wrong, 75
Fireside Fairies. By Susan Pindar, 44
Good in Every Thing. By Mrs. Barwell, . . . . 50
Leisure Moments Improved, . . 17
Life of Punchinello, . . . 74

## LIBRARY FOR MY YOUNG COUNTRYMEN.

Adventures of Capt. John Smith. By the Author of Uncle Philip, . 38
Adventures of Daniel Boone. By do. 38
Dawnings of Genius. By Anne Pratt, . 33
Life and Adventures of Henry Hudson. By the Author of Uncle Philip, . 35
Life and Adventures of Hernan Cortez. By do. 38
Philip Randolph. A Tale of Virginia. By Mary Gertrude, 38
Bowan's History of the French Revolution. 2 vols. 75
Southey's Life of Oliver Cromwell, 38

Louis' School-Days. By E. J. May, . 75
Louise; or, The Beauty of Integrity, 25
Marryatt's Settlers in Canada, 52
   "   Masterman Ready, 63
   "   Scenes in Africa, 63
Midsummer Fays. By Susan Pinder, 68

## MISS McINTOSH'S WORKS.

Aunt Kitty's Tales, 12mo. 75
Blind Alice; A Tale for Good Children, 38
Ellen Leslie; or, The Reward of Self-Control, 38
Florence Arnott; or, Is She Generous? 36
Grace and Clara; or, Be Just as well as Generous, 38
Jessie Graham; or, Friends Dear, but Truth Dearer, 38
Emily Herbert; or, The Happy Home, 37
Rose and Lillie Stanhope, 37

Mamma's Story Book, 75
Pebbles from the Sea-Shore, 37
Puss in Boots. Illus. By Otto Specter, 25

## PETER PARLEY'S WORKS.

Faggots for the Fireside, 1 13
Parley's Present for all Seasons, 1 00
Wanderers by Sea and Land, 1 13
Winter Wreath of Summer Flowers, 3 00

## TALES FOR THE PEOPLE AND THEIR CHILDREN.

Alice Franklin. By Mary Howitt, 38
Crofton Boys (The). By Harriet Martineau, 38
Dangers of Dining Out. By Mrs. Ellis, 38
Domestic Tales. By Hannah More. 2 vols. 75
Early Friendship. By Mrs. Copley, 38
Farmer's Daughter (The). By Mrs. Cameron, 38
First Impressions. By Mrs. Ellis, 38

Hope On, Hope Ever! By Mary Howitt, 38
Little Coin, Much Care. By do. 38
Looking-Glass for the Mind. Many plates, 38
Love and Money. By Mary Howitt, 38
Minister's Family. By Mrs. Ellis, 38
My Own Story. By Mary Howitt, 38
My Uncle, the Clockmaker. By do. 38
No Sense Like Common Sense. By do. 38
Peasant and the Prince. By H. Martineau, 38
Poplar Grove. By Mrs. Copley, 38
Somerville Hall. By Mrs. Ellis, 38
Sowing and Reaping. By Mary Howitt, 38
Story of a Genius. 38
Strive and Thrive. By do. 38
The Two Apprentices. By do. 38
Tired of Housekeeping. By T. S. Arthur, 38
Twin Sisters (The). By Mrs. Sandham, 34
Which is the Wiser! By Mary Howitt, 31
Who Shall be Greatest! By do. 38
Work and Wages. By do. 38

### SECOND SERIES.

Chances and Changes. By Charles Burdett, 38
Goldmaker's Village. By H. Zschokke, 38
Never Too Late. By Charles Burdett, 38
Ocean Work, Ancient and Modern. By J. H. Wright, 38

Picture Pleasure Book, 1st Series, 1 25
   "   "   "   2d Series, 1 25
Robinson Crusoe. 300 Plates, 1 50
Susan Pindar's Story Book, 75
Sunshine of Greystone, 75
Travels of Bob the Squirrel, 37
Wonderful Story Book, 59
Willy's First Present, 7
Week's Delight; or, Games and Stories for the Parlor, 75
William Tell, the Hero of Switzerland, 50
Young Student. By Madame Guizot, 75

# Miscellaneous and General Literature.

An Attic Philosopher in Paris,
Appletons' Library Manual,
Agnell's Book of Chess,
Arnold's Miscellaneous Works,
Arthur. The Successful Merchant,
A Book for Summer Time in the Country, 50
Baldwin's Flush Times in Alabama, 1 25
Calhoun (J. C.), Works of. 4 vols. publ., each, 2 00
Clark's (W. G.) Knick-Knacks, 1 25
Cornwall's Music as it Was, and as it Is, 50

Essays from the London Times. 1st & 2d Series, each, . . . 50
Ewbanks' World in a Workshop, . 75
Ellis' Women of England, . . 50
"  Hearts and Homes, . . 1 50
"  Prevention Better than Cure, 75
Foster's Essays on Christian Morals, 50
Goldsmith's Vicar of Wakefield, . 75
Grant's Memoirs of an American Lady, . . . . . 75
Gaieties and Gravities. By Horace Smith, . . . . . 50
Guizot's History of Civilization, . 1 00
Hearth-Stone. By Rev. S. Osgood. 1 00
Hobson. My Uncle and I, . . 75
Ingoldsby Legends, . . . 50
Isham's Mud Cabin, . . . 1 00
Johnson's Meaning of Words, . 1 00
Kavanagh's Women of Christianity, . . . . . . 75
Leger's Animal Magnetism . . 1 00
Life's Discipline. A Tale of Hungary, . . . . . 63
Letters from Rome. A. D. 138, . 1 90
Margaret Maitland, . . . 75
Maiden and Married Life of Mary Powell, . . . . . 50
Morton Montague; or a Young Christian's Choice, . . . 75
Macaulay's Miscellanies. vols. . 5 00
Maxims of Washington. By J. F. Schroeder, . . . . 1 00
Mile Stones in our Life Journey, . 1 00

## MINIATURE CLASSICAL LIBRARY.

Poetic Lacon; or, Aphorisms from the Poets, . . . . 38
Bond's Golden Maxims, . . 31
Clarke's Scripture Promises. Complete, . . . . . 38
Elizabeth; or, The Exiles of Siberia, . . . . . 31
Goldsmith's Vicar of Wakefield, . 38
"  Essays, . . 38
Gems from American Poets, . 38
Hannah More's Private Devotions, 31
"  -  Practical Piety. 2 vols. 75
Hemans' Domestic Affections, . 31
Hoffman's Lays of the Hudson, &c. 38
Johnson's History of Rasselas, . 38
Manual of Matrimony, . . 31
Moore's Lalla Rookh, . . 38
"  Melodies. Complete, . 38
Paul and Virginia, . . . 31
Pollok's Course of Time, . . 38
Pure Gold from the Rivers of Wisdom, . . . . . 38
Thomson's Seasons, . . . 38
Token of the Heart. Do. of Affection. Do. of Remembrance. Do. of Friendship. Do. of Love. Each, . . . . . 31
Useful Letter-Writer, . . 38
Wilson's Sacra Privata, . . 31
Young's Night Thoughts, . . 38

Little Pedlington and the Pedlingtonians. . . . . 50

Prismatics. Tales and Poems, . 1 24
Papers from the Quarterly Review, 54
Republic of the United States. Its Duties, &c. . . . . 1 00
Preservation of Health and Prevention of Disease, . . . 75
School for Politics. By Charles Gayarre, . . . . 75
Select Italian Comedies. Translated, . . . . . 75
Shakespeare's Scholar. By R. G. White, . . . . 2 50
Spectator (The). New ed. 6 vols. cloth, . . . . 3 00
Swett's Treatise on Diseases of the Chest, . . . . 3 00
Stories from Blackwood, . . 50

## THACKERAY'S WORKS.

The Book of Snobs, . . 50
Mr. Browne's Letters, . . 50
The Confessions of Fitzboodle, . 50
The Fat Contributor, . . 50
Jeames' Diary. A Legend of the Rhine, . . . . 50
The Luck of Barry Lyndon, . 1 00
Men's Wives, . . . 75
The Paris Sketch Book. 2 vols. . 1 00
The Shabby Genteel Story, . 50
The Yellowplush Papers. 1 vol. 16mo. . . . . 50
Thackeray's Works. 6 vols. bound in cloth, . . . . 6 00

Trescott's Diplomacy of the Revolution, . . . . 75
Tuckerman's Artist Life, . . 75
Up Country Letters . . 75
Ward's Letters from Three Continents, . . . . 1 00
"  English Items, . . 1 00
Warner's Rudimental Lessons in Music, . . . . 50
Woman's Worth, . . . 38

## Philosophical Works.

Cousin's Course of Modern Philosophy, . . . . 3 00
"  Philosophy of the Beautiful, . . . . 62
"  on the True, Beautiful, and Good, . . . 1 50
Comte's Positive Philosophy. 2 vols. . . . . 4 00
Hamilton's Philosophy. 1 vol. 8vo. . . . . 1 50

## Poetry and the Drama.

Amelia's Poems. 1 vol. 12mo. . 1 25
Brownell's Poems. 12mo. . 75
Bryant's Poems. 1 vol. 8vo. Illustrated, . . . . 3 50
"  "  Antique mor. . 6 30
Bryant's Poems, 2 vols. 12mo. cloth, . . . . 2 00
"  "  1 vol. 18mo. . 62
Byron's Poetical Works. 1 vol. cloth, . . . . 2 00
Antique mor. 4 50

Burns' Poetical Works. Cloth, . 1 00
Butler's Hudibras. Cloth, . . . 1 00
Campbell's Poetical Works. Cloth, 1 00
Coleridge's Poetical Works. Cloth, 1 25
Cowper's Poetical Works . . 1 00
Chaucer's Canterbury Tales, . . 1 00
Dante's Poems. Cloth, . . 1 00
Drydon's Poetical Works. Cloth, 1 00
Fay (J. S.), Ulric; or, The Voices, 75
Goethe's Iphigenia in Tauris. Translated, . . . 75
Gilfillan's Edition of the British Poets. 12 vols. published. Price per vol. cloth . . . 1 00
Do. do. Calf, per vol. . . 2 50
Griffith's (Mattie) Poems, . . 75
Hemans' Poetical Works. 2 vols. 16mo. . . 2 00
Herbert's Poetical Works. 16mo. cloth, . . 1 00
Keats' Poetical Works. Cloth. 12mo. . . 1 25
Kirke White's Poetical Works. Cloth, . . 1 00
Lord's Poems. 1 vol. 12mo. . 75
" Christ in Hades. 12mo. . 75
Milton's Paradise Lost. 18mo. . 38
" Complete Poetical Works, 1 00
Moore's Poetical Works. 8vo. Illust. 8 00
" " " Mor. ext. 6 00
Montgomery's Sacred Poems. 1 vol. 12mo. . 75
Pope's Poetical Works. 1 vol. 16mo. 1 00
Southey's Poetical Works. 1 vol . 3 00
Spenser's Faerie Queene. 1 vol. clo. 1 00
Scott's Poetical Works. 1 vol. . 1 00
" Lady of the Lake. 16mo. . 38
" Marmion, . . 37
" Lay of the Last Minstrel, . 25
Shakspeare's Dramatic Works, 2 00
Tasso's Jerusalem Delivered. 1 vol. 16mo. . 1 00
Wordsworth (W.). The Prelude, 1 00

## Religious Works.

Arnold's Rugby School Sermons, . 50
Anthon's Catechism on the Homilies, . 06
" Early Catechism for Children, . 06
Burnet's History of the Reformation. 3 vols. . 3 50
" Thirty-Nine Articles, . 2 00
Bradley's Family and Parish Sermons, . 2 00
Jotter's Mass and Rubrics, . 38
Coit's Puritanism, . . 1 00
Evans' Rectory of Valehead, . 50
Greyson's True Theory of Christianity, . 1 00
Gresley on Preaching, . 1 25
Griffin's Gospel its Own Advocate, 1 00
Hacker's Book of the Soul, . 1 00
Hooker's Complete Works. 2 vols. 4 00
James' Happiness, . 25
James on the Nature of Evil, 1 00
Jarvis' Reply to Milner, . 75
Kingsley's Sacred Choir . 75

Kehle's Christian Year, . . 37
Layman's Letters to a Bishop . 25
Logan's Sermons and Expository Lectures, . 1 12
Lyra Apostolica, . . 50
Marshall's Notes on Episcopacy, . 1 00
Newman's Sermons on Subjects of the Day, . 1 00
" Essay on Christian Doctrine, . 75
Ogilby on Lay Baptism, . 55
Pearson on the Creed, . 2 00
Pulpit Cyclopædia and Ministers' Companion, . 2 50
Sewell's Reading Preparatory to Confirmation, . 75
Southard's Mystery of Godliness, . 75
Sketches and Skeletons of Sermons, 2 50
Spencer's Christian Instructed . 1 00
Sherlock's Practical Christian, . 75
Sutton's Disce Vivere—Learn to Live, . 75
Swartz's Letters to my Godchild, . 38
Trench's Notes on the Parables, . 1 75
" Notes on the Miracles, . 1 75
Taylor's Holy Living and Dying . 1 00
" Episcopacy Asserted and Maintained, . 75
Tyng's Family Commentary, . 2 00
Walker's Sermons on Practical Subjects, . 2 00
Watson on Confirmation, . 06
Wilberforce's Manual for Communicants, . 38
Wilson's Lectures on Colossians, . 75
Wyett's Christian Altar, . 38

## Voyages and Travels.

Africa and the American Flag, . 1 25
Appletons' Southern and Western Guide, . 1 00
" Northern and Eastern Guide, . 1 25
" Complete U. S. Guide Book, . 2 00
" N. Y. City Map, . 25
Bartlett's New Mexico, &c. 2 vols. Illus., . 5 00
Burnot's N. Western Territory, . 2 00
Bryant's What I Saw in California, . 1 25
Coggeshall's Voyages. 2 vols. . 2 00
Dix's Winter in Madeira, . 1 00
Huc's Travels in Tartary and Thibet. 2 vols. . 1 00
Leyard's Nineveh. 1 vol. 8vo. . 1 25
Notes of a Theological Student. 12mo. . 1 00
Oliphant's Journey to Katmandu, . 50
Parkyns' Abyssinia. 2 vols. . 2 50
Russia as it is. By Gurowski, . 1 00
Russia. By Count de Custine, . 1 25
Squier's Nicaragua. 2 vols. . 5 00
Tappan's Step from the New World to the Old, . 1 75
Wanderings and Fortunes of German Emigrants,

| | |
|---|---|
| Williams' Isthmus of Tehuantepec. 2 vols. 8vo. | 3 50 |

## Works of Fiction.

### GRACE AGUILAR'S WORKS.

| | |
|---|---|
| The Days of Bruce. 2 vols. 12mo. | 1 50 |
| Home Scenes and Heart Studies. 12mo. | 75 |
| The Mother's Recompense. 12mo. | 75 |
| Woman's Friendship. 12mo. | 75 |
| Women of Israel. 2 vols. 12mo. | 1 50 |

| | |
|---|---|
| Basil. A Story of Modern Life. 12mo. | 75 |
| Brace's Fawn of the Pale Faces. 12mo. | 75 |
| Busy Moments of an Idle Woman, | 75 |
| Chestnut Wood. A Tale. 2 vols. | 1 75 |
| Don Quixotte, Translated. Illust. | 1 25 |
| Drury (A. H.). Light and Shade, | 75 |
| Dupuy (A. E.). The Conspirator, | 75 |
| Ellen Parry ; or, Trials of the Heart, | 63 |

### MRS. ELLIS' WORKS.

| | |
|---|---|
| Hearts and Homes ; or, Social Distinctions, | 1 50 |
| Prevention Better than Cure, | 75 |
| Women of England, | 50 |

| | |
|---|---|
| Emmanuel Phillibert. By Dumas, | 1 25 |
| Farmingdale. By Caroline Thomas, | 1 00 |
| Fullerton (Lady G.). Ellen Middleton, | |
| "     "     Grantley Manor. 1 vol. 12mo. | 75 |
| "     "     Lady Bird. 1 vol. 12mo. | 75 |
| The Foresters. By Alex. Dumas, | 75 |
| Gore (Mrs.). The Dean's Daughter. 1 vol. 12mo. | 75 |
| Goldsmith's Vicar of Wakefield. 12mo. | 75 |
| Gil Blas. With 500 Engr's. Cloth, gt. edges, | 2 50 |
| Marry Muir. A Tale of Scottish Life, | 75 |
| Hearts Unveiled ; or, I Knew You Would Like Him, | 75 |
| Heartsease ; or, My Brother's Wife. 2 vols. | 1 50 |
| Heir of Redclyffe. 2 vols. cloth, | 1 50 |
| Heloise ; or, The Unrevealed Secret. 12mo. | 75 |
| Hobson. My Uncle and I. 12mo. | 75 |
| Holmes' Tempest and Sunshine. 12mo. | 1 00 |
| Home is Home. A Domestic Story, | 75 |
| Howitt (Mary). The Heir of West Wayland, | 50 |
| Do. A Tale of the Ancient Fane. 12mo. | 75 |
| The Iron Cousin. By Mary Cowden Clarke, | 1 25 |
| James (G. P. R.). Adrian ; or, Clouds of the Mind, | 75 |

| | |
|---|---|
| John ; or, Is a Cousin in the Hand Worth Two in the Bush, | 25 |

### JULIA KAVANAGH'S WORKS.

| | |
|---|---|
| Nathalie. A Tale. 12mo | 1 00 |
| Madeline. 12mo. | 75 |
| Daisy Burns. 12mo. | 1 00 |
| Life's Discipline. A Tale of Hungary, | 38 |
| Lone Dove (The). A Legend, | 25 |
| Linny Lockwood. By Catherine Crowe, | 50 |

### MISS McINTOSH'S WORKS.

| | |
|---|---|
| Two Lives ; or, To Seem and To Be. 12mo | 75 |
| Aunt Kitty's Tales. 12mo. | 75 |
| Charms and Counter-Charms. 12mo. | 1 00 |
| Evenings at Donaldson Manor, | 75 |
| The Lofty and the Lowly. 2 vols. | 1 50 |

| | |
|---|---|
| Margaret's Home. By Cousin Alice, | |
| Marie Louise ; or, The Opposite Neighbors, | 50 |
| Maiden Aunt (The). A Story, | 75 |
| Manzoni. The Betrothed Lovers. 2 vols. | 1 50 |
| Margaret Cecil ; or, I Can Because I Ought, | 75 |
| Morton Montague ; or, The Christian's Choice, | 75 |
| Norman Leslie. By G. C. H. | 75 |
| Prismatics. Tales and Poems. By Haywarde, | 1 25 |
| Roe (A. S.). James Montjoy. 12mo. | 75 |
| "     To Love and to Be Loved. 12mo. | 75 |
| "     Time and Tide. 12mo. | 75 |
| Reuben Medlicott ; or, The Coming Man, | 75 |
| Rose Douglass. By S. R. W. | 75 |

### MISS SEWELL'S WORKS.

| | |
|---|---|
| Amy Herbert. A Tale. 12mo. | 75 |
| Experience of Life. 12mo. | 75 |
| Gertrude. A Tale. 12mo. | 75 |
| Katherine Ashton. 2 vols. 12mo. | 1 50 |
| Laneton Parsonage. A Tale. 3 vols. 12mo. | 2 25 |
| Margaret Percival. 2 vols. | 1 50 |
| Walter Lorimer, and Other Tales. 12mo. | 75 |
| A Journal Kept for Children of a Village School, | 1 00 |

| | |
|---|---|
| Sunbeams and Shadows. Cloth, | 75 |
| Thorpe's Hive of the Bee Hunter, | 1 00 |
| Thackeray's Works. 6 vols. 12mo. | 6 00 |
| The Virginia Comedians. 2 vols. 12mo. | 1 50 |
| Use of Sunshine. By S. M. 12mo. | 75 |
| Wight's Romance of Abelard & Heloise. 12mo. | 75 |